Structures of thinking

International Library of Sociology

Founded by Karl Mannheim

Editor: John Rex, University of Aston in Birmingham

Arbor Scientiae
Arbor Vitae

A catalogue of the books available in the **International Library of Sociology** and other series of Social Science books published by Routledge & Kegan Paul will be found at the end of this volume.

Structures of thinking

Karl Mannheim

Text and translation edited and introduced by
David Kettler, Volker Meja and Nico Stehr

Translated by
Jeremy J. Shapiro and Shierry Weber Nicholsen

Routledge & Kegan Paul
London and New York

First published in 1982
by Routledge & Kegan Paul Ltd
11 New Fetter Lane, London EC4P 4EE

Published in the USA by
Routledge and Kegan Paul Inc
in association with Methuen Inc
29 West 35th Street, New York, NY 10001
Set in Times
and printed in Great Britain by
Redwood Burn Ltd, Trowbridge, Wiltshire
Reprinted 1986

© Routledge & Kegan Paul 1982

Library of Congress Cataloging in Publication Data

Mannheim, Karl, 1893–1947.
Structures of thinking.

(International library of sociology)
Translation of: Structuren des Denkens.
Includes bibliographical references.
1. Culture   2. Knowledge, Sociology of.
I. Kettler, Davis.   II. Meja, Volker.   III. Stehr,
Nico.   IV. Title.   V. Series.
HM101.M26213   306   81–13824

ISBN 0 7102 0730 1

Contents

Editors' preface

The texts to be presented in this edition had been in the possession of the late Dr Paul Kecskemeti, who was a close associate of Karl Mannheim and a distinguished social scientist in his own right. The published version rests upon a photocopy of the typescripts, which Dr Kecskemeti allowed to be made some years ago. In preparing the texts for publication, almost sixty years after their composition, the editors have been governed above all by their conviction that Mannheim's reflections on cultural sociology have value beyond their interest as documents for a representative intellectual biography. The objectives have accordingly been to preserve the methodological structure and substantive content of the works while putting out of the way linguistic and grammatical obscurities which could only serve to distract the attention of readers. This has meant, especially in the case of the less finished later text, a certain amount of editorial retouching, especially of syntactical patterns occasionally reminiscent of Mannheim's native Hungarian. But every care has been taken to avoid meddling with Mannheim's conceptualizations, rich in metaphors Mannheim hopes to revitalize, as well as deliberate tautologies and ambiguities. These are methodical, systematized notes, preparatory to the carefully wrought essays which were Mannheim's chosen means of public expression. To burden the edition with an apparatus detailing editorial changes would render the contents less accessible and would imply unwarranted claims for the historical weight of these texts. Specialists can consult the complete, unedited typescripts in the libraries of the Universität Konstanz and Trent University, where they are also available for reproduction.

The texts were preserved in several typewritten copies separately assembled in binders. In the one, there is a title page, with

1

the title, author's name, and the notation 'Sulz am Neckar. Begonnen September, 1922', followed by three pages of fairly detailed table of contents, and 183 consecutively numbered pages of text, of which the last eight are devoted to footnotes. The second typescript is longer, and the pagination more complex. The title page is limited to the title and sub-title, and the one-page table of contents contains only the headings of the major sections. After a three-page *Vorwort,* the pagination begins again. The first part runs from page 1 to page 50. The second part is numbered from page 1 to page 136, but there is an error in the count. After page 56, the numbering returns to 50 and runs once more through 56 before going on. There is no sign in the text that this is anything more than a simple mistake in pagination, consistent with other signs of this being an unrevised early draft. The third part is a twelve-page fragment, breaking off in mid-sentence with a half-line of periods followed by a note about topics for continuation. In the edited version, most of this last part has been included as an Appendix. Both texts, in the original, employ marginal summary headings; and these have been removed. The table of contents for the earlier text includes almost all these headings, making for a sort of analytical outline. The editors have used many of the headings from the later text in a similar way, to construct a comparable table of contents.

The typescripts appear to have been typed on the same machine, perhaps a portable, not equipped with the German sharp *s* or umlaut; but there is no reason to suppose that the texts were re-drafted after their original composition, and every reason to suppose the contrary.

Since the German publication of these materials in *Strukturen des Denkens* (Frankfurt: Suhrkamp, 1980), the Dutch sociologist Henk Woldring has generously put at our disposal a second copy of the text of the second manuscript, and this copy has some corrections in Mannheim's hand, enabling us to solve a few textual riddles. It has also allowed us to include page 97 of the manuscript, which was missing from our earlier copy. More important, the state of the manuscript gives very good reason for believing that Mannheim reviewed the text as late as 1945 or 1946, since he noted a 1945 edition of a psychology book on the cover sheet, seemingly in the same manner of writing (which did change over the years). And at that late date, it seems, he found it appropriate to make very few, largely grammatical or narrowly stylistic changes. To maintain the historical integrity of the text, we did not reproduce the three changes which affect the substance, although even these are barely perceptible adjustments in nuance.

The editors wish to thank the departments and research committees in their home universities for valuable assistance. Special thanks go to Professor Kurt H. Wolff of Brandeis University, who has all students of Mannheim and Mannheim's subjects in his debt and who has been a special goad and inspiration to two of the editors.

David Kettler
Trent University

Volker Meja
Memorial University of Newfoundland

Nico Stehr
University of Alberta

Note on the translation

In his own work on the translation of *Ideology and Utopia*, Karl Mannheim experienced the dilemmas facing any translator of work like his own, where the German terms chosen are meant to resonate within a dense cultural atmosphere and the meaning is carried as much by overtones as by the primary denotations. Mannheim, we are told, took desperately heroic measures: he required his youthful English assistant, with the language skills of a talented undergraduate, to try her hand at colloquial equivalents with nothing more to help her than hearing him read the German words and phrases. The present editors and translators have been more timid, though not less perplexed. We have tried to respect the need to avoid a merely technical jargon, precisely because the theoretical work being translated belongs to an intellectual movement which thinks of itself as breaking through the impasses of technical philosophy by restoring the descriptive powers of attentive observation and language. But we have also tried to meet the requirements set by the fact that Mannheim means to have us consider aspects of things which our most familiar common-sense vocabulary encourages us not to distinguish, and which indigenous English theorizing has also commonly neglected. Not even the powerful poetic diction of a Samuel Taylor Coleridge, wrestling with similar tasks a century ago, could properly naturalize the concepts needed. We have no illusions about our own success.

Our primary rule has been to use words in ways which connect with colloquial English usage, although the meanings intended may be third or fourth in the Oxford English Dictionary, and the contexts in which certain usages occur may sometimes surprise the reader. We hope that readers will at least consider, if something pulls them up short, that there may be an insight available to them

5

if they give the editors and translators the benefit of the doubt and try to find a reason for a word that may jar or a repetition that may annoy. A secondary rule has been to let readers with professional interests follow, so far as this can be done consistently with the primary rule, the author's variations on technical terms within the tradition. As an aid, we have noted the German equivalents where we thought this would be helpful, notwithstanding the paradox involved in technicizing terms which were often originally chosen or coined for their anti-technical, evocative, descriptively rich qualities and associations.

Closely related to the problem of words are problems of syntax and style. Mannheim uses, and indeed exploits, the capabilities of German usage for bringing the reader to consider a number of things all at once, with qualifications, antithetical comparisons, and accumulated appositions. As noted in the introduction, this lets him advance his argument by rhetorical moves he considers necessary with regard to matters which do not admit of evidentiary proofs in the normal sense, and it lets him signal unmistakably what things he wants the reader to keep in suspense because he means to leave them unresolved. We have stretched the norms of ordinary style to reproduce as much of this as possible, where we thought that the intellectual gain would compensate for the strain on the reader's attentiveness.

To identify the most important terminological decisions, it may be useful to anticipate a very few points about the tasks and operations of 'thinking' and 'knowing', as Mannheim wants us to recognize them. First of all, it should be noted that these are to be seen as activities and that the concern in the work is to characterize the structure of these activities and not the products of such activities alone. We have emphasized this by translating *Denken* almost everywhere as 'thinking' rather than 'thought', and *Erkennen* as 'knowing' rather than 'knowledge'. Where Mannheim speaks of *Erkenntnis,* of course, 'knowledge' will commonly be employed. Where *Erkenntnis* occurs as a modifier, as in *Erkenntnissoziologie,* we have said 'cognitive sociology' rather than 'sociology of knowledge', however, in order to hold fast to the somewhat technical point that Mannheim never used the expression *Wissenssoziologie* in these texts; and it is, of course, the latter term which is so importantly associated with his subsequent work and its translations.

The activities of thinking and knowing, together with other activities which Mannheim and the traditions informing his work considered outward expressions of distinctively human capabilities, formed the domain of *Geist.* Wherever it is possible to render this word as 'spirit' without risking absurd misunderstanding, we have done so. Our major exceptions, made with regret because the shift in language deprives us of an association we need in order to get the full message, are 'intellectual history' for *Geistesgeschichte* and 'humanistic sciences' for *Geisteswissenschaften.* Distinctly human energies in their inner conformation are *die Seele,* and we have not shied away from 'soul', although we have rendered the adjectival form as 'psychic'. What Mannheim would have us consider is a world in which actors possessing the attributes of soul, at least potentially, move among a multiplicity of entities displaying a coherence whose character is not obvious. They regard or encounter or experience these things amid others doing the same. The conceptual problem is to designate the major constituents and processes in this world in such a way as to let us notice, for example, when an actor truly becomes an actor, rather than a passive victim, or even when an encounter becomes an experience. More difficult for us is the need to fix stages in the development of the entities entering into these relationships. Following Hegel, Mannheim wants us to observe the formed entities which inhabit the domain of spirit without trying to decide whether they are truly formed, in some world 'out there', or whether we impose form on them ourselves as we notice them. Accordingly, he speaks often of *Gebilde* and *Gestaltungen,* using words which are reminiscent of the activities of formation, while they are also quite ordinary words for constructions of various sorts. We have used 'formations' and 'formed entities', despite the slight strain on English, except where the development of Mannheim's argument has specified the characteristics of *Gebilde* in some portion of the spiritual cosmos enough to let us speak of 'cultural creations' or 'social arrangements'. *Gestaltung* often appears also as construction or production. When Mannheim wants to emphasize the interconnections among elements whose constitution cannot yet be specified, he speaks of *Zusammenhänge.* This term has to do hard work in the first of the two manuscripts, where interconnected packets of experience are observed in their interplay with formations in order to work up some understanding of 'knowing' and 'thinking'. We have often used 'configuration', hoping to enlist some of the wealth of associations of 'figure' to help us convey the process and its direction. Elsewhere we have preferred 'contexture' or 'context', as seemed appropriate.

The most general sort of outer event in the spiritual domain is an *Erlebnis,* which translates as 'experience' and forms the basis for compounds and adjectival forms, to identify configurations and contents, for example, which are to be examined as they must be

7

supposed to appear to experience without the help of linguistic or other contextualizing aids. *Erfahrung* also has 'experience' as counterpart, but generally focuses on that portion of the connotative spectrum of the word, where we are talking about 'know-how' and the accumulated weight of discrete experiences: we occasionally use 'learning' as equivalent, making it clear that we are not suggesting anything remotely like scholarship. In one extended discussion, Mannheim relies on the noun form of the adjective *gegenüber* to point at the indeterminate somethings which human actors can be said to encounter, before these can be further specified, to the extent of designating them as objects or Others. The word ordinarily means 'on the opposite side' and has been translated by the comparable French expression, which has been naturalized into English as *vis-à-vis*.

It is Mannheim's central conviction that actors do not experience things without turning towards them in some way which can be characterized in detail. His words for this turn towards formed entities are distinguished from the somewhat analogous psychological notions which we find more familiar, in that they deliberately avoid reference to the motive forces, desires or impulses we would be inclined to invoke. He says *Intention,* but we have tended to use language emphasizing the element of attentiveness and structured focus rather than the cognate English word, associated so closely with a presumed motive force. A closely related class of terms in Mannheim's German derive from Riegl's concept of *Kunstwollen,* employed to designate a patterned mode of artistic understanding common to some school or time, without specifying whether or how individual actors are moved by it. Mannheim uses the term *Wollen* in combination with *Denk–* (thought), *Erkenntnis* (cognition) and *Welt* (world), as well as *Kunst* (art). We have decided against coining a class of technical terms to render these, preferring to use a variety of translations. Quite often, *Wollen* becomes 'project', because we can build on the fairly widespread acceptance of this Sartrean version of the concept. We thus have artistic, intellectual and even cosmic projects. These are, respectively, the designs some collective subject may have on art, on thinking, and, most generally, on the world as a whole. Because 'cosmic project' moves so far from the visceral associations of the original *Weltwollen,* we have occasionally preferred an English equivalent more directly reminiscent of the classical source in Schopenhauer and Nietzsche and have spoken of a 'will to the world'. Where Riegl himself is under discussion, we have opted for 'artistic volition', as is more common, despite our misgivings about 'volition' for *Wollen* and our unwillingness to perpetrate anything like world or intellectual volitions. A last key term to do with the ways in which actors organize experiences by attending to them in certain ways is *Einstellung,* whose meaning here can best be rendered by the slang expression 'being tuned in'. We have used 'directedness' and 'attitude', and hope that the latter will be taken in its positional rather than the emotional sense. To have a certain 'attitude', in the sense intended here, is to turn in a certain way and to be receptive to certain aspects of things. It is not necessarily to have certain feelings or emotion-charged beliefs. If the mode of conduct associated with being turned in a certain direction is also to be signified, Mannheim will often use *Verhalten,* and this has been rendered by the slightly dated 'bearing'. Moving away from the moment of action, we find the now familiar class of terms derived from ways of seeing, which have been translated pretty straightforwardly as perspective, world-view, point of view, etc. Equally important, and related, are the powerful metaphors, derived from seeking one's way: orientation, situation, starting point, and the rest. Again we have been able to follow obvious usage, and note the matter here simply to call attention to the fact that we do not consider the metaphors altogether dead and have taken some pains to transmit them.

The last preliminary point about our language concerns logical terms. Mannheim speaks of *prinzipielle* considerations or sciences, but does not as a rule intend what we mean by a 'matter of principle'. He means to designate the quality of being fundamental, usually to science, and can often be translated on this point by 'logical'. It is worth noting, however, that he thinks that logic in a narrow sense is inadequate as a fundamental framework, and that he means to include ontological and/or phenomenological ways of grounding and ordering inquiry. His own use of logical terms must consequently be rendered so as to avoid a false impression of a rigorous deductive system. Terms like *Funktion* and *Bestimmung* are used on the model of mathematical rather than empirical usage and so indicate a logically explicable structured interdependence rather than causal necessity; but they do not provide mathematical rigour either. Accordingly, the former has sometimes been assimilated to the latter in our translation, with both rendered as 'determination'. In all cases 'determination' should be understood to leave unresolved the precise nature or stringency of the relatedness intended. As further sign of that, Mannheim uses *Bedingung* and its variants as equivalent to *Bestimmung,* and this refers to a relationship of 'conditioning' or 'influencing' which is far from rigorous determinacy.

It would be unfair to Mannheim to elaborate these preliminary

9

notes on his concepts because, as he teaches, such notes must come ever closer to the matter of the work. And we have determined to let readers encounter that for themselves.

The Editors and Translators

Introduction: Karl Mannheim's early writings on cultural sociology

David Kettler, Volker Meja and Nico Stehr

Dialectical thinking typically links the content and form of its investigations. When Karl Mannheim set out, first in 1922 and then again a few years later, to reflect on the intellectual activities he grouped together as 'cultural sociology', he quickly made a transition from taking them simply as subject matter to applying their method. Like Martin Heidegger, whose lectures he repeatedly cited, Mannheim sought a method for '"listening in" to what is already "going on"'; and this 'method's reflexive involvement with this subject matter of what is already "going on" is a "going along with it and after it"'.[1] Accordingly, Mannheim does not call cultural sociology into question in his studies; he experiments with the discipline upon the discipline, while paying close attention to what he is doing.

This attention does not always yield clarity, and it rarely finds altogether satisfactory answers to the questions it remarks. The worth of these papers lies above all in their openness. It is troubling to realize, then, that they have been shut away, perhaps for that very reason, that they have had to wait almost sixty years for publication; and it is distressing to think that this delay has had to do with the obstacles to openness created by career and forcible relocation and then by the posthumous stereotyping of claims to recognition. Although available evidence provides no direct answer to the question why Mannheim chose not to publish these texts or why they have been left in manuscript since his death, it seems likely that they were not found compatible with the design, at least partly imposed by harsh circumstances, of having Mannheim appear as an authoritative and professional academic sociologist, rather than as a suspiciously philosophical speculator.[2] But this is not the place for lugubrious inquiries into Mannheim's own reasons for withholding these essays or into those of his literary executors. Let it be said that the manuscripts did not merit this fate and that they can still help, not only with the understanding of Mannheim's project but also with contemporary reflection on sociological interpretation.

The opening reference to dialectical thinking is not meant to suggest that Mannheim has somehow applied a superior logic that overcomes difficulties and builds a finished theoretical system. The characteristic feature of Mannheim's thought, nowhere more clearly shown than in these essays, is a willingness to reopen questions prematurely closed by others, to leave alternative possibilities in suspension, to let difficulties find solution later. This is true within each of the studies to be presented here; it is even more strikingly true of the relations between the two works. Everywhere Mannheim looks, it seems, he finds antithetical pairs which must be somehow brought into structured coexistence. But this can only happen in time. Mannheim expressly makes the intellectual time and place present in his writings, and he assigns them an active part in continuing as well as starting the work he is doing.

When Mannheim tried to characterize in 1921 the cultural situation in Heidelberg, where he found himself after the defeat of the Hungarian Soviet interrupted his precocious literary career in Budapest, he displayed this characteristic intellectual propensity. Writing to a friend, he reported that 'the intellectual life of Heidelberg can be measured according to the opposition of its two poles'. One extreme consists of the sociologists, following the model of the recently deceased Max Weber, and the other consists of the poet Stefan George and his disciples. 'On one side,' he wrote, 'is the university, on the other the boundless literary world.'[3] A review of Mannheim's history to that point, not to speak of the highly 'literary' character of the letter itself, might lead to the expectation that he would gravitate toward the pole opposed to sociology; and so we must pause briefly to consider how it came about that Mannheim, beginning in these years, was to make sociology his lifelong care, that he was to await resolution of the contending tendencies within this field.

Mannheim, born in 1893, grew up in Budapest amid contrasting intellectual tendencies in some respects similar to the polarities he found in Heidelberg and, indeed, strongly influenced by German developments. The Social-Scientific Society under Oscar Jaszi translated European sociological texts and generated proposals for reform and social development through sociological analyses of Hungarian backwardness, while Georg Lukács propagated cultural renovation with the help of a group for humanistic studies inspired by intellectual currents antithetical to the positivism predominant among the sociologists. Mannheim drew close to Lukács before he was twenty, and he was allowed to speak for the humanistic group during its most prominent public appearance, in the later years of the First World War.[4] Mannheim's comments on the Stefan George Circle in Heidelberg suggest an important difference between the literary anti-positivist movement within which Mannheim came of age and what he found in Heidelberg, and they indicate some of his reasons for turning instead to Max Weber's brother, the cultural sociologist, Alfred Weber. He claimed that the George circle, despite its many merits and accomplishments, failed to contribute, in the end, to the transformation of life and radical renewal of spirit he considered necessary. Their humanism proved too literary and conventional:

> The George community . . . is a well-intentioned experiment of lonely intellectuals trying to solve the various problems of spiritual homelessness. . . . They deceive themselves with the feeling of having ground under their feet. They have drawn inward, covering themselves with the blanket of culture, leaving the world out and becoming lost in themselves. Life in Heidelberg, protected by the hills all around, makes them feel that they exist and that they are important and effective; only a thunderstorm is needed and they become the symbols of a past age.[5]

For Mannheim, as for Lukács, the involvement in culture was bound up with a conviction that the old cultural contents had become obsolete and lifeless and thus with a passionate attention to history as locus of radical renewal. The problem was to find the historically apt way of attending to history. In his 1917 lecture on 'Soul and Culture' Mannheim insisted that aesthetic criticism and the exploration of formal structures was all that could be done, despite the radical 'inadequacy' of such cultural activities, and that this restrictive phase would somehow be brought to a drastic overturn by the closure which such inadequate cultural work would somehow provide.[6] This had been Lukács's position too, until he became convinced that the Communist revolution signified the promised redemptory crisis. Mannheim never followed him in this, but he also suspected that the destiny of culture was linked to the social and political awareness of those who were to carry it forward. In his brief account of Max Weber in the cultural letter of 1921, he admires his 'limitless' social and economic knowledge and evident calling for a career as a 'political leader', and regrets that confinement in the university and town blocked his energies and led to his being known 'only as a scientist'.[7] Eventually, Mannheim

13

tried to break through this blockage, in his proposal to bring together the political and scientific vocations into a politics as science to be brought about by an intelligentsia freed from the bonds of locality. But that project was only foreshadowed in the early years in Heidelberg. In the language he then preferred, it can be said that he believed it necessary to master the forces which rendered what the spirit had made impervious to the needs of the soul for self-expression and community, and that the discipline required for such mastery was in some sense sociology. Certainly in comparison with the illusory cultural haven inhabited by the Stefan George group, sociology must have appeared to Mannheim as a place for historical understanding and practical development.

Sociology itself was a strong and growing spiritual power, and for that reason alone merited attention. Yet, from Mannheim's point of view and in the light of his own earlier development, there was much about it that was threatening. It had originally appeared as a force dedicated to modes of social progress hostile to what he understood by spiritual renovation, and it had propagated standards and methods of knowledge which scorned the spiritual structures constituting cultural works. The question is whether it is possible to have a sociology that will serve culture, a study of man in his socialized being and development which will not strengthen the forces of social objectification but rather make intellectuals 'feel that they exist and that they are important and effective', without deceptive shelters from the world, like those which secluded the followers of Stefan George. The idea of a *cultural* sociology, then, involves a puzzle, if not a paradox. How can a sociology comprehend culture, when sociology appears as the organon of mental methods hostile to culture? A cultural sociology, in a sense Mannheim would consider proper, cannot simply be a sociology about cultural subject matter. It must be a way of relating to culture which is consonant with the genuine forces making for culture, a sociology partaking of culture and indeed serving to renovate it. The two essays before us represent two phases of Mannheim's reflections on these questions.

Mannheim takes as starting point the failure of the old idealism and the discrediting of the antithetical materialism corresponding to it, which appeared as evident to him as it did to many others of his generation, and which he had already delineated in his Hungarian writings.[8] The cultural crisis which he believes attends these developments is no occasion for sceptical demoralization or mere 'impressionism', however, but opportunity for beginning anew. This can only be realized by working on the problems most immediately and most urgently raised, with the cultural resources which have become available. But the problems which form the heart of the crisis – the *relativism* accompanying the recognition that 'truths' change in time and the *reductionism* implied by the conviction that the history of such changes can only be comprehended by uncovering underlying material or biological or economic causes – seems to be only exacerbated by the characteristically modern historical and sociological treatments of cultural creations, which are now given as the way to work on the problems themselves. This is the challenge which Mannheim states and accepts, although in different ways, in both of the essays introduced here; and the project he initiated here is to inform all his subsequent studies.

Mannheim began writing 'The distinctive character of cultural-sociological knowledge' in a village in the Neckar valley in September 1922. By then, he had been in Germany for three years; he had published a review of Lukács's *Theory of the Novel* in the prestigious journal, *Logos*, an investigation of the concept 'world-view' in a journal of art history, an extended German version of his doctoral thesis on the 'structural analysis of epistemology' in *Kant-Studien*, and a review of a technical work on the classification of the sciences and thus on the distinction between humanistic and natural sciences in the foremost social science journal, the *Archiv für Sozialwissenschaft und Sozialpolitik*.[9] Mannheim was no longer a mere beginner. The position taking shape in these writings is that the variety of phenomena, whether in the sciences or in other cultural domains, can be referred to an underlying 'logic' or 'systematization' appropriate to each domain, and that this logic must be shown in turn to rest upon some deeper reality. In two of these early writings, the reality appears to be accessible to an ontological mode of investigation adapted from the researches of Edmund Husserl; in the other two, to a philosophy of history like that which Lukács adapted from Hegel before his turn to Marx. In either case, Mannheim rejects the claims of epistemology or methodology generalized from the structure of modern physical science, while he also insists that mere intuition which disregards structures cannot secure controllable knowledge. The questions he brings to cultural sociology, therefore, are not only whether it can talk about culture without obscuring its dependence on the world (as the George circle does) or undermining its character as culture (as positivist sociologists do), but also whether this investigation can uncover a logic of cultural objects and show the inner relationship between that logic and an ultimate spiritual reality.

The 1922 essay reflects the indecision of the publications immediately preceding it. In the first two sections, dealing fairly systematically with the contrast between philosophical and sociological considerations of culture and so directly with the question of relativism, Mannheim distinguishes 'immanent' from 'non-immanent' interpretations of cultural objects. Immanent interpretations address the explicit or implicit claim of the object to be 'valid': as a law which obliges, a verified theoretical proposition, a beautiful aesthetic object, a just moral action, or something of that sort. Non-immanent interpretation puts aside questions of validity while it regards some other aspect of the object, placing the object in a context other than the one indicated by its manifest meaning. As an example of such interpretation, sociological interpretation can neither confirm nor deny the truth of statements about the world, which it treats as cultural objects having a certain social significance. Mannheim insists that 'it will never be possible to construct a sociological critique of human reason'.[10] Anticipating critics of his own later writings, who will speak in this connection of 'Mannheim's paradox', Mannheim challenges one of Marx's important programmatic statements about the social nature of ideas. Marx contradicts himself in this characteristic formulation of his theory of ideology, Mannheim contends, because he does not consider that he can hardly make philosophical or scientific claims for his own statements if he states, without distinguishing levels of interpretation, that such statements are nothing but reflexes of socioeconomic determinants.[11] When such errors are corrected and the necessary distinctions made, according to Mannheim, cultural sociology neither implies nor fosters relativism. Validity is directly accessible to us by phenomenological methods which uncover the ontologically grounded principles we require. And these principles provide the framework for immanent interpretation.

Such methods make possible an immanent interpretation of cultural sociology itself and permit assessment of its validity. Sociological interpretation, according to Mannheim, has as its deep experiential foundation a human capacity to grasp the 'functional' aspect of human doings, to discern their place in the experienced world of social actions and relationships. This account of a fundamental human capacity is not to be understood as an empiricist psychological theory of primary perceptions which enter into the formation of 'ideas', but rather as insight into a primal structure of knowledge which serves as ground for subsequent theoretical development. Mannheim's use of the term 'function' derives from mathematics and is linked to other mathematical metaphors he uses to indicate the *logical* character of the relationships between social and intellectual configurations. The sociological interpretation whose development he is reconstructing does not inquire into the functions of ideas *in* society, but rather their character as functions *of* society. Such development into a disciplined study of cultural sociology takes place after philosophy, having dissolved the claims of several competing values to be supreme, discovers 'culture' as the process of creating value and makes it the supreme organizing principle, after sociological concepts come to express the social world, and when the interplay between this world and the cultural domain is being comprehended.

Mannheim devotes much of the remainder of the essay to showing that this interplay cannot be understood by causal and reductionist theories of base and superstructure. And it is in the course of this presentation that Mannheim manifests the indecision already noted, creating uncertainties about the continuing centrality of the distinction between immanent and sociological interpretation. To appreciate this shift, it is necessary to trace Mannheim's argument. Reductionism is to be avoided first of all because cultural sociology, whatever it may sometimes claim, cannot interpret cultural objects by referring them to some underlying, non-spiritual complex. What cultural sociologists actually do, according to Mannheim, is to find a congruence between the 'style' or principle underlying a given cultural production and the 'world-view' appropriate to some social condition or location. 'Spirit' is related to 'spirit'; and the interpretation of world-views mediates between the two terms of cultural sociological interpretation. Such interpretation does not claim causal necessity for the relationships it uncovers: the interpreter's movement between the cultural object and the social configuration yields an understanding of the social factors as a 'constellation' (almost in the astrological sense) which renders the cultural formation 'possible'.

This way of situating an object in its logically appropriate place and time, Mannheim suggests, takes its departure from the older philosophy of history exemplified by Hegel. While the cultural sociologist does not claim to have a systematic metaphysical explanation for the 'logic' or 'structure' he finds in the intermeshing and development of things, and while he does not have a concept of qualitative progress toward some end of history, he nevertheless gains the ability to offer the sorts of elucidations (*Deutungen*) that the old metaphysicians attempted. Cultural sociology does not offer mere positivist explanation. World-views are interlinked and changing, and in their historical development constitute a 'higher' reality to which the cultural sociologist refers the matters he interprets. In this discussion, as in the papers on Lukács and on the interpretation of world-views which it follows, there seems to be ever less occasion for an immanent encounter with cultural objects: the

17

historical 'reality' comprehended by philosophy of history appears ever more as the ontological reference point all understanding seeks.

As the work moves toward conclusion, however, Mannheim hedges his bet by turning from the direct structural analysis of cultural sociology to a classification of different types of sociology and of the different types of cultural sociology which correspond to them. In this typology, the approach linked to philosophy of history is classified as 'dynamic' and put alongside two other types which are also said to have some continuing importance. There is a 'pure' cultural sociology, derived from Kantian influences, and a 'general' cultural sociology, carrying forward positivist tendencies. Pure cultural sociology, as developed by Simmel and continued by phenomenological writers, has special interest for Mannheim; indeed, his account of it sometimes comes close to depicting it in turn as a complete way of encountering and reconstructing culture. This sociology follows after and interrogates the cultural work of socialized man, longing ultimately for something purely human and spiritual, that which transcends social determination. This metaphysical longing cannot attain its ostensible object, Mannheim contends, because there is no genuine home for pure human spirit in any cultural production, except in the heroic acceptance of homelessness, and so in the sociological work which is a form of this acceptance. Paradoxically, then, the search for the purely cultural leads to the subtle explication of the social and historical constitution of cultural phenomena. The terms of this analysis are strongly reminiscent of his comments on the Stefan George group and on their illusion that they have ground under their feet and have found a home.

More mundane is his treatment of the generalizing sociology of culture, which tries to derive causal generalizations from comparative historical studies. Despite his earlier criticism of the methods and assumptions of such an approach, he simply accepts that this is also one of the modes of that cultural sociology whose actual ways he is trying to follow and understand, and that it must consequently be based on some aspect of things which may properly be so approached.

The second and longer work, written several years later, retains some of this presumption in favour of achieved substantive work, regardless of its fit within the overall theoretical design, but departs in principle from the earlier acceptance of a world richly pluralistic in incommensurable realities and the diverse modes of knowing appropriate to them. Internal evidence suggests that 'A sociological theory of culture and its knowability' was prepared after Mannheim completed the essay on 'Historicism' published in 1924,[12] and before the essay on 'Problems of a sociology of knowledge,' published a year later. The latter work introduced new terminology which Mannheim subsequently employs, beginning with the expression *Soziologie des Wissens* in the title, and concerns itself with writings – especially the essay by Max Scheler published in 1924, which also seems to be the source of the new terms – that could not have been ignored if they had been available at the time of writing 'A sociological theory of culture'. The paper on 'Historicism', repeatedly cited in the manuscript, clearly prepared the way for a reconsideration of cultural sociology. In this essay, Mannheim decides that a dynamic-historical philosophy of life secures a foundation for the interpretation of all philosophies, as well as providing a dynamic metaphysics to serve in place of epistemology to define knowledge. With this he seems to resolve the indecision still found in the 1922 manuscripts: philosophy cannot be understood to provide a universal method for exploring a timeless domain of validity; it explicates the world-view of its time and itself develops dialectically as historical development proceeds.

The problems of philosophy of history, then, are the problems put to present-day thinkers by history. They include the need to devise and ground a conception of truth which will be as adequate to the new historical modes of knowing as were the Kantian reasonings to the seemingly timeless science of Newton; and they include the need for a synthesis between 'spirit' and 'life', which are both seen as the medium in which the essential dynamism proceeds. This reformulates the problems of relativism and reductionism by calling for a new philosophical way of understanding the things which the old philosophy comprehends in these terms. These and related issues, Mannheim maintains, are as inescapable for his generation as were the questions posed by the Sophists for another age; and their resolution will prepare the way for the new dynamism which he sees as an impending destiny.

Extending this thesis, the first part of 'A sociological theory of culture' opens with the claim that there cannot be a purely philosophical or immanent doctrine of method or knowledge. Methodological doctrine arises from reflection upon methodical inquiry: an observer or the investigator himself asking what the investigator, going about his work in a given society, is about. Such reflection will yield sociological orientation or self-orientation for the investigator, locating him within a structure ultimately to be comprehended by philosophy of history. This offends against the modes of reflection decreed by conventional philosophy; but the methods and criteria upheld by professional philosophers as universally valid and authoritative derive from an incomplete, unhistorical understanding of physical science. They can now be even more deeply understood as expressions of the will which the capitalist bourgeoisie brings to the world. When the philosophers dismiss as relativistic and therefore self-contradictory any doctrine which accepts the validity of historically conditioned knowledge, they are trying to enforce against historical-social understanding of cultural reality the rationalistic prejudices associated with limited experience of some other sciences. Mannheim here disavows the line of reasoning he himself adduces against Marx in the first of the manuscripts.

Mannheim concedes that the knowledge to be given recognition may be considered 'relativistic' in some sense, but he denies that this harms its claims to be knowledge, for two mutually inconsistent reasons. He insists first, that, for certain critical matter at least, such knowledge bound to time and place is all that can be attained, and that it is therefore meaningless to call it relativistic, a designation given meaning only by an irrelevant contrast-model of universality. Second, however, he grants the existence of relativism but looks forward to its reversal, by means of a philosophy of history which will, when uncovered, locate the many complexes of meaning and knowledge within a unified developmental sequence. But this reversal cannot be forced; it must be allowed to happen. As in his 1917 lecture on 'Soul and Culture' Mannheim considers it necessary to follow the road he finds indicated in his time, a road through relativism, to pursue lines of inquiry which do not themselves yield new substantive cultural values but which move, he contends, towards a drastic turning, when such values will be revealed.

While the inquiries to be pursued, as well as the reflections upon these inquiries, will not and cannot conform to the supposedly universal logic abstracted from physical science, they will not be romantic effusions of intuitive imagination. Cultural interpretation and the theory of such interpretation have as their ground the structured thinking of everyday life. The application and explication of structure is a disciplined, conceptual undertaking, and it cannot be achieved by mere feeling. As in everyday life, there is trust in sources of belief which a narrow rationalism considers irrational; but such rationalism is mistaken in supposing that either the trust or the sources work in an erratic, incomprehensible way. The understanding of culture is the work of the 'whole man', and not only of the special capacities involved in bourgeois calculation and its theoretical counterparts.

The historical possibility of such understanding, according to

Mannheim, is given by the interplay between the old anti-capitalist spirit, carried forward in traditionalist and conservative social strata, and the new anti-capitalism of the proletariat, attuned to bourgeois rationalism while also anticipating a revolutionary and utopian discontinuity in that order. The reference to social groupings, as Mannheim explains at greater length in the unfinished last part of the work, is not meant to suggest that modes of understanding can be reduced to effects of class interests. Cultural sociology does not deal in causal analyses, in his view, and Mannheim distinguishes between the bias doubtless often produced by interest, when thinking is inauthentic, and the essential perspectivism which is to be imputed to a socially shared mode of experiencing the world, engaging oneself to it, willing a world fit for one's socialized existence. This distinction presupposes Mannheim's account of the constitution of thinking, which takes up most of the manuscript. And this account also seeks to lay out the innermost connection between culture itself and its sociological-historical interpretation.

Drawing on phenomenological thinkers, and especially on the distinctive version of that approach presented in Heidegger's unpublished lectures, Mannheim describes all knowing as an appropriation of something encountered, which makes it possible for us to orient ourselves to it and to respond adequately. There is always a directedness in our knowing: that which we encounter presents itself to us in some perspective, which is associated with the will we bring to the world in and outside ourselves. We come upon it in the course of our own movements. Mannheim pairs the visual metaphors of perspective with the language of touching and tasting. He claims that touching and being touched are central to the experience which grounds knowledge, and he chooses the term 'conjunctive knowledge' to designate all knowledge which is close to this deep source and which serves vital orientation, shaping and interpreting a world within which we are at home. Such knowledge is inherently qualitative, judgmental, situational – and it belongs neither to the isolated individual nor to any universal human faculty. Conjunctive knowledge pertains to communities, constitutes communities, is borne by communities. In the abstract model of related single individuals which Mannheim develops in order to expound his conception, conjunctive knowledge is a function of contagion between two, a function of shared and exchanged experiences accumulated while following wills becoming ever more common. Apart from the model, in historical concreteness, generations are initiated into conjunctive communities, and any novel departures they may make gain meaning by reference to the conjunctive knowledge of those communities.

21

The structure of knowing, then, has at least three levels, according to Mannheim. The deepest is the primordial contagious encounter with some reality met as we act on the will we share with a community; the second is the structuring of an orienting response to that encounter, commonly by means of language and always with communal resources; and the third, conceptual and even theoretical in character, reflects on the direct knowingness of the second level, the knowingness which actually constitutes the various cultural formations and the stylistic systems which they in turn comprise. Mannheim says that it is the second level, the inner understanding which orients participation in the collective representations of the culture, which is properly to be called *Verstehen*. Whether the third level, theoretical interpretation, will adequately interpret *Verstehen* at any time depends on the requirements of the cultural system as a whole. According to Mannheim, theoretical knowledge serves to prepare the 'next step' in the inner development of a given stylistic system, arising out of what has been done, and the adequacy of the interpretation will be determined by what is needed to make that step.

It may consequently happen that interpretative theory will gain the ability to interpret things in a past age better than those active during that age could do, if the newer interpretative theory achieves a more profound depth of penetration in response to the requirements of its own age. So, to take the example crucial to the argument, although all cultural systems are subject to change, as their own accomplishments help to change conditions which in turn set new requirements, many systems have not required a theoretical awareness of historical development. Crucial symbols and other structured relationships underwent a process of meaning-change without any recognition of the process itself, and stories of olden times were told as if the past were simply an adjoining room. Now, in contrast, the dynamic character of things is everywhere evident; and, according to Mannheim, we can understand the pasts better than those who lived them or first tried to recollect them.

In the context of this structural analysis, Mannheim never expressly says just why it is that we must now understand historicity in order to prepare the 'next step'. But the continuation of his account implies an answer. Culture must understand itself as historical because culture has spawned a mode of knowing, a way of relating to vital realities, which threatens the very possibility of community and the continued creation of values which is culture. Without an historical interpretation, there cannot be any conception, under the sway of this new way of knowing, that there can and must be a 'next step'. To bring this potent but threatening knowledge within his account of thinking, Mannheim relates it to the possibility of a language serving to connect participants in different conjunctive communities who do not have in common the experience requisite to mutual conjunctive understanding. Devised to secure and express the narrow shared understanding required for certain limited objectives, especially practical ones, such a language will be restricted to the narrowly material or utilitarian aspects of things. This language constitutes, through its immanent logic, what Mannheim calls 'communicative knowledge', which is the knowledge found in physical science, technology, commerce, utilitarian calculation – in short, the elements of society rather than community (Tönnies), civilization rather than culture (A. Weber). Historical theorizing will not expunge communicative knowledge, of course, but it will locate it within a wider context of developing meaning and it will accordingly contribute to the formation of that next step which the present generation, according to Mannheim, appears destined to prepare, the reconstitution of cultural community on the basis of new will and spirit.

Mannheim then considers how such theoretical interpretation is possible. Mannheim cannot doubt that it is, because he believes that he has been doing it, 'going along' with 'what is going on' among cultural sociologists, inquirers into ideology, interpretative psychologists, historians of artistic styles, and others. Underlying this theoretical work he finds participation in a common cultural formation he calls *Bildungskultur*, which comprises individuals from diverse social groupings, including especially such 'outsiders' as the Jews and members of groups as yet little affected by the spirit of communicative culture, who have come together in activities which are conditioned by the older cultural education they share. The experiential bases upon which they found theoretical reflections derive from the life-situations of the groups represented in their intermingling or apprehended by the special sensibility which such intermingling brings about. Because they are dependent upon such grounding experiences, they cannot be said to be truly 'free-floating'. Nevertheless, the distancing derived from the very fact of intermixture and furthered by the distinctive education which is *Bildung* does make for the possibility of comparisons, combinations, and choices which justify speaking of this group as one which can be comparatively detached. What the *Bildungskultur* does, it seems, is to extrapolate from the possibilities generated by cultural experiences and to reflect on the interplay among such possibilities. What it cannot do is to generate new possibilities of its own.

Mannheim's discussion at this point is full of tensions, as he struggles for the first time at length with the problem of intellectuals, which he takes to be also the central problem of his own self-understanding and self-orientation. Already, in the 1921 letter about Heidelberg quoted earlier, he had written that he felt compelled to concentrate on the groups around Weber and George, despite some discomfort about the fact that intellectuals always attend only to other intellectuals, because he had to understand himself in this way. In that letter there is also considerable assurance that these 'beneficiaries and victims of spirit', as he calls them, can define and accordingly profoundly alter other worlds. Now the matter appears much more difficult. The intellectuals produce what is needed for the next step, but the transmutation of their historical and structural studies into a philosophy of history able to constitute new cultural action and creation appears to be out of their hands. Such philosophy can only come into being at some incalculable turning point. In this, as in so much else in the essay, Mannheim cannot choose between the active and passive voice: repeatedly he describes things twice, once as the effect of actions and again as the product of happenings. If it is correct to say that Mannheim sought an alternative to the way in which the George group made intellectuals 'feel that they exist and that they are important and effective', he succeeded better in the first than in the second half of his undertaking. The issue which Max Scheler formulated as 'the impotence of the spirit' is not resolved here. Yet he is confident that he has taken the right turning.

The historical and interpretative studies, to be relevant, must link up to the way in which all other groups increasingly experience their lives, and so they must relate what they are studying to the social and economic shape of things, which have become experientially central. The conjunctively apt mode of proceeding within the novel and imperfect sort of conjunctive community formed by *Bildungskultur*, accordingly, relies on sociology, thereby unavoidably partaking of the mode of knowing generated by communicative knowledge. But cultural sociologists do not employ this system of thought in the same manner as do ordinary sociologists, who have fashioned it on the model of natural sciences. In seeking qualitative interpretation rather than causal explanation, these studies aim at a cultural rather than a civilizational sociology.

Mannheim asks at last how the claims and findings of such interpretations, including his own, can be judged. Mannheim insists that validation in this case cannot involve the sort of proof appropriate to mathematics or natural science, which he calls *Beweis*, but rather a showing (*Aufweis*), and that this showing can only be properly appraised by connoisseurs from within the conjunctive community (or by others who come to have a genuine *Verstehen*). This applies to the validation of any sort of conjunctive knowledge and implies no denigration of the validity so ascertained. In particular, the validity of an interpretation is established, for those who have conjunctive access to it, by means of three tests. First, there is said to be a profound evidentiary feeling which arises when an account of something has got to the heart of the matter. It is, second, possible to review the authenticity of an interpretation, to ascertain the extent to which the interpreter has allowed interest to bias his reading of things. And, third, a valid interpretation will establish itself in time among connoisseurs and will last. But in the end, these tests are not decisive. Whether an interpretation provides knowledge depends on its ability to orient those who grasp it and to let them respond adequately to their reality. And this can only be known by a future interpretation, itself subject to no other sorts of checks.

As his subsequent work shows, Mannheim was not satisfied with so uncertain a standard. It threatened to cast the sociological investigator into that 'boundless literary world', which had appeared to him antipodal to the university, when he first examined Heidelberg. In the essay on historicism, written just before the 'A sociological theory of culture', he depicted a 'spiritual divide' within contemporary German thought

> between a brilliant, often very profound world of independent scholarship and aestheticism, which often loses itself in untestable vagaries, however, because it lacks inner or outer constraining bonds, on the one side, and, on the other, a scholarly world constrained by its academic positions and mastering its materials, but distant from the living centre of contemporary life.[13]

He has been talking about Ernst Troeltsch, and he ascribes to him the aim of unifying these into a synthesis, which, he approvingly adds, 'is truly needed'. But such an effort exacts costs: 'Inwardness is destroyed.' As epitaph for Troeltsch, then, and perhaps as epigraph for his own project, Mannheim writes:

> He sacrificed what was best in him because he did not want to be better than it is possible to be at this time, if one also wants to be genuinely and vitally bound to the present.[14]

At the sacrifice of his own 'inwardness' and speculative perseverance, Mannheim chose the university and a new, contested academic discipline as locus for his future work and as limiting and legitimating framework for his further investigations. This choice

25

put him at some distance from the connoisseurs of the *Bildungskultur* addressed at the conclusion of his 'Sociological theory of culture'. While his later work repeatedly pushes against the boundaries of academic sociology, it tends to equivocate between the sorts of imprecise, audacious standards delineated earlier and criteria more ordinarily implied by norms of academic and professional competence. With this came some shift back towards the pluralism of the earlier of the two manuscripts here presented. One sign of this renewed and continuing irresolution is ambivalence about Max Weber, the patron of academic sociology, and long, inconclusive preoccupation with his work. Between 1928 and 1933, Mannheim kept a publisher in expectation of a study of Weber entitled 'Spirit and Society', which he evidently never completed and quite likely destroyed. In the last phases of his English career, after his hopes of reforming academic sociology there had been frustrated, Mannheim presented himself to his associates in the Christian intellectual group, where he had found an influential audience, as master of an empirical sociology which had command of the actual course of things, and which left it to the Christian thinkers to provide the deep counter-current of reflection on ultimate meanings.[15] The interplay between these forces, controlled by neither, would determine events. Mannheim's work cannot be understood without attention to the overlapping and cross-cutting dualisms which engage it, and without recognizing that he had chosen to meet these engagements within the boundaries of academic sociology.

Mannheim never published anything except essays, and he repeatedly insisted that their essayistic character exempted him from requirements for theoretical completeness. In a letter written during the last year of his life, he replied to some critics who had complained about 'Mannheim's paradox' in his sociology of knowledge. Any 'contradictions or inconsistencies' which may be found in his essays and among them, are due to the fact that he makes 'a point of developing a theme to its end, even if it contradicts some other statements'. Taking up once more the historical theme from his earliest writings, he continued:

> I use this method because I think that in this marginal field of human knowledge we should not conceal inconsistencies, so to speak covering up the wounds, but our duty is to show the sore spots in human thinking at its present stage. In a simple empirical investigation or straightforward logical argument, contradictions are mistakes; but when the task is to show that our whole thought system in its various parts leads to inconsistencies, these

inconsistencies are the thorn in the flesh from which we have to start.[16]

Mannheim goes on to describe this contradictory starting point as the clash between empirical findings concerning the perspectivism and historicity of beliefs, however methodically established or rigorously defended, and the philosophical requirements of an epistemology which links validity to universality. Within this account, expressed in language Mannheim deemed comprehensible to English-speaking professional sociologists – and it is worth noting how this clashes with the imagery of wounds, sore spots, and thorns which opens the discussion – we can recognize the familiar themes of relativism and reductionism. The two earlier works, now published for the first time, represent a more systematic and more forthcoming statement of the ways in which Mannheim understood these issues, not least because they could be cast in a language more congenial to his thought. These are papers full of hope. The astonishing thing is that Mannheim closes his letter twenty years later, despite all tragic disappointments, with an appeal to 'our whole generation' to carry forward the work of synthesis, which is 'one of the most exciting tasks of the near future'. Many sociologists active today in the study of culture would argue that Mannheim's project of synthesis is fundamentally misconceived and that Mannheim went wrong when he abandoned the distinction between 'immanent' and 'sociological' modes of interpretation. The texts before us let us review the considerations which led him to his new starting point, as well as some of those which kept moving him back towards the old.

Notes

1 Robert Denoon Cumming, *Starting Point. An Introduction to the Dialectic of Existence*, Chicago: University of Chicago Press, 1979, p. 147.
2 The relationships between Mannheim's changing circumstances and his writings are explored in David Kettler, 'Rhetoric and Social Science: Karl Mannheim Adjusts to the English-Speaking World'. Paper presented at the meetings of the International Society for the Sociology of Knowledge (ISSK) in New York (August 1976).
3 Letter from Heidelberg (1921), *Tuz* (Vienna), 1, 1921, pp. 46–50. English translation by Charles Cooper, 'The Hindu Prince: A

Sociological Biography of Karl Mannheim, 1893–1947', vol. II: Appendices (unpublished typescript), p. 75.

4 David Kettler, *Marxismus und Kultur. Lukács und Mannheim in den ungarischen Revolutionen 1918/19*, Neuwied and Berlin: Luchterhand, 1967. English: 'Culture and Revolution: Lukács in the Hungarian Revolutions of 1918/19', *Telos*, 10 (1970).

5 Letter from Heidelberg (1921), in Charles Cooper, *op. cit.*, p. 80.

6 Karl Mannheim, 'Seele und Kultur', in Kurt H. Wolff (Hrsg.), *Karl Mannheim: Wissenssoziologie*, Neuwied and Berlin: Luchterhand, 1964, pp. 66–87. Cf. David Kettler, 'Sociology of Knowledge and Moral Philosophy: The Place of Traditional Problems in the Formation of Mannheim's Thought', *Political Science Quarterly*, 82, 3 (September 1967), pp. 399–425.

7 Letter from Heidelberg (1921), p. 70.

8 In his 1917 lecture ('Soul and Culture'), Mannheim cites as models for himself and for others in his 'generation' Dostoyevsky, Kierkegaard, the German periodical *Logos*, the Hungarian periodical *Szellem*, the philosophers Lask and Zalai, the art historians Ernst and Riegl, Cézanne, the *Nouvelle Revue Française*. The theme of participating in a generational movement is a recurrent one in Mannheim's thought; cf. Karl Mannheim, 'Das Problem der Generationen' in Kurt H. Wolff, *op. cit.*, pp. 509–65. English: Paul Kecskemeti (ed.), *Essays on the Sociology of Knowledge*, London: Routledge & Kegan Paul, 1952, pp. 276–322.

9 Review of Georg Lukács, *Die Theorie des Romans. Ein geschichts- philosophischer Versuch über die Formen der grossen Epik*, in *Logos*, 9 (1920–1), pp. 298–302. Reprinted in Kurt H. Wolff, *Karl Mannheim: Wissenssoziologie*, pp. 85–90. English: Kurt H. Wolff (ed.), *From Karl Mannheim*, New York: Oxford University Press, 1971, pp. 3–7. 'Beiträge zur Theorie der Weltanschauungs-Interpretation', *Jahrbuch für Kunstgeschichte*, I (XV), 4 (1921–2), pp. 236–74. English in Kurt H. Wolff, *From Karl Mannheim*, pp. 8–58. 'Die Strukturanalyse der Erkenntnistheorie', *Kant-Studien Ergänzungsheft* No. 57, Berlin: Reuther und Reichard, 1922. English: Karl Mannheim, *Essays on Sociology and Social Psychology*, ed. Paul Kecskemeti, London: Routledge & Kegan Paul, 1953, pp. 15–72. 'Zum Problem einer Klassifikation der Wissenschaften', *Archiv für Sozialwissenschaft und Sozialpolitik*, 50, 1 (1922), pp. 230–7. Reprinted in Kurt H. Wolff (Hrsg.), *Karl Mannheim: Wissenssoziologie*, pp. 155–65.

10 'The distinctive character of cultural-sociological knowledge', in this volume, p. 82.

11 'The same men who establish their social relations in conformity with their material productivity produce also principles, ideas and categories, in conformity with their social relations. Thus these ideas, these categories are as little eternal as the relations they express. They are historical and transitory products.'
Karl Marx, *The Poverty of Philosophy*, Moscow: Progress Publishers, 1950, p. 122. The contention that Mannheim's own mature theory is

paradoxical in this way is developed, e.g., in Ernst Grünwald, *Das Problem einer Soziologie des Wissens*, Vienna and Leipzig: W. Braumüller, 1932. Mannheim always insisted on the contrast between relativism and the epistemological consequences of his own approach.

12 Max Scheler, *Versuche zu einer Soziologie des Wissens*, Munich and Leipzig: Duncker & Humblot, 1924.

13 'Historismus', *Archiv für Sozialwissenschaft und Sozialpolitik* 52, 1 (1924), pp. 1–60. Reprinted in Kurt H. Wolff, *Karl Mannheim: Wissenssoziologie*, pp. 246–307. English: Karl Mannheim, *Essays on the Sociology of Knowledge*, pp. 84–133.

14 *Ibid*.

15 David Kettler, 'Rhetoric and Social Science', *op. cit.*

16 Quoted in Kurt H. Wolff, 'The Sociology of Knowledge and Sociological Theory', in Llewellyn Gross (ed.), *Symposium on Sociological Theory*, Evanston, Ill.,, White Plains, N.Y.: Row, Peterson, 1959, pp. 571–2.

Part one

The distinctive character of cultural-sociological knowledge

Contents

1 The sociology of sociology

1 Why cultural sociology first came into being in our era

The topic of these investigations is a distinctive way of regarding the phenomenon of culture. Gaining increasing awareness of themselves by theoretically reflecting upon their own proceedings, these investigations seek to shed light upon the problem of what it may mean to subject culture to sociological investigation. Cultural sociology is not a finished, fully developed discipline. Considered from the standpoint of philosophy of history, its point of origin belongs in the present epoch. Anyone attracted by the prospect of observing a science while it is *in statu nascendi* could not find a better opportunity than an investigation of the present state of this discipline.

But it is not only cultural sociology that is of very recent origin. The related disciplines comprising philosophy of culture are creations of this age as well. As though guided by an invisible hand, the entire apparatus of present-day humanistic science is at work on the effort to grasp the phenomenon of culture, in its historical course as in its systematic properties.

Before we proceed to the investigation of our principal question about the actual meaning of cultural sociology, then, it is necessary to consider how it has come about that the phenomenon of culture is now an organizing principle for spiritual life. Of course, if one projects the current attitude towards things into the past, one can say that there have always been sciences of culture: philosophy, history, philology, etc. have always occupied themselves with cultural manifestations. Against this opinion, however, it must be objected that they did not take them *as* cultural manifestations. Which is not to say that the new concept of culture appeared out of the blue: it stems from an altogether novel experiential attitude towards realities of the spirit, and it is this which first made the constitution of this concept possible. It shall be our preliminary task to set forth the distinctive kind of experiential relatedness which underlies the fact that formed entities are grasped as not only self-sufficient and complete in themselves but also regularly as phenomena of culture. Together with a phenomenological description of this focus on cultural significance, we shall try at the same time to specify in a systematic way the concept corresponding to it; which is to say that we shall inquire which other concepts present together with it co-determine the specific meaning of the modern concept of culture.

But before entering upon the two-fold task of this introductory chapter, we must first characterize, however briefly, the process of cultural movement itself which first made it possible that a novel attitude towards spiritual contents and the concept of culture corresponding to it could arise at all. It must be asked, then, prior to phenomenological and systematic analysis, what had to have happened before there could arise a novel relationship of the subject to spiritual formations such that these latter became recognizable *as* cultural phenomena and gained their ultimate significance from exactly this 'as' -status? What occurred within the cultural process itself, we want to begin by asking, that made it possible for the concept of culture in our sense to constitute itself and to take possession of the highest hierarchical place in our life-system?

Considered sociologically, what is central to any operative world-view is by no means the value which some system produced by thought makes into the pivot of its theoretical design; at the centre are, rather, the substrata in the construction of life which are valued as ultimate in 'lived life'. Because of his spiritual structure, man not only thinks but also experiences hierarchically. That is to say that there is always present a 'system' of inner- and outer-worldly things, not usually intellectualized, by which one orients oneself in acting, living, and experiencing, an ordering of worldly but also of other-worldly things, in which some part or an entire domain of things is taken as highest and given special emphasis. And the remaining elements of what is present order themselves by reference to this and derive their ultimate meaning from it. Intimately connected with this hierarchical structure of experiencing, furthermore, is the fact that while valuations may be derived from one another and justified by one another, the ultimate valuation, the one that is hierarchically most valued, must, as it were, provide its own warrant. That which presents itself as origin and beginning in the system produced by thought and which there falls beyond any theoretical justification, receives its self-warranty within the historical life-process from the collective consciousness present at a time, and it can be kept unproblematical only by this. In the Middle Ages this ultimate value emphasis fell on something transcendent, on God. As long as this valuation was actually supported by collective consciousness, the other realities bound themselves organically together and the image of the world rounded itself out to a relatively stable completion. At the moment, however (though it is an abrupt leap only when viewed systematically, since factually it is a development which proceeds gradually in historical time), when this hierarchical highpoint drops out of experience, as it were, due to a change in the social process and accordingly in the 'spirit of the age', and when it becomes problematic, all spiritual factors begin to move. The possibility is given of a re-ordering in the hierarchical relationships among spiritual realities.

At first, this movement presents itself as a struggle of the cultural spheres for autonomy.[1] Once each sphere (as, for example, art, science, as well as economic, political, and even purely sensual life) had got out of the systematic attachment in which it gained its whole sanction and specific meaning from a central life-value, each sought to constitute itself as self-sufficient, as end in itself. Here, too, it was in life that this process of becoming independent first manifested itself; and theory appears as a reflexive sanctioning, after the fact, of a result which has already been achieved by the historical process. To exemplify this, we may recall that a theory of the autonomy of reason followed after the liberation of science and philosophy from the status of handmaiden to theology, a differentiation which is a typical phenomenon in the cultural process and began as early as the age of magic. Similarly, a theory of the autonomy of art, which found expression in the aesthetics which then first constituted itself, could come forward only after art had freed itself, during the Renaissance, from its restriction by religion.

Parallel to these autonomy strivings on the part of the cultural spheres runs a simultaneous struggle among them for supremacy. Always under the primacy of a different cultural factor, it is repeatedly attempted to initiate a new organization of the image of the world on the basis of a new hierarchy. Scientific, aesthetic, and ethical cultures stand opposed to one another as different attempts at solution, as types of life- and world-design. None ever established itself definitively. Their endeavours to bring into being a regroupment of the constituent elements of world-view prove unable to succeed. This tension, which appears unresolvable, seems to receive an unexpected and, at first glance, paradoxical solution as the outcome of this process. Amid this struggle of spiritual realities contesting for autonomy and primacy, a new element has asserted itself: the cultural process itself, in its characteristic liveliness, so plainly apparent, in contrast to the medieval state of things. Since the scale of valuations and interpretations no longer presents itself as a fixed and stable reality, as if grown to the things themselves, but becomes graspable as valuations and interpretations undergoing change which can be followed within the lifetime of a single generation, the presence of this process comes itself to be accessible to observant reflection. This visibility of the cultural process has associated with it, first, a growing and deepening sensibility for bygone culture, and later, a scientific-historical activity of knowing, which continues to bear fruit in the historicism which lives on at the present. If the process of dissolution was so deep for the whole of the time up until late in the nineteenth century that, as we saw, none of the individual cultural forces could establish themselves as the force to organize life, then there could be no other solution to the problem of finding some place for the value-emphasis which had been cast adrift than to attach it to the phenomenon of culture as such, and to sanctify culture as the highest meaning, taking it either as a timeless, abstract force or in its growth and change.

In this struggle modern consciousness brought forth stabilization of world-view of three main types: the enlightened, the romantic, and the dynamic. The enlightened solution, proceeding out of an unhistorical, timeless consciousness, attempts somehow to justify culture as an end in itself. The design here is to transfer the dispossessed value-emphasis to the general phenomenon of culture. If God was once philosophy's supreme care, philosophy, as the most thoroughgoing expression of this struggle, now turns completely into cultural philosophy. This type attains in Kant's philosophy a formulation which is comprehensible, self-aware, and powerful, even though Kant remains influenced by the transient ascendancy of ethical primacy, by the ethical culture of the Enlightenment. The cultural totality, which Rousseau had made problematical precisely upon ethical motives, becomes the exclusive theme of philosophy; it becomes a power whose value is unconditional, to be justified on the basis of timeless reason. From this supratemporal stabilization of culture itself, a straight line leads to the contemporary formulation of this thought in *Wertphilosophie*, the philosophy of value. The timeless cultural values proclaimed by this philosophy, which are supposed to be acknowledged as warranting themselves, prove to mean, when subjected to sociological scrutiny, that the value-emphasis has been shifted to the phenomenon of culture itself, taken as being in a state beyond time.

40

The 'enlightened' solution we have associated with Kant is tied to a consciousness of a state beyond time, and, by virtue of this consciousness, it sanctions the very concept of culture as ultimate. For the other two kinds of solution, however, it is the historical rather than the suprahistorical which counts as experiential substratum. It is change itself and not the identity persisting within change which is treated as highest value, as end in itself. Just as divinity was once visible, or a nature permeated by ascribed meanings of a fantastic kind, history now comes truly alive. It is the source from which man draws life. Increasingly it becomes the new-found substratum for experience. Man has always lived in history, of course, and unhistorical ages are perhaps more traditionalist – which is to say, more thoroughly attached to the past – than historical ones. But in unhistorical ages, man has simply lived *in* history; he did not experience it *as* history. In romantic and dynamic consciousness, in contrast, the past is experienced *as* history. The romantic attempt at solution begins by comprehending as historical nothing more than a certain phase of the past, in its plenitude of culture and value. It seeks to transplant this structure, which has become transparent with regard to its historicity, into the present, and to make it into a determinant of new life. In this striving, however, it has within it all the seeds of a paradox and, in the end, of self-dissolution. Inasmuch as romantic consciousness recognizes the past as historical, it must also grasp its absence of contemporaneity. In the case of a consciousness in which the sense of history has not yet arisen and which deals with past productions of life as with present ones, it doesn't matter much if it regards these productions as present powers. But for a consciousness which has already experienced the historicity attaching to the past and which grasps all the elements injecting themselves into these productions from a buried world as *having* this antiquated character, it must mean an insoluble contradiction to regard them as powers in the present. A second contradiction which romantic consciousness contains is that, distinguished as it is by a sense for the quality of having 'grown', which marks formed entities and cultural epochs, it nevertheless seeks to achieve a condition antecedent to knowledge by means of knowledge, to bring about an organic growth of the present by means of 'organization'. Romantic consciousness experiences the historical in only one specific historical period; its contact with it, it might be said, leaps over time.

The third mode of solution, however, which resembles a synthesis of the other two, does, first of all, experience change, becoming, and development, but it transforms exactly this very process of becoming different into the highest value, the end in itself: the ultimate value emphasis is not laid upon a suprahistorical concept of culture but upon something else which is itself also beyond time, the historical transformation of culture in itself. This mode is a unification of historicism with timeless systematics, and can be found in its purest form in the Hegelian system. As a sequel, out of the crumbling of many a theoretical thesis while the underlying life-system is held fast, historicism arises. In its theoretical formulations, however relativistic they might be, historicism experiences, willingly or not, the becoming of culture and culture in its becoming as ultimate value.

These have been the outlines, only briefly to be sketched here, of the process within the dimension where world-view and culture are linked, which has had it as its outcome, as already remarked, that all of our science (except for the natural sciences) has become cultural science, and all of our philosophy has become cultural philosophy.

2   Characteristics of the modern concept of culture

This whole process of culture whereby culture was itself, so to speak, discovered, must be before us, if we want to understand why every effort in the sciences of the present day is directed to cognitive mastery of this phenomenon. It is a consequence of the struggle for autonomy and supremacy within the various cultural spheres and of the shift in value-emphasis to the phenomenon of culture itself, that a concept of culture has constituted itself for science as well.

We shall now attempt to work out the elements which appear to us as the essential determinants of the modern concept of culture,[2] paying particular attention to the following six, some of which have already been mentioned, which combine with the older ones in the course of the modern development:

1 The reciprocal relativizing of the individual cultural spheres, whereby the value emphasis falls on the whole.
2 Awareness of the relativity and transitoriness of every historical manifestation of the phenomenon of culture.
3 Awareness of the essentially processive character of culture.
4 Experience of culture as such in a cultivated way, the ideal of cultivation (*Bildungsideal*).
5 The antithetical drawing apart of the concepts of culture and nature.
6 Awareness of the social character of the phenomenon of culture.

We have already put forward the first three elements constitutive of the modern concept of culture, considered within the course of development just depicted. At this point, before discussing the latter three in greater detail, we simply want to add several remarks summing up what has gone before. The first precondition for the modern concept of culture, we asserted, was that its distinctive synthesis could only come into being by virtue of the reciprocal relativizing of the individual cultural spheres. This was not possible so long as one sphere – the religious, for instance – was singled out from the others, and thus successfully claimed for itself the primacy which, as a primacy of the cultural totality as such, is essential to the modern concept of culture. It is not that there had never been comprehensive synthetic concepts before, generated by some complex of problems, which could have embraced in their own way all matters of the spirit. It is just that this earlier synthesis occurred on the basis of one particular individual sphere of culture, which thereby moved out of culture, to a certain extent, and even into contrast with it. Since a correlative part fixes the constitutive meaning of its counterpart, the universalist meaning of the contemporary concept of culture was not available. So, for example, the Middle Ages also had expressions to designate what man in his spiritual capacity is able to achieve (i.e. they had synthetic concepts), but these expressions arose out of a problem complex which was different because it was religious. When Meister Eckhart[3] speaks on the 'work', for example, and counterposes it to mystic absorption, it appears at first glance that an inclusive comprehension of all spiritual and other activities which are possible, similar to that achieved by 'culture', has been attained. But this synthesis materializes out of a problem complex which simply runs counter to the contemporary concept of culture. The mystical-religious bearing is here expressly removed out of the series of 'cultural appearances'; the entirety of things remaining, in contrast to the religious bearing, is comprehended from a height from which neither its inner differentiation nor its organic unity can be grasped, as does happen in our concept of culture. It required the overthrow of religion before an attitude towards 'works' could emerge, in which all spiritual realities, homogenized in a manner of speaking, allowed themselves to be unified, and inner interest redirected itself towards the whole.

There was still another relativization required in order to arrive at the present-day concept of culture, and that was the relativization of every specific historical conformation of culture. The stability-mindedness of an age which thinks in a metaphysical-ontological way is necessarily predestined to grant its own cultural

43

environment some sort of ontological preference and not to experience it as a merely transitory form. That brings us to the third characteristic, and that is the processive aspect of the modern concept of culture. We imagine the spiritual cosmos not only as changing and fluid, but also in the form of a process, in which no historical phenomenon stands alone, but rather each secures its determinate place from those that go before and those that follow after. The times are not interchangeable; one cannot simply wander about the past as one does in the present; one cannot deal with the powers of the past as with those of the present. A thorough transformation of attitudes, standards, and concepts is necessary in order to relate to the past. It is obvious that for this there must be a prior relativizing of one's own spiritual environment: only the man who has somehow renounced his own absolute rootedness can leave his self behind and turn empathetically towards the past.

We have already incorporated the first three determinants within this course of development. The element mentioned fourth and now to be discussed may be said to be their product. We have a different relationship towards all the spiritual forces which happen to compose the culture of a community than do the epochs which relate to their spiritual formations as to entities which simply exist, and not, as we do, as to formations created by unconstrained will (*Kürwillen*). One may state this difference as a contrast between cultivation-experience and primeval experience,[4] or between culture as experienced in society and in community.[5] A radical difference in the relationship of the subject to spiritual formations is epitomized in each of these antitheses.

As long as culture is not experienced as culture, cultural creation takes place, so to speak, behind the back of the creative subject. The subject knows nothing about actuation or spontaneity; he lives on the inside of his formations, his interpretations, as in a second reality, a second nature. Significance and the attachment of meanings are like a casing over things, and the relationship of the phenomenological subject to them is ontological. Cultivational experience, in contrast, is characterized by the fact that the attachment of meanings detaches itself from things, so to speak, and that it is experienced as product of the creative subject. (The Kantian theory of knowledge represents a strange over-extension of this attitude, applying it to nature.) The receptivity of the phenomenological subject to formed entities combines two signals. Primeval directedness is an absorption, a nature-like submission to the effects of the formed entity upon oneself (as a man might let a ray of sunshine affect him). But this is crossed by an 'afterthought', an 'after-feeling', that the formation is a 'work', something shaped, creation and not being, expression of another and not self-realization. As a cultural creation, it is experienced as having value and not as simply existent, as assessable and judgeable and not as something to be simply taken in. In prayer, one is directed towards religion, not God; in thinking towards the advancement of knowledge, not primarily the result; in the picture, towards art, not that which is to be portrayed. The character of the creations as culture is experienced together with their primary existence. This second directedness constantly increases in force, represses the first, and increasingly supplants it as dominant. It is only where cultural creations are experienced as cultural creations, where the attitude towards them has already transformed itself as described, that it is possible to distinguish this region for itself, so to speak, conceptually and as a distant sphere. A given cultural experience has already vanished when the concept of culture emerges: the organic growth of culture-as-being has ceased. If works were earlier experienced as if they were nature, now even the cultural realities caught up in organic, non-deliberate growth (language, custom, etc.) are experienced as if they were works. Culture becomes a value where it has ceased to exist as being; it is little more than a projection into the past, although an unavoidable one, when one characterizes organic cultures as themselves directed towards value.

Only where the cultural, the meaningful no longer lies in the sphere of being has it become a value. Then it can be called into question and tested for its worth (Rousseau). Dependent on our will, our suppositions, it can be comprehended as movable, calling for reform.

Once the value-emphasis has shifted from religion to the totality of culture, this shift can take one of two forms: either one sees something in the totality of the creations produced by cultural life which warrants itself as possessing ultimate value; or one anchors the value of the creations in something which has being, in humanity, for the sake of which the creations ultimately exist. Creations are given sanction on the basis of their function of ennobling humanity, a conception given classical formulation in the humanistic ideal. If we are to grasp the concept of culture in its modern meaning, we must also bear this subjective sense in mind.

The characterization of the concept of culture would not be complete, if we did not contrast it with the decisive correlate concept, the concept of nature. The designation of culture as non-nature became genuinely concrete and internally consistent only because being and meaning, actuality and value were experienced as having parted from one another. It would make no sense to trace here all

45

the changes and differentiations undergone by the concept of nature. Needless to say, a metaphysical conception of nature, which posits it as effectual potency, is altogether left out of consideration here. The concept of culture developed by something like the doctrine of natural law was also nothing more than a precursor for the concept of nature relevant here. In that doctrine, 'nature' still stood for an attribute befitting all men in all ages in identical form; and it was an intrinsically evaluative concept. It retains that character in Rousseau, for whom it expresses a longing for directness, simplicity, and goodness. Finally, the distinction between cultural and natural science, which is methodologically constituted in essence, cannot be more than secondary, compared to the experiential contrast between nature and culture which is at issue here.

The nature which makes up the contrast to the modern 'culture', its correlate, then, is something that is only a bare ground for possible meanings, being itself devoid of meaning or value. It gathers together the accumulation of all the qualities which do not pertain to the cultural. Nature is thus that which cannot be penetrated by the spiritual, that which is indifferent to value, that which is not subject to the spiritual-historical course of development.

And at this point a remarkable expansion of the concept of culture must be noted. The more man becomes aware of his historical constitution, the less is it possible for him to comprehend what presents itself to him in his inner or outer world as stable in the way that nature is.

Even though the steadily mounting historical sense quickly made everything in the environment mobile, so to speak, which is to say that it showed that nothing remains identical to itself, eternally fixed, and that everything is subject to constant change – as is the case with political forms, art, religion, science – belief in the eternal sameness of human nature persisted for a long time. And it was this alone which made possible such a thing as a static psychology. But the more the concept of culture is conceived as essentially historical, the more the historical way of looking at things, and then historicism enters as well into consideration of the inner world. It becomes apparent that even what seems to be most exclusively our own – our emotional life, our desires, the forms of life and experience – actually belongs to exactly the same meaningful sphere as does, for example, the world of works. The concept of culture takes in more and more in its expansion, and what is left as remainder is a minimal hylostratum, our instinctual life and our sensuousness. This alone is now called nature – but by virtue of its divorce from meaning and its ahistorical character, and not by way of evaluation.

3 The social determination of cultural creations

With the analysis of the constituent of the modern concept of culture which was listed last, the element of social determination in it, we enter into the domain which is more narrowly that of cultural sociology.

The social determination of cultural creations did not emerge as a problem until the most recent phase of spiritual development. This problem could arise only after consciousness of the social process had come into being, displaying all the features which we have been noting until now with regard to the cultural process, or, in other words, until after the social process as such had actually come into view. It is striking that the problem of culture first constituted itself for reflective theory at about the same time as the problem of society. This suggests that the same general grounds, constellations, were at work in the latter as in the distinguishing of the phenomenon of culture. Here too, theory – let us take autonomous economic theory as an example – only follows after the rise to prominence and the coming into view of the sphere in question; here too, there first emerged a static depiction (classical economics) and it came to a dynamic conception of the economic and social systems only later, after here too there had occurred a relativizing of the individual phases as merely historical figurations. Here too, it was only after social life had become mobile that the social and the economic were comprehended as such. The movement of society, correspondingly, was made visible not only by the changing course of history which, impelled by the dissolution of the feudal life-order, brought about a constant ferment and a series of revolutions. At least equally involved was a fact that may have been even more important here: religious attachments of meaning in the social sphere, which, being everywhere grown together with social reality, had in the Middle Ages completely obscured the actual character of that reality, were now stripped away. The way to a purely sociological inquiry lay open.

There is an extensive analogy here to the general constellation out of which modern science arose. Pure quantification of nature became possible only when nature emerged from its magical-mystical integument. As long as one could grasp social units only by way of religious meanings and they were visible only in so far as they could be associated with the mystical body of Christ, a theory of society in the modern sense could not arise. But the exposure of society did not occur at one stroke and without transitions.

Towards the end of the Middle Ages, a juristic conception of

47

social formations takes the place of the representation of society as hemmed in, as it had been during the Middle Ages, by a theocratic context. Most notably, state and society were viewed as 'corporations' and comprehended by means of all the determinants available within the juristic conceptual dimension of the time (e.g., legal personality, contract). This conception originates in the penetration and ascendancy of ancient natural jurisprudence in the Middle Ages. At the outset of this development, the theocratic system of society infuses itself into the justification of the jurisprudential system. But this latter system then emancipates itself and sets itself up in opposition to the theocratic conception, as counterpole. The theocratic system, in turn, survived after its defeat, as spiritual systems generally do, as an undercurrent and it flourished again, most notably in the Reformation.[6]

It is well known that the conception of society in our sense, detached from the juristic-political concept of the state, first entered into theoretical consciousness with Saint-Simon. Simultaneously we find a tendency to situate the forms of sociation by reference to the economic system; and the concept of class immediately takes the place of the juristic conception. The tendency to situate society by reference to the economic sphere and to derive the forms of society from there, asserts itself in full measure with Marx and his followers. It is only in the most recent time that the movement, which seeks to work out a conceptual apparatus for comprehending the social, as far as possible independent of the juristic and economic ones, has got under way. Foremost in this movement have been Simmel,[7] Kistiakowski,[8] and Max Weber.[9]

Only when a process of social formation stripped free of relations of meaning became visible as a reality, and, correspondingly, when a distinctive conceptual dimension had constituted itself, could a sociology take shape which then in addition opened up the possibility for the latest discipline, cultural sociology. But it is only the possibility of a sociological consideration of cultural creations that is offered by sociology as a doctrine of society; no necessity is before us as yet.

For cultural sociology to be able to arise at all, there had to be a new kind of attitude towards spiritual formations. This is commonly called genetic; and it will be one of our principal tasks to consider a specific type of this kind of attitude, viz., the socio-genetic. A related example is already to be found in the discipline of history, inasmuch as genetic historiography, in the sense in which Bernheim,[10] for instance, contrasts it to narrative and pragmatic ones, has only broken through since the second half of the eighteenth century. Not every kind of genetic scrutiny was unknown to the

48

ancients; but that specific kind of genetic scrutiny which establishes itself in modern times with the psychological as well as sociological explanation of the contents of meaning, i.e. to attempt to explain spiritual formations by reference to real formations which are as far as possible devoid of meaning – this is peculiar to modern thinking. In a metaphysical-religious epoch, men are attuned to the immanent qualities of the contents of meanings (and this is the more true the more deeply and widely the epoch is spiritualized). The aim is interpretation, not explanation. And interpretation always consists in making one meaning understandable by reference to another. Something appears interpreted when its *topos noetos* within a more comprehensive system has been established, when one has somehow shown the place proper to that which is to be interpreted, by reference to a religious metaphysics. Once the experiential ground has been removed from under such metaphysics, there remains for the explanation of spiritual formations only an 'interpretability,' as it were, by reference to a reality bereft of meaning. If we can call the interpretation of spiritual formations by reference to more comprehensive spiritual totalities (e.g., the interpretation of the phenomenon of the state by reference to the theocratic system) an interpretation *downward from above*, we could call this kind of elucidation of formations, which explains by reference to formations which are simpler because at least comparatively empty of meaning, an explanation *upward from below*. At first this kind of interpretation gains the upper hand in sociology and cultural sociology (as well as in other fields): the more complex formations are to be explained by reference to the more simple, by reference to their elements. Only after this tendency of atomization had arrived at the most extreme exaggeration was it possible to recognize that the attempt made in this field, to explain adequately something which has meaning by reference to something which has none, and the more complex by reference to the more simple, contains an inherent paradox.

As we shall see, efforts are under way in cultural sociology at the present time which, while they do not go back to the antiquated metaphysics, now quite obsolete, generally seek to renovate and utilize, in many things, that which is methodologically meaningful in its structure.

4 Distinctive characteristics of a cultural science

In what has gone before we have sought to trace in outline, starting from a perspective which links sociology with philosophy of history, the process of cultural movement itself by which cultural

49

sociology has become possible at all. This obliged us to direct our attention, on the one hand, to the coming into view of the phenomenon of culture and, on the other, to the emergence of the sociological viewpoint in general. A second major question that we posed, equally cultural-sociological, was this: which spiritual realities present together with it give the modern concept of culture its distinctive meaning?

This way of considering a science may appear eccentric at first glance, since we are accustomed to proceeding purely logically-methodologically in ascertaining the distinctive character of a science. We limit ourselves, as we get under way, to the logical structure of the scientific exposition, as we encounter it at a given stage of development; we consider this stage of development as paradigmatic; and we hope to apprehend, as if statically, the timeless structure of the science concerned, within this stage. As justified as such a static view may be, and as much as it will in fact find application, in part, in our study as well, we believe, nevertheless, that the determination of the distinctive characteristics, of a *cultural* science, above all, is complete only when the immanent logical analysis of the knowledge it yields is complemented by ways of looking which are prior to inquiry governed by questions strictly of logic.

In a merely logical-methodological analysis of the cultural sciences, two altogether essential moments are either completely overlooked or wholly neglected on purpose: first, the fact (and the methodological consequences of this fact) that cultural sciences are themselves part of the process they are describing, that, accordingly, in this case the subject and object of science in a sense coincide; second, the fact (and the methodological consequences of this fact) that the subject of cultural-scientific knowledge is not the mere epistemological subject, but the 'whole man.' If it was Hegel who first expressed the first of these ideas and Dilthey, above all, who expressed the second, it is now time to take these ideas really seriously in the structural investigation of the humanistic sciences.

Stated in a simple formula, what follows from these two ideas? This much anyway: that one may not apprehend spiritual realities as if they were things, and that one may not, in the course of methodological reflection, falsify the knowledge relating to them, by analogies drawn from the natural sciences (which, more or less explicitly, dominate our reflections).

First of all, cultural phenomena are not something fixed, and knowledge of them is not something static, always remaining the same. This is, first, because new kinds of reality are constantly coming into being in the course of the process of culture. But furthermore, and as a result of this, it is not only that the objects of possible knowledge are always new, but also that the concepts by which these objects are grasped are in change. And this is because the newly arising concepts are never anything but a derivative of the changing cultural basis, which extends far beyond the theoretical. We traced this in the analysis of the concept of culture, in the course of which it became evident to us that this concept is dependent, with respect to the contents which variously fill it, upon the general spiritual state of things from which it has arisen. On a logical-theoretical plane, this was evidenced by the fact that the concept proved itself dependent upon the remaining spiritual factors already conceptually fixed, which determined its specific meaning by virtue of being correlatively posited together with it.

When speaking of a thing-like object in nature, let us say a stone, it is possible to maintain that it was equally a stone 500 or 1,000 years ago; i.e. that the stones of that time were stones in the same sense as the present ones are. But it cannot be said of a spiritual reality which constitutes itself in consciousness (and, as a matter of fact, in the historically determined consciousness of human individuals and communities) that it has always been there and in a comparable sense, in the way that we experience such phenomena today and conceptually comprehend them.

A cultural philosophy which chooses not to occupy itself with these shifting differences and which emanates from the contemporary complex of problems, which always corresponds to the prevailing attitude towards spiritual realities, may attempt to elaborate, by means of these inadequate concepts, some eternal structure of culture, perhaps in regard to its systematization of values.

A sociological examination, however, which is trying to bring out precisely that which has been deliberately passed over and neglected in such philosophical systematizing, must do justice, in its conception of the concept of culture, to the dynamic change within the object of this concept; and it must not seek to explain the change on the basis of the concept, but rather the emergence and specific meaning of its concept on the basis of the process of change. It must ask itself which spiritual forces helped to bring it about that a concept specified in just this way took form and established itself.

We have attempted to meet this requirement for a dynamic, cultural-sociological examination in what has come before, and to identify the most essential factors in its emergence and present state. And in this we have, so to speak, retraced the way leading to cultural sociology in its present structure. Accordingly, our treatment will be a static one from now on. But we can carry out even this seemingly systematic task only in part by the usual logical-methodological means. In our view, a characterization of the cultural sciences which tries to grasp their structure from the objective side alone (as by setting forth the distinctive features of its concept-formation) can only solve a part of the problem. This is because the constitution of knowledge of a cultural-scientific sort is always distinguished by the attitude with which the whole subject approaches the spiritual reality it aims to investigate scientifically.

For it is here that the circumstance mentioned second among those emphasized as important with regard to cultural sciences becomes relevant; and that circumstance is that the subject of cultural science is not the epistemological subject but the whole man, and that the 'whole man' substantially projects into the knowledge which is acquired, inasmuch as we arrive at altogether different determinations of spiritual creations as we proceed towards the formations out of different attitudes.

Spiritual realities are not like things, not only by virtue of the fact that only certain realities are present or visible for any given age – that, in brief, they have their birth and their demise within the spiritual process – but also by virtue of the fact that it is in being experienced that they constitute themselves and that, therefore, the attitude of the experiencing subject projects into their inner structure. And this applies not only to the creative subject, from whom the spiritual contents first arise, but also to the receptive subject seeking to understand the creations which have at some time come into the world. This understanding can be effected from various attitudes, and the distinctive character of the attitude will find expression in the product of the understanding, in the logical formulation of what is understood.[11]

The understanding of a work of art, for example, varies with the different phenomenological types of receptive subject, among whom G. Lukács[12] has specifically distinguished the naively receptive, the essayist, the aesthetician, and the historian. These types are not to be taken in an empirical-psychological sense, because they describe the structural properties of constitutive, typical possibilities for a conscious approach to spiritual realities and not actually existing subjects according to their empirical-psychological dispositions. After such a typology in accordance with pure structures has been extrapolated from actual experience, it is possible to ascertain that certain ages have not as yet actualized certain attitudes or that they give special preference to others.

That the structural types are brought back to historical actuality in this manner and the undeniable fact that the further course of history will prepare new attitudes and new types of receptivity with regard to understanding cannot alter the fact that the types which have been grasped in their purity by an intuition of essences (*Wesensschau*) are by no means mere generalizations derived from induction.

By way of such phenomenological analysis, it may be noted, one penetrates, in the case of each of the various types, to a structure which exhibits inner necessity; everything having its source in mere facticity is stripped away from them. It is in this sense that we shall seek to make evident the attitudes which alone make 'sociological interpretative understanding' possible at all.

The analysis of the phenomenological subject of cultural-sociological interpretation does not suffice by itself, naturally, to provide a fully valid characterization of cultural sociology. Since cultural sociology is not simply a direct understanding but is at the same time a *knowledge* of spiritual formations founded upon this interpretative access, methodological problems like those of any other science come up at this point, where the question becomes one of transposing that which has been experientially grasped into the conceptual sphere.

But the methodological analysis of a scientific discipline can also be undertaken in different ways. It is possible to formulate the methodological analysis and the classification of different tendencies within a science by reference to its auxiliary sciences,[13] or it is possible to group the tendencies by reference to research hypotheses,[14] etc.

Since these kinds of classification yield nothing more than a superficial arrangement of the tendencies possible within a science, it is methodologically more fruitful to classify the sciences in general as well as the different varieties of the same science by reference to their concept-formation (Rickert). For the whole of a methodology is implicit, so to speak, within the concept-formation.

We too will, accordingly, put principal stress in the analysis of sociology and of cultural sociology in particular upon concept-formation; but we believe that this must be expanded into a complete structural analysis of this discipline. In this, it is a matter of reproducing, in theoretical self-examination, the total cognitive intent of cultural sociology and, with the help of this guideline, of setting out the distinctive manner in which the object (cultural formations) presents itself in the sociological conceptual dimension, as well as the distinctive manner in which the sociological attitude transposes itself into conceptual operations.

Our overall task can thus be divided into two parts: a phenomenological analysis of the subjective side – which is to say, an analysis of the attitude specific to cultural sociology – and, on the other

53

side, a methodological knowledge of culture. This investigation forms the subject matter of the chapters to come.

But first (in the first five sections of the next chapter), we must attend to several basic points, especially concerning the relationship between sociology and cultural sociology. The principal topic of the next chapter, nevertheless, is the distinction between immanent and cultural-sociological ways of regarding cultural phenomena.

2 Immanent and sociological consideration of cultural phenomena

1 Science of society and cultural sociology

Sociology can be the science of the construction, organization, and transformation of life as it renders itself social, or, alternately, the science of the embeddedness of cultural formations within social life. In the former case, we shall speak of sociology as *science of society* (*Gesellschaftslehre*), and in the latter, of *cultural sociology*. Despite this differentiation, the unity of sociology is not destroyed. The 'union of the crowns' within the researcher is also conceded as an empirical matter of fact, as he is in constant alternation in his approach to things, sometimes with the one set of questions and sometimes with the other. We are here concerned only with a distinction in principle which results from the distinctive attributes of the different objectivities and from the difference in the problem complex adhering to each.

The inner kinship between the two branches of sociology, then, remains intact. It is guaranteed by the close ties between their subject matter: society is always a factor which forms culture (and its forms, the forms of sociation, may themselves be considered, in a certain sense, as cultural formations); and cultural formations, once they have emerged and achieved a state of being 'in themselves', become socializing factors in turn. But it is quite a different matter to investigate the part that 'social-historical reality' (Dilthey) plays in the emergence of cultural formations, how deeply it enters into their inner constitution, than it is to ask what sort of cultivation these formations signify for social life, once they are in being, how far they prove themselves, reacting in turn, to be socializing factors. Cultural formations rise up out of social life and they return to it. They are one of the functions of society, but it is also (in a different sense) one of their functions to have a socializing effect. In this latter respect they are matter for sociology as science of society. The subject matter of the science of society is the social process, with all the changing forms within which the association among individuals and the integration of each take place. Cultural formations are of interest to this discipline only in so far as they are socializing. In contrast, it is *culture* that is the subject matter of cultural sociology. Sociological consideration of this phenomenon, moreover, only extends as far as the social enters into the constitution of cultural formations and they can be considered societal.[15]

2 Cultural sociology and cultural philosophy

The interest of the cultural sociologist is primarily directed to the phenomenon of culture; cultural sociology may be regarded as a specific type of interpretation of cultural formations. The cultural sociologist, however, shares this interest with other investigators, including above all the cultural philosopher, for whom the phenomenon of culture also serves as focal theme. But while the cultural philosopher approaches the phenomenon of culture with philosophical points of view, the sociologist ventures forth with sociological ones. A difference in concept formation parallels this difference in points of view, and, accordingly, we shall encounter different concepts for the same cultural phenomena in cultural philosophy and cultural sociology.

3 Fundamental phenomena and concepts

It is quite evident from the preceding analysis that we shall have to distinguish between *fundamental phenomena* (*Grundphäno-mene*), on the one hand, and, on the other, the different concepts which, corresponding to the differences among the disciplines from which they originate, nevertheless refer to the same phenomenon. An instance of a fundamental phenomenon is thus culture itself, in its state of being in itself, prior to any science. Its concept in cultural philosophy differs essentially in construction and contents from its concept in cultural sociology. We shall also have to distinguish between a discipline as a *fundamental science* (*Grundwiss-enschaft*) and its appearance as method, in so far as it offers points of view for comprehending objects which lie outside of its immediate domain.

As science of society, sociology is a fundamental science; as cultural sociology, it is a method, a point of view for considering, up to a point, a phenomenon which lies outside of its domain proper.

Corresponding to the various fundamental phenomena are the various fundamental sciences; i.e. levels of concept-formation from which a phenomenon may be most adequately comprehended in theory, levels from which it really constitutes itself for conceptual consideration. The concept of society constitutes itself in this way within sociology, but the concept of culture, in philosophy. For it is obvious that synthesis of the most varied spiritual formations which we call 'culture' does not have its logical source in the science of society itself; in so far as it appears within that science, while it has been thoroughly adapted to the structure of sociological consideration and operated upon with sociological methods, all this is nothing but a reworking of something which has its origin elsewhere.

Let us show just such a relationship in the case of a different science. Psychology is the science of psychic processes; it is a fundamental science because it has a fundamental phenomenon as its basis: no other than the life of the soul, as it is constrained within the flow of time and manifested in psychic acts. But as psychology of art, it is method: i.e. it considers the work of art with the methods of psychology, in so far as it is also a psychic phenomenon. It could not constitute the concept of a work of art by its own resources, because the psychic process as such does not yield a criterion for distinguishing a work of art. The concept rather constitutes itself elsewhere, in aesthetics; and the psychology of art is nothing but a selective emphasis upon the psychic phenomena which are connected with the experience of art. As such, psychology of art investigates, on the one hand, psychic life in so far as it is directed towards artistic formations at all, and, on the other, it takes it upon itself to explain all those things about an individual work of art that can be grasped on the basis of the general lawfulness of psychic life.

It goes without saying that the concept of art is refashioned in the course of this consideration: only certain aspects of the fundamental concept, 'art', are considered here; namely, the extent to which the further course of psychic life is affected by it, or so far as psychic processes (association, fantasy, etc.) enter constitutively into the work of art.

What makes up psychological consideration of art, then, is that one approaches the phenomenon with the conceptual apparatus of psychology and with the problem complex contained therein; the subject matter of psychology is initially determined in accordance with its concept, and this has been adequately constituted elsewhere, in aesthetics. Analogously, sociological consideration of culture consists of moving towards culture from the sociological

57

conceptual level, on the basis of the concept of culture as constituted within cultural philosophy.

4 Limits of pure methodologism and intuitionism

It is already becoming apparent that one cannot approach with the methods of a given science simply any object external to it that one happens to prefer. It makes sense to pursue sociology and psychology of art and culture; but there is no meaningful prospect of pursuing chemistry or physics of art. At most, one could investigate the canvas of the artwork or its marble; but with this, the work of art itself would completely fade from consideration. In an inadequate consideration, in contrast (like a psychological view of art or a sociological view of culture), only certain parts of the phenomenon as a whole are neglected. From this it can be seen that not even a methodology can be generated from an exclusively methodological attitude; i.e., when the ontic background is not taken into consideration. We must therefore assume the existence of certain fundamental phenomena as prior to their constitution in concept; it can only be due to their distinctive character that material resistance against arbitrary expansion of the various points of view sets in. We must possess a pre-scientific (experiential) access to these fundamental phenomena, which extends into theoretical work so as to be able to subject it to some control.

We must also assume that there are ontic connections between such fundamental phenomena as 'society' and 'culture', or 'psychic life' and 'art'; and that it is only such connections which allow us to approach the second in each pair with the methods of sociology or psychology as well as with those of their respective fundamental sciences. If it is right, then, to stop short of any exclusive logicism, which claims that we possess these phenomena only in concepts and propositions, we must also bear it in mind that these phenomena are comprehended and matter in science only in so far as they have been taken up in concepts, and that the conceptual constitution does not correspond directly, as its copy, to the 'reality' of the 'fundamental phenomenon', but always has its contents co-determined by the correlations out of which the concept arose. As has been earlier noted, legality, custom, culture, art, etc. have only so much meaning to science as the concepts – or, more broadly, the entire conceptual system – which have been already worked out at the given state of knowledge, have inwardly comprehended. The concepts of capital and ground rent, for example, are not simply copies of the 'realities' they designate, but depend in their contents on the existing state of the systematization of national economy as

58

a science; and even someone who employs them unreflectively, vulgarly, presupposes this altogether self-contained conceptual set of an economic theoretical level.

The ultimate presupposition of our standpoint (and such ultimate presuppositions of a view should always be given prominence, because all thinking has them and its representations cannot be thoroughly understood without them) is thus a middle way between intuitionism and logicism. We assert, in sum, that we do begin with a completely atheoretical access to realities, and to spiritual ones above all, by virtue of the fact that we participate with them in the spiritual process, that we are attached to this process by all of our sensoria (which include sensuality, empathy, will, artistic sensibility, etc.), and that we experience life and its fundamental phenomena, so to speak, in the instance of ourselves, within ourselves, not without ourselves; but we also assert that we only *know* the phenomena to the extent that we have worked out concepts for them. And these concepts are not simply descriptive; i.e., their contents are not merely determined by the pre-theoretical phenomena in an immediate way, but rather depend most closely on the state of the entire conceptual systematization and the problem complex anchored there. And for this reason we believe that while a purely phenomenological description is not without meaning, it does not possess the same immediate relationship to the phenomenon as the original experience of it. (By original experience should be understood the adequate, pre-theoretical attunement to the formation, such as, for example, a purely religious, immersed relationship to religious phenomena.) In the phenomenology of art, just as in the philosophy or sociology of art, it is possible to derive theoretically from the phenomena only as much as is permitted by the problem constellation of the time, which has its precipitate in the conceptual systematization. The onward movement of the humanistic sciences, then, always depends on two factors, and its state at any time is to be measured by the growing or declining pre-theoretical sensibility for the phenomena being considered and by the state of its conceptual systematization, which has its own logical laws of movement.

5   Summary and objectives

As we turn back to our original problems from this excursus, it appears, in keeping with our distinctions, that cultural sociology is a science which considers the fundamental phenomenon of culture from the sociological conceptual level. It is evident that a foundation for this discipline is called upon, first, at least to make evident the availability of a sociological conceptual level, and, second, to work out the distinctive constitution of the sociological concept of culture; i.e., to establish what changes, what shifts each cultural formation or the concept pertaining to it undergoes by virtue of the fact that it is subjected to sociological consideration, and what distinctive attitude towards the phenomenon corresponds to this conceptual shift.

6 The sociological concept of law

To comprehend the kind of concept formation characteristic of cultural sociology, it is more rewarding to study this with regard to a concrete cultural formation than with regard to the general concept of culture as such. Taking the sociological concept of the law (*Rechtsbegriff*) as our example, we want to investigate the changes and shifts to which this concept, constituted elsewhere, is subjected at the sociological conceptual level. In this, we have it in mind to observe the sociologist, so to speak, at his work.

Max Weber has undertaken to specify the sociological concept of law; and here we have an instance where such a transfer of a concept derived elsewhere to the sociological plane is carried out with consciousness and reflection, upon grounds of principle:

> In speaking of 'law', 'legal order', 'legal dictum', it is necessary to pay particularly strict attention to the distinction between juristic and sociological modes of consideration. The former asks: what possesses validity as law in the realm of ideas? In other words, what significance, what *normative meaning ought properly* to pertain in logic to a linguistic formation presenting itself as a legal norm? The latter mode of consideration asks, in contrast: what *actually takes place* by virtue of the *probability* that persons who take part in societal transactions – and among these especially those who hold in their hands a socially relevant measure of actual influence upon these societal transactions – *subjectively* regard certain regulations as valid and treat them as such, which is to say that they orient their own transactions by reference to them?[16]

For our purposes, the following points to be found in this passage must be selected for emphasis:

(a) The distinction between two modes of consideration. This corresponds entirely to the distinction which we have expressed by 'different points of view' and 'different conceptual levels'.

(b) Second, we want to call attention to the fact that in the formulation, 'In speaking of "law" ... it is necessary to pay particularly strict attention to the distinction between juristic and sociological modes of consideration', it is presupposed that law is a 'fundamental phenomenon' even apart from the modes of consideration. It is, however, not taken into account – and on this point our position differs from the Weberian one – that these points of view and the sciences corresponding to them are distinguishably more or less adequate in relation to the fundamental phenomena. In our view – and this is not intended to be a distinction of worth – juristic consideration grasps more of the distinctive character of the fundamental phenomenon, 'law,' than does the sociological. The juristic concept of law constitutes itself on the basis of the *experience of law*: this experience, it might be said, shows it the way. And it is precisely the 'element of obligatoriness' which distinguishes the experience of law, even at the level of 'original experience'. Juristic consideration, although proceeding from a theoretical attitude, wholly retains this element of obligatoriness.

(c) But it is precisely in the falling away of the normative element that Max Weber quite rightly sees the shift which the concept of law undergoes within the realm of sociology. The normative character which continues to be given effect in immanent-juristic consideration is 'put in brackets' within the sociological realm. For sociology the law which has been bracketed turns into a matter of fact. And in this condition, it can equally become something factual for other disciplines, notably for psychology.

What are the concepts, it must next be asked, which are inter-related with the concept of law within Max Weber's system, so as to render that concept sociological? Once bracketed with regard to its validity, law becomes something factual inasmuch as:

(1) it becomes a *subjectively intended meaning*
(2) in the *consciousness* of many individuals; and
(3) is able to operate there as a causally efficacious motive for transactions since it is a possibility for each of the socialized separate individuals that all the others will also orient themselves by the contents of the same intended meaning.

These determinants correspond to the following ones, which appear when the phenomenon is viewed juristically:

(1) Meaning-contents in the realm of ideas, which
(2) direct themselves to the *legal subject*,
(3) who is under *obligation* to *actualize* them,
(4) in a way that is logically-juristically *correct*.

The guiding concepts of Max Weber's sociological mode of consideration, i.e., the constituents of the sociological conceptual level which is being brought to bear on the juristically conceived phenomena, are social community, plurality of real individuals, actual course of experience, subjectively intended meaning, motive, transaction, 'orienting himself'. These concepts are already laid down in the definition of sociology, which states:

> Sociology (in the present sense of this word, which is so often used in equivocal ways) shall mean: a science which seeks to understand societal transactions interpretatively and which seeks thereby to explain them causally in their course and consequences.

'Transaction', moreover, is to mean human conduct (regardless of whether it is a deed, an omission, or a sufferance, and regardless of whether it is internal or external) when and in so far as those engaged in the transaction attach a *subjective* meaning to it. '*Social* transactions, moreover, is to mean transactions which have reference to the conduct of *others* in the meaning intended by the transactor(s), and which are oriented to this reference in their course.'[17] The conceptual dimensions here laid down are in fact adhered to by Weber; all other factors, such as validity, correctness, etc. are consistently translated so that they can be accommodated within this 'cosmos'. Anything else that may be knowable about them (because comprehensible through different modes of consideration) has no place in this system.

Now there are several features of the axiomatic system thus laid down which are peculiarities of Max Weber's sociology, such as his extreme nominalism, which recognizes nothing but the individual as social reality and does not acknowledge any sort of group formation, any form of socialization, as social reality in any sense (not even in the broadest sense of the word), but consistently reinterprets them into existing 'possibilities' for certain sorts of transaction oriented to meaning. We must not bind our own analysis to such methodological presuppositions dictated by a world-view: we shall see how it is possible to approach the same phenomena upon a realist (universalist) basis. Our present concern has been primarily to see how valid formations are bracketed by the sociologist with regard to their validity, in order to be able to be confronted with the realities as they occur here within sociology. Max Weber speaks about this as well:

> It is obvious that these two modes of consideration set themselves altogether heterogeneous problems and that their 'subject matters' cannot come into contact with one another without mediation; that the 'legal order' as it appears in the

realm of ideas, which pertains to jurisprudence, has nothing to do directly with the cosmos of actual economic transactions, since they lie upon different levels: the one upon the level of what ought to be valid, in a realm of ideas, and the other, upon the level of real happenings. If it is nevertheless the case that the economic and the legal order stand in a most intimate relationship to one another, this is because the latter is not understood in this context in its juristic but in its sociological sense: as *empirical* validity. The meaning of the expression 'legal order' changes completely in this case. It does not designate a cosmos of norms which can be logically deduced as 'correct', but a complex of actual determining grounds for real human transactions.[18]

The legal order became a social fact by virtue of being placed within a set of such concepts as real individuals, transactions, determinacy, etc.

7 Immanent and non-immanent consideration of formations

We have proceeded at some length with the analysis of Max Weber's concept of law because it offered an opportunity for showing upon a concrete example what we have in view when we speak of *shifting* the contents of a concept previously constituted on to a level foreign to it. In this example, we were also able to render concrete the case of 'bringing a foreign conceptual level to bear' upon a phenomenon previously constituted. We could, moreover, observe in this example what must be understood by the bracketing of the quality of validity of a normative realm, as occurs, for example, in considering the juristic realm from a sociological level.

To this extent, then, the example served to confirm what was said before. Now we want to pursue one point which has surfaced in the course of our analysis and which is well-suited to take us further in our inquiry. As was already pointed out in the course of the analysis of the example from Weber, systematizations which refer to the same fundamental phenomena do not all possess equal adequacy with regard to it; it is rather the case that there are some which comprehend the phenomenon in immanent consideration. Now a 'consideration' that was adequate to a phenomenon in every respect and most authentically immanent would actually be an experiential implementation of the phenomenon. If I am embroiled in a legal dispute, make pleadings, adduce legal dicta, etc., a theoretical attitude is not involved, despite the isolated conceptual contents which I employ. In a reversal, actually quite common, thinking here enters into the service of an extra-theoretical relationship, which is legal life, in this case. A conceptual attitude like legal thinking cannot be properly called 'knowing'; there is available to us the most suitable expression, 'engaging in argumentation'. Although such arguing (in the sense of the law) is a process comprising conceptualization, in its overall meaning it is something extra-theoretical, because it is a function of a more embracing attitude: the experience of law. The element of validity is *implemented* in the original experience of law, but it is not subjected to knowledge. If we want to be precise, we may accordingly say that the phenomenon is *grasped* under such circumstances, but not that it is being *considered*, let alone *known*. We may thus speak of adequacy here and of 'being on the inside', but not of an adequate immanent consideration. What is required for consideration or for knowledge is distance, in the broadest sense of the word. But distance may be more or less great. There is one distance from which the element of validity remains visible (legal philosophy), and another from which it disappears from view. This is not to say that the knowledge at greater distance has no value or meaning. Adequate knowledge has the advantage of offering the fundamental phenomenon in its purity (and we are always bound to refer back to this original experience by which phenomena are given); the non-immanent consideration of the more distanced view, in contrast, has the value of revealing the entire phenomenon at once, as it is interwoven with the whole of life and experience and as it is indebted to them.

From within the legal attitude, for example, it would never be possible to see that a legal attitude precedes legal phenomena: it is precisely when we are attuned to its meaning-contents and enclosed within its sphere of validity that we cannot grasp its character. Nor could it be seen that the entire sphere, and also every single legal act, are also a function of the whole experiencing subject and of the societal community which stands behind him. If one is attuned to an artwork in the original way, there is only the insular, self-enclosed work. The attitude towards it disappears, as does the functionality of the sphere. Sociological consideration of culture is a kind of non-immanent consideration, which seeks out the functionality of every cultural formation.

8 Attitude and concept-formation

We are obliged to make evident the existence of different attitudes towards spiritual contents, because the ultimate difference between immanent and sociological consideration of cultural formations could only be derived from these differences in attitude. Philosophical consideration corresponds to the theoretical-immanent, sociological to the non-immanent consideration of spiritual formations. A difference in attitude towards the phenomena within the subject corresponds to what we were able to observe at first as a 'shifting', as a bracketing of validity. If cultural formations did not possess the quality of being directly present to us, without reference to individual and social processes of experience, a philosophical mode of considering such formations would be impossible. A theoretical proposition has perfectly understandable meaning without our having to know the condition and inner world of the subject to whom it corresponds. An artwork denies its genesis in time and its functionality by presenting itself to us in its quality of being objectified and thoroughly wrought. In so far as expressive elements, messages, and confessions are contained in it, they ask to be regarded as parts of this work, detached from all functionality, and not as functions of some individual life. They are perceived as needed or as superfluous, as justified or as intrusive foreign objects by reference to the compositional and meaning-giving centre of the work. 'I have forgotten my own grounds,' every formation seems to say to us, in so far as it finds us in the original attitude. But just as philosophical consideration of culture would be impossible if the possibility for immanent consideration able to be durably sustained were not given within the phenomenon itself, so no sociological conceptual level would be possible if the experiencing subject did not simultaneously have a capacity for experiencing the functionality of all these formations. There is an attitude attuned to the functionality of every single spiritual formation, in relationship to individual as well as to collective life. This attunement to functionality is a pre-theoretical attitude, not a theoretical one; and for this reason the subject of social cognition is not merely the theoretical (or aesthetic, etc.) subject but (as Dilthey calls it) the 'whole man', or (as we shall later render this term precise) social man.

Cultural sociology as a science corresponds to an altogether original attitude towards cultural formations, just as cultural-philosophical consideration corresponded to a distinctive, objectivist, immanent attitude. We can accordingly say that even though cultural sociology can be best defined logically and structural-analytically by reference to the premises (conceptual level) which it brings to bear upon phenomena constituted elsewhere, it can be best characterized by reference to the attitude corresponding to it; and this is an attunement to the social functionality of cultural formations.

9 Attunement to functionality

What we understand by a pre-theoretical attunement to the functionality of a formation must be shown by an example. First, we want to show this pre-theoretical character of such attunement in the case of *individual* life. Take the following case: A stray shot strikes a sentinel in the woods; he is wounded and cries out loudly in pain. This first cry is not a communication, sign, or anything of the kind. The cry is rather a direct continuation of the uninterrupted psycho-physical changes brought about in this man by the shot: the cry pours from his throat like the blood from his veins. But it is possible that in a moment the same cry, quite likely without change in sound, turns into a call for help, a communication. A world divides these two phases of the same sound. The first phase is a natural occurrence; in the second, the alien self, society is posited as premise. The cry now addresses itself to the human surroundings, no matter how far these may be removed, even if they are beyond the reach of any cry. The first phase of the cry is a biological-organic occurrence; the second, an occurrence in the domain of consciousness.[19] It contains a 'turning towards', a 'need to be apprehended'.[20]

And in this second phase of the cry (which has become a call and perhaps has already assumed the form of articulated speech and may consist in the sentence, 'I have been wounded') one can already phenomenologically distinguish two constituent elements: on the one hand, that which has been externalized from the inner life, the pure objectification (and this is already present in the cry and not first in the articulated sound-complex, since the cry which has become a call is in this event equivalent to the statement, 'I am wounded'); and, on the other, the functionality of this call, by virtue of which it is more than an objectification, by virtue of which it does not comport itself centrifugally towards the experience but upholds and asserts its connectedness to the life situation and to the stream of life. The ultimate meaning of a call for help is so deeply embedded in its functionality and that which is objective is so minimal that, on cursory consideration, functionality seems to cover everything. But the seed of detachability from the situation, from the stream of experience, is nevertheless given in the call; the call bears the mark of a certain generality and accordingly of sociability.

For our present consideration, this objective dimension has far less importance than the functionality, which far outweighs it anyway in this instance (which is why we deliberately chose this example). In its predominant functionality, as in its objective sense, the call can be understood only by a receptive subject who has access to this functionality. This presents no special difficulty in the case of a cry by a wounded person: every human being has sufficient sensibility to understand the characteristics of functionality in such an easy case. But if the call or articulated complex of sounds arises out of a more complicated life-situation, the 'theoretical man' will understand only as much of the communication as has been objectified in theoretical terms within it, but the sensitive person (who has a developed sensibility for functionality) will always grasp the functional relatedness to experience along with the 'objective meaning'.

This state of things is most commonly explained by the theory of empathy; we don't want to go into the insufficiency of that theory in this place, but simply refer to Scheler's discussion of it.[21] But whether through empathy or by direct perception (the distinction does not matter in our present context), it is one thing to understand objective contents and quite a different matter, in either case, to enter into their functionality.

To comprehend functionality in these cases means to grasp, on the basis of the transmitted objective contextures (which may be a long speech, a sequence of deeds, or indications which are merely discontinuous), the individual experiential contextures as a function of which the objectifications confront us. Acquaintance with the external condition and course of life may be helpful in grasping this experiential contexture, but such features are not strictly external in this case, since they come into consideration as striking symbol of the 'inner' experiences that pertain to them. Once grasped as functionality, even the most isolated cry instantly transports us into a whole constellation of inner – and outer – worldly experiences.

In order to bring the atheoretical character of the experience of functionality more fully into relief, we want to recommence our exemplification another layer deeper. The call has already been overloaded with functionality; in the following, we choose an example in which a functionality which can only be grasped irrationally predominates even more, so that what we understand by this concept will emerge as clearly as possible.

Let us assume that I am teaching someone how to load and prime a gun, or I am teaching him how a knot is to be tied. It is well known how awkward and ultimately, even impossible it is to put these 'technical directions' and 'rules of thumb' into concepts. One would have to fill up many pages in order to convey to someone how to tie a knot or a binding, without illustrating it directly or by pictures. As soon as one has an opportunity of showing how the thing is done, in contrast, one can transmit the whole operation in no time at all. And this is due to the fact that a grasp of the 'objectivity', knot, depends completely on an adequate grasp of the functionality which belongs to it. One 'understands' the phenomenon, knot (as yet, we shall not come close to the matter of comprehending the knot as means to some end, etc.) by virtue of the fact that one becomes aware of the movements of the organism, with the motor sensations associated with them, as the 'resultant' of which the knot appears before us. This example shows us functionality within a stratum very different from that of the previous example. While the call is also something comparatively primitive, functionality in that instance nevertheless lies within the higher realm of psychic contents; the functionality that manifests itself in the knot, however, lies in the realm of organic sensations – or, more accurately, sensations of movement – which is to say, in a layer in which the physical and the psychic cannot be distinguished from one another even in abstraction. The exclusively intuitive character of the grasp of functionality which goes along with every phase of the visible process (i.e., tying the knot) is not to be recognized as clearly anywhere as it is in this example: one comprehends the knot as knot (i.e., as yet free from any association of purpose or meaning) only in so far as one understands organic functionality. If one wishes, one can also distinguish objectivity (the completed knot) from functionality (the embeddedness of the organic movements appropriate to it within the configurations of our organic repertory) in this case. One can come to a theoretical comprehension of the entity (the knot as resultant of certain movements) only in so far as one breaks it down into phases and follows the conceptual description and instruction with illustrations which picture the individual phases in the formation of the knot; but even then, each illustration makes sense only to the extent that one rouses in oneself the organic sensation corresponding to each phase, which also signifies the embeddedness of the functionality pertaining to it. The technical phenomenon 'knot', in short, possesses comprehensibility in its functionality alone. What stands in place of the 'objective' (what corresponds to the literal meaning of a proposition, an artwork, etc.) is nothing but the knot as resultant, in this case, and by 'resultant' is to be understood the storing up of the processes producing the formation. 'Meaning', in the broadest sense, in contrast, designates something distinct from the resultant, and it can be grasped only by means of a distinctive attitude. Functionality is stored up in the call, an artwork, etc. as well – to that extent they are also resultants. But they are also comprehensible apart, about their own centres, without recourse to the functionality stored up in them; and for this reason, they can be reached by immanent consideration. This discussion shows that we do not associate the phenomenon of functionality with the realm of organic sensation alone, but see its structure reappearing within all higher manifestations of consciousness as well.

It is not our aim to erase real differences by these claims. A knot is quite a different thing from a call, an artistic creation, an ethical transaction, etc. We are merely asserting that each of these formations is marked by a layer which contains functionality and thus retains a similarity to organic functionality, and that the higher psychic functionality located in symbolic objectifications can also, in the last analysis, be only intuitively grasped.[22] The kind of intuition here is certainly different from the intuitive grasp of organic functionality proper to a knot; but this intuition is nevertheless just as 'meaningless' in essence as is the comprehension of organic functionality.

In the case of the higher formations (theoretical proposition, artwork, ethical transaction, etc.), each has a dual aspect. It is resultant, accumulated psychic functionality,[23] and it is something constituted out of elements contained within the resultant but which is nevertheless something novel, a meaning which can be grasped in itself. This double character, this superimposition of two strata within the formation, can even be observed in the case of the knot, a binding, when, for example, the knot is seen not only as a technical formation (as mere resultant of certain organic movements) but also in an aesthetic-ornamental sense. In such an event, all the lines shaping the knot, a binding, are grasped in their own ornamental-aesthetic worth as well as in their organic functionality. That it may happen that certain embedded organic sensations may also be the grounds for objective aesthetic comprehension (i.e., that they may enter into the aesthetic ornamental relationship as such), is nothing more than a complication, and at the same time also a confirmation of our analysis.

There are drawings in which the rhythm of the hand movement preserved in the shape of the line functions as aesthetically effective movement, where organic movement does not merely enter into the resultant but where it is also associated with the aesthetic value of the drawings and thereby an integral part of the meaning which can be comprehended objectively. In such cases, the relationship of functionality is simultaneously a constituent part of meaning. In a similar way, a higher psychic element, such as a feeling, may possess the character of functionality while it is also a part of meaning. As functionality it is expression of the soul and part of the resultant; as component of significance, it is part of the objective meaning.

10 The comprehension of functionality

It has been repeatedly observed that these examples merely serve to illustrate the actual phenomenon of functionality. We want to insist once more that we are far from wanting to transfer organic functionality to higher regions unchanged or to draw analogical inferences from it. It is only a related structure which recurs in the higher formation; and the descent to organic sensation was only necessary in order to show in a gross instance how functionality is situated within a formation which is objectively self-contained. Although this functionality was already placed within the higher psychic realm in our first example (that of the 'call'), this example was still only designed to represent the comprehension of functionality in relation to the psychic organization of the individual. What we said in this connection consequently remains within the domain of an interpretative psychology concerned with individual psychic life. Such a study will attempt to comprehend a cultural formation (an artwork, for example), not objectively, like the disciplines which are attuned to immanent meaning (art criticism, aesthetics, philosophy, etc.), but genetically, from a non-immanent attitude, by considering the formation in its functional relationship to the psychic life of the creative individual.

The fortunes of sociology (and especially of interpretative sociology) are most closely bound up with those of interpretative psychology: just like psychology, it does not choose the standpoint of immanent consideration, the standpoint of objective analysis, but attempts instead to comprehend cultural objectifications with regard to their functionality. In contrast, though, it directs its attention towards the functionality of the work in relation to the 'societal process', not the psychic life of the individual, and comprehends cultural formations as a function of that process.

It is now our task to show that there is such functionality in relation to the societal subject (and not only in relation to the experiential contextures of individuals) and that it can be apprehended by means of a spiritual act attuned to it.

Once it has been granted that cultural formations can stand in a relationship of functionality with regard to the creative-individual subject, once the relationship of functionality as such has, in short, been granted, it is only a matter of showing whether it is at all possible to speak of functionality in this other regard, and how far it is possible to do so.

The individual does not live alone and for himself: that which emerges out of the contexture of his experience as a distinguishable formation is not a function of his own experiential stream alone. The individual possesses a great part of his stock of experience in common with other individuals. These experiences, which are simultaneously present in all the individuals who belong to the same entities constituted by processes of socialization and community-formation, must be mutually interconnected in structure in a way similar to that which obtains among the experiential parts of an individual stream of experience. That is to say that it is altogether unsatisfactory, in portraying the experiential contents common to a group in a certain historical period, for instance, to conceive of them as a sum of experiential components present at the same time within separate individuals, monadically closed to one another. My membership in a group does not consist in my agreeing, fortuitously and occasionally, on the basis of my own pattern of motives, with the experiential contents of other individuals belonging to the same group, but rather in being able to complete a considerable stretch of patterned experience in common with the other members of the group. We are brought into community (*vergemeinschaftet*) only to the extent that and in so far as we communally put such common stretches of experience behind us. This can be easily clarified by an example. A political party consists of many different sorts of individual. It is possible, after all, to arrive at the same conception of political events and the same mode of response to them on the strength of the most varied individual fortunes and patterns of experience. But an agreement among many individuals which has it as a consequence that the different individuals chance to come together on more points and are again united on another occasion, like a convergence of happy accidents, would not generate a collective consciousness, however frequently the fortuitous sequence were to recur. Nor would communal association come about by way of a predetermined harmony which had the monadically isolated individuals running in parallel by means of a well-regulated psychic clockwork. Communal, collective experience arises only where and when different individuals execute within themselves an identical pattern of experience, at least with regard to some portion of their external fortunes (in our example, it was with regard to the political). The formations called political ideologies, party programmes, etc. grow up out of these collectively concluded stretches of experience, which the individual, in such cases, quite explicitly does not experience as his own but rather as belonging to the collectivity.

In the emergence of such ideologies and party programmes, where there is awareness of the collective way in which they are raised up, every individual experiences within himself the functionality of these ideas in relation to the community. When the individual acts not only in his own name but in the name of all, when he takes part in argumentation in the name of all,[24] he is aware that he is running more than his own course of life and that the emerging formations must be taken as functions of the communal stream. In this state, all motivational patterns having their source in other ranges, as for example in his accidental individual existence, are automatically rendered without effect; with a portion of his ego, the individual lives the existence of the communal stream;[25] he grasps the functionality of the ideas as that of the communal stream, as functionality in relation to a certain condition of the inner and outer constellation of communal fortunes. This is the point, then, at which the functionality of certain ideologies is already experienced in terms of the fortunes of the collectivity and not in terms of the fortunes of the experiencing individual.

The way that we have just followed consisted, first of all, in our attempting to show that every formation subject to objective understanding may also be seen as function of a pattern of experience, which it was at first necessary to represent as belonging to individual life. Once there is insight into the fact that all objective contents have a double meaning – one that is purely objective and another that is functional in relation to the individual configuration of experience – and once it is grasped clearly enough that this attunement towards functionality is a distinctive attitude, it only remained to show that there is also a functionality in relation to communal experiences. But such functionality can exist only in relation to patterns or contextures of multiple experiences; there cannot be functionality in relation to some single item out of the contents of the soul. It was therefore necessary to show that there are not merely isolated experiences which happen to occur at the same time and to have the same contents, but that there exist stretches of experience which are genuinely collective, as a function of which one grasps certain contents, which one imputes to this collective contexture of experience rather than to oneself as soon as they manifest themselves. Sociological consideration thus has two presuppositions: first, the capacity to see objective intellectual contents as functions of conditions of life and contextures of experience at all, and, second, the capacity to grasp certain functionalities expressly in relation to a communal stream as such and not only in relation to individual destinies and experiences.

11   The social structure of consciousness

The functionality of a spiritual formation in relation to a collective stream of experience was most easily comprehensible where an experience manifestly belonging to a group was, so to speak, immediately within reach, where the individual may be said to be forced, by the spatial and temporal simultaneity of experience among many, to comprehend a portion of the contexture of experience as not belonging exclusively to himself, and to experience the formation emanating from there (the collectively formulated decision, the party programme, etc.) in their functionality with regard to the psychic state of the group.

It is here that the individual has the original experience of how a collective 'position in life' or 'mood' transposes itself into a formation, and the prototypical sociological instruction (*soziologische Urerfahrung*) concerning the functionality of certain information with regard to collective experiences imposes itself. It is not psychic contagion or imitation (which must by no means be denied as psychic facts, as factors in the constitution of the mass), but the contexture of experience given collectively, and the collectively grasped situation, which forge masses into unity and make out of the isolated individual a microcosm which contains the social macrocosm. All theories which construe the mass as a multitude made up of atoms (whereby the unity or similarity among individual parts is supposed to arise from imitation, interaction, and the like) are only applicable in the explanation of mass demonstrations, popular assemblies, etc., and they break down as soon as what is wanted is an explanation of phenomena that extend in time or space beyond a transitory gathering. But man is a social being, no matter how isolated he may seem to be – even when he leaves a mass assembly, when he has nothing but objects before him ('The human being is in the most literal sense a *zoon politikon*, not merely a gregarious animal, but an animal which can individuate himself only in the midst of society': Marx[26])

How social determination can occur under such circumstances can only be explained if, even in the explanation of mass experience, we do not limit our consideration to psychic contagion proceeding from one individual to another, but already here put our emphasis upon the 'social structure of consciousness' as such. The task is to establish that by far the greatest part of the individual's contextures of experience (even when he appears isolated) proceeds along tracks which are characteristic for a group or an age as a whole. Even when the individual departs from the political assembly and experiences the latest constructs of external existence by himself, he experiences by far the greater part in a typical way, i.e., as continuation of the situations, constellations, problem sets, emotional attitudes which were also characteristic during collective experience. Once he has been directed along the track of an experiential contexture, it is only possible for experiences which are no more than *comparatively* new to present themselves. An age (or a social stratum within it) which is attuned to tragic experiences, and another, which is pointed towards relativistic conceptions of life and therefore deals with things so as to emphasize the experiences themselves, will gain fundamentally different impressions from circumstances of life which are externally very much alike. But the cohesiveness of a group constitutes itself precisely in the fact that the range of possible modes of apprehension and attitudes with regard to fortunes in prospect is, as it were, predetermined on the basis of collective contextures of experience in the past. Where the preceding contexture of experience has constituted itself collectively, only a comparatively small margin for deviations and differences of opinion is possible. The differences are relatively slight because, however far opinions may seem to diverge from one another, they still rest on the basis of a common experiential foundation, which is, after all, required to make disagreement possible at all. But if the actual consciousness of the individuals is shot through with experiential schemata which operate even when the group which belongs to these schemata is not physically present, the imputation of certain ideas to certain groups is in order under such circumstances as well. A functionality in relation to collective contextures of experience subsists even when the individual, to all appearances, acts only on his own volition, when he thinks of himself as acting on his own behalf and not as representative or member of a group. Individual transactions and creations will be group-conditioned to a considerable extent even when the group is not physically present.

If it is indeed the case that the seemingly isolated individual will always bear with him an encompassing stock of experience in his consciousness and that a large number of his dealings and spiritual objectifications will be connected with this originally social current of consciousness, this is not to say that the experiencing individual is always aware of this. Quite to the contrary, the naive, unreflecting individual will always be inclined to impute his spiritual objectifications to his own individual stream of experience, with regard to their functionality. The problem, whether experienced spiritual contents are to be imputed as function to individuality or to groups in the background, will only surface as problem when groups (e.g., as units of status, class, or race) confront one another and when,

74

with regard to the subject belonging to a different group, that which attaches to him by virtue of that group distinguishes itself from the accidentally individual. Cultural-sociological knowledge is closely linked, as noted earlier, with the coming into view of the social movement. In a half-reflected way, the social aspect of 'conducting oneself' is already present in consciousness of social rank, where it is a matter of the individual knowing that he must conduct and bear himself in a certain way, that he must think a certain way because this alone befits his rank. A relationship of functionality is already apprehended in this idea of suitability to rank, although it is not developed into sociological knowledge. Sociological knowledge of the functionality of spiritual formations has its source in this kind of learning from life (arising out of a struggle for social existence).

12 The relevance of cultural-sociological knowledge

What follows from all this, with regard to the distinctive character and relevance of cultural-sociological knowledge?

First, that it is only man as he has been socialized who is able to pursue, understand, and test cultural sociology. While natural-scientific knowledge presents itself so that, at least in principle, it abstracts from all anthropomorphic reference (hence its tendency to translate all quality into quantity), cultural sociology wants to involve man, not only as creaturely, corporeal being as such, but also as social subject, and it must do so. The socialized individual is knowing subject as well as subject matter of sociology.

It should be said that this refers only to the cognitive *sources* of cultural-sociological knowledge and not to its *presentation*. Presentation, showing, and proof must be carried on with conceptual means, as in other sciences; as far as access to cultural-sociological knowledge and the experiential foundations of this knowledge are concerned, however, it is not only the human individual but also the socialized individual who is more closely touched by reference to the social.

Second, it follows from the distinctive circumstance that socio-genetic consideration of cultural formations is actually a mere extension and consistent sustaining of an attitude which belongs to the 'everyday experience of life',[27] that it cannot and should not depart from this basis without the greatest care. Many who have been surprised and overwhelmed by the remarkable successes achieved in the natural sciences in consequence of Galileo's deed, are of the opinion that the cultural sciences, above all the social sciences, will also come to full flowering only when this same detachment from the attitudes of everyday life comes to predominate here as well.[28] This tendency has repeatedly led to the vain effort to graft the methods of the natural sciences on to the cultural sciences. Nothing has come of this except a positivist blindness with regard to the most obvious facts about things of the spirit: the attempt has been made to silence all the methods and approaches which everyday experience has so richly elaborated within the living life of culture. The natural sciences have indeed abandoned all parts of the attitude which everyday life has towards natural things, except for the technical attitude; but this is impossible with regard to cultural formations which are sought to be understood. What would become of cultural science if, for example, it attempted to break completely with the naively artistic attitude, for the sake of 'exactness'? But just as there is an original, not further reducible way of being attuned to the experience of art, which is the ultimate source of every 'exact' science of art, so there is an original way of being attuned to the social, and especially to the sociogenesis of spiritual formations, and this way is constantly in effect in the course of living. It must form a special problem for cultural sociology to investigate the phenomenon of what is called 'prescientific learning from experience', which is constantly being treated as a rudimentary form of knowledge, yet to develop into science.

Against this view, it is necessary to bring to attention and treat as a problem whether it might not be possible that only one of the capacities for creating knowledge possessed by the human spirit is invoked by natural-scientific knowledge and immanently carried to its final conclusion by it, but only in a certain direction, while the remaining capacities for knowledge lie fallow, indiscriminately intermingled in the womb of all knowledge, in the 'experience of everyday', not utilized on behalf of science. All the cognitive approaches to spiritual realities, which have developed themselves within pre-scientific knowledge, through the tasks set by everyday life, to a marvellous state of refinement, have been discredited by the unwarranted extension of natural-scientific method. Clearly indicative of this state of affairs is the current crisis in psychology. Natural-scientific psychology has not been able to satisfy with its methods the expectations which the humanistic sciences brought to it. It proved itself incompetent for the explanation and interpretation of higher psychic phenomena.

Abandoning the natural-scientific way, however, means treading the path of interpretative psychology, which, if it is not simply a return to the methods of pre-scientific learning from experience is at least a far-reaching openness to them. This turn came about because, among other things, it simply became too apparent that, while natural-scientific psychology kept on producing results which were at least irrelevant to the understanding of spiritual forma-tions, untutored psychology and characterology were able to grasp the most subtle connections between works and creators, between experiences and contents. What followed from this was no straight-forward return to pre-scientific learning from experience; it was rather the case that attention was directed to the fact that methods and sensibilities lay fallow within the attitudes of everyday, the util-ization and 'perfection' of which could take the place of precisely that which has come to be missing from the immanent development of science. Sociology has nothing to be ashamed of in its origin in and constant connectedness with the pre-scientific 'whole man', but should rather acknowledge both of these among its presup-positions.

In the *third* place, then, this pre-scientific origin of socio-genetic knowledge does not in any way signify an invitation to inexactness. That social man is a presupposition for socio-genetic knowledge does not signify the uncertainty of sociological knowledge any more than the circumstance that musical receptivity is a presuppo-sition for musical science renders this science uncertain: no relativi-zation of the validity of its theory inheres in this. Musical science is science by virtue of the fact that it renders musical experience in concepts and, where possible, ascertains lawfulness in music. But it does not imply any unverifiability of these cognitive findings that these propositions can be grasped and tested only by someone who has an 'ear' for the musical evidence. And it is only in this sense that the sociological attunement to functionality is required and permitted to be a pre-theoretical presupposition of sociological theory.

13 Immanent and genetic interpretations

Our description of the distinctive socio-genetic focus on the func-tionality of cultural formations will only be complete when we have compared it with other genetic approaches. Just as there are several kinds of immanent interpretation of cultural formations, so there are several kinds of genetic interpretation. In what follows we shall attempt to indicate the most important kinds of each by using the example of various possible interpretations of a philo-sophical system.

A philosophical system is grasped *immanently* when it is as far as possible seen in its own terms, in terms of its own doctrinal contents. This implies that one is able to interpret the tenets of the system for oneself or for the reader by developing every statement from the ultimate presuppositions and axioms of the system. Often the author has already done this himself, and the interpreter, usually guided by pedagogical considerations, merely rearranges the doctrine's parts and points of departure, and so regenerates the author's train of thought from a different standpoint.

A second kind of immanent interpretation draws certain consequences that are implicit in the author's doctrine and carries out his thought to its logical conclusion ('understanding Kant better than he understood himself').

A third kind of interpretation consists of understanding the author from the point of view of another system (cf. the various kinds of Plato interpretation by modern thinkers). While the doctrinal content of the system in its systematic totality is exceeded in this case, it nevertheless remains an immanent interpretation, inasmuch as the interpreter maintains a systematic standpoint and merely juxtaposes a different system to the one to be interpreted. All these kinds of interpretation must be regarded as immanent because they focus on the signified content and do not consider the genesis of this content.

Interpretation in terms of the history of ideas occupies an intermediate position between the immanent and genetic interpretations. It is genetic because it breaks through the self-contained unity of the finished work by following the historical development of the various intellectual motifs that enter into the system and unite themselves into it. But because it leaves the immanence of meaning of these motifs untouched, it must still be understood as an immanent interpretation. The history of ideas as it tends to be practised today is still in the chronicle stage,[29] since, in the final analysis, it simply follows the path of the intellectual motifs, and thus seeks neither to explain how individual motifs are anchored in broader cultural contexts nor tries to find the reason for changes in meaning in terms of larger totalities. Thus it merely describes the external fate, so to speak, of fragments of ideas. In art history, the history of styles corresponds to the history of ideas,[30] either as purely iconographic-historical study or as narrowly formal history of style.

A form of interpretation of meaning that goes deeper but remains on the borderline between genetic and immanent interpretation is interpretation of the genesis of meaning (*sinngenetische Interpretation*). This form of interpretation attempts to explain not the empirical emergence of the motifs contained in a system but rather their point of departure, by giving a purely typological list of the motifs possible (within the relevant sphere) and the immanently decisive grounds for the particular choice made. If one attempts to interpret a specific philosophical resolution of a problem by means of a general typology of possible solutions,[31] and thereby to determine the source and the logical place of the specific solution attempted, then one has given a genetic explanation which under certain circumstances may go deeper than a merely psychological or merely historical study of the motifs. But however genetic this kind of interpretation may be, in leaving behind the closed circle of the given system, it nevertheless remains immanent, like the previous one, in that it does not transcend the sphere of meaning as such. It may happen that the genesis of meaning will be quite different from the way in which the philosopher actually came to his specific solution; but what is known by such an interpretation is nevertheless a genesis in that the specific is comprehended in terms of its derivation from the structure of the philosophical sphere as a whole. The ancients were already familiar with this sort of genetic thinking, and in the most diverse forms it has sustained its own existence, from cosmogonies and mythologies to the transcendental deduction. This sort of interpretation is not limited to the theoretical sphere; in art history, for example, it is also possible to use historical material to set up disjunctions of problem solutions from the viewpoint of the genesis of meaning. Thus one can attempt to understand a doorway or a cupola in terms of the possible artistic solutions of what is in the last analysis a technical architectural problem, and to understand whereby the specific solution differs from other possible solutions.

At the opposite pole to interpretation which refers to genesis of meaning is purely causal explanation invoking psychological factors,[32] which must under no circumstances be confused with explanation referring to functionality. Explanation in terms of genesis through psychological causality is not actually concerned with explaining the signified contents of cultural formations of a work, but rather attempts through the methods of natural science to give a purely causal explanation of those mental processes whose product is the cultural formations before us. This form of interpretation includes, among others, Freudianism,[33] which tries to reconstruct the genesis of those experiences necessary for the creation of the work by substituting for the various cultural formations, as they present themselves in their immanent meaning, psychological complexes remote from such meanings and comprehensible in generalized terms, such as 'repression' and 'sublimation', and by explaining the former by means of the latter. This procedure is justifiable in itself; but it is not a method of interpretative understanding but rather a form of causal explanation, which may reach the natural process of experience but never the meaning itself.

Between causal-genetic explanation and pure meaning-genetic explanation are the two modes of understanding phenomena by reference to functionality: explicative (*verstehende*) individual-psychological interpretation and explicative social-psychological interpretation. The two are similar in that they grasp the cultural formation as 'result' (in the sense already explained), that is, having arrived at an immanent understanding of the meaning, they immediately give it up in order to bring out the stored-up functional relationship to the experiential whole.

Both modes of understanding recur to the subject behind the work: the individual-psychological interpretation to the creative individual, the social-psychological to the group subject of the experiential whole. They are similar in that they do not, as causal-genetic interpretation does, dissolve the meaning of the cultural objectifications into processes without meaning accessible to the methods of the natural sciences. These modes understand the meaning-contents in their meaningfulness as a fragment of the broader totalities called 'world-views'. In the one case it is a question of the world-view of an individual, in the other of the world-view of a group or historical period. The totality identified as a world-view is placed in a functional relationship to the corresponding experiential wholes, which can then be characterized not as devoid of meaning but as related to meaning. Individual psychology calls these experiential wholes which are related to meaning spiritual types;[34] sociology in contrast tries to conceive them as social group types.

14   The discrepancy between genetic and immanent interpretations

In this study we have approached our problem from two directions. First we tried to discern the distinctiveness of the sociological approach in its sociological concept-formation. Then we attempted to characterize the attitude of consciousness which underlies any socio-genetic approach to cultural formations. In the first approach we found that we can observe in sociological concept-formation a certain shift, a shift we may describe as 'bracketing the validity aspect'. The second approach revealed that the subject to be ascribed to the sociological perspective is placed in an attitude which is altogether different from that of the subject who experiences the cultural formation immanently, from the inside, an attitude which we described as oriented toward the functionality of the formations.

It is evident that our two approaches do not exist in a state of complete separation from each other, but that the first is somehow connected with the second. On closer examination one sees that the validity contents of the formations after bracketing – that is, the remainder that has been abstracted from the complex of meanings – is nothing but the relationship of functionality stored up in the entities. This we call the result. It is precisely the fact that the formation is a result, a stored-up experiential contexture which can always be evoked in the receptive subject, that makes it possible to examine it in terms of its functionality. It is the fact that the formation is also more than a stored-up experiential contexture, and precisely that by which it is more, that makes possible an approach directed at this balance. But this means at the same time that a genetic view can explain a formation only to the extent to which it is a result; namely, the result of a social-psychological experiential contexture.

The discrepancy between the genetic and the immanent approaches, between a focus on the result and a focus on the meaning-contents, is never so striking as when it is a question of a genetic, and especially a socio-genetic investigation of *thought* itself. It is evident that not only law, morals, forms of life, art, religion, etc. can be examined in their socio-genetic functionality, but that the process of thinking and knowing, as well as the structure of intellectual formations and the concrete intellectual contents of an age can be understood in terms of their socio-genetic functional relationship in several ways: as a function of broader psychic constellations, of the world-view of any particular individual, or as a function of the pursuit of economic and social power by groups. In both respects the most general forms of thought (such as abstraction, analysis, synthesis, etc.) as well as the concrete contents of thought (such as the idea of freedom, universality, etc.) are conceived as *results* of extra-theoretical constellations. But this genetic approach gives rise to a conflict for the thinker of these thoughts (whether or not he is aware of it), a conflict which can be explained precisely from this duality of attitudinal possibilities. Let us cite as an example the following thesis by Marx: 'The same men who establish their social relations in conformity with their material productivity, produce also principles, ideas and categories, in conformity with their social relations. Thus these ideas, these categories, are as little eternal as the relations they express. They are historical and transitory products.'[35]

If one takes a closer look at this proposition, one immediately

81

discovers in it the contradiction with which philosophy has always reproached relativism and pragmatism; namely, the contradiction between the contents of this proposition and its own character as a proposition, that is to say, with the propositional form. The proposition's contents proclaim the relativity of all knowledge, because knowledge is merely the 'product' of ever-changing environmental relations in its intellectual contents as well as in its categories. But the same proposition as a proposition appears to us nevertheless necessarily in apodictic form, that is, it makes a claim to truth and thus asserts the timeless validity of the idea it expresses and of the categories employed. It thereby involves itself in contradictions which clearly make it untenable.

Any sociology of cognition (*Soziologie der Erkenntnis*) will need to construct propositions of analogous structure. For even if one does not, as Marx does, always in the end derive ideological factors from the relations of production, every sociological investigation will nevertheless in some form attempt to derive theoretical configurations from extra-theoretical constellations. The circumstance leads to a contradiction, since the sociologist of cognition here finds himself maintaining a dual attitude toward the 'theory'. As a *sociologist* he is focused on the functionality of thought, and therefore gives a *non-immanent* consideration to the domain of theory. As *thinker* and theorist, however, in the capacities in which he advances his propositions, he attends to the immanent in the theoretical domain, he acknowledges the titles of validity that press upon him here, he is compelled to posit them himself.

But this duality of attitudes (which is the real basis of the paradox) does not lead to an ultimate contradiction. For, as we have seen, sociology can comprehend only as much of the formation to be interpreted as has gone into it in the form of a 'result'. What one arrives at in an immanent approach, the meaning-contents and their validity (that surplus of which we spoke) does not enter into the sociological view and thus can be neither confirmed nor doubted. This also means, however, that sociological or other genetic explanation can neither confirm nor refute the truth or falsity of a proposition or of the entire theoretical sphere. How something came to be, what functionality it may possess in other contexts, is entirely irrelevant to its immanent character of validity. This implies that it will never be possible to construct a sociological critique of knowledge or, as has recently been asserted, a *sociological critique of human reason*.[36] Conversely, it is completely impossible to refute the possibility and justification of socio-genetic study through logical objections (as, for example, by saying that it leads to self-contradictions). Logical insights and arguments cannot refute findings of specialized sciences. With reference to our example, this implies that only historical, sociological facts can establish or refute whether the categories through which we understand events change in time, and whether certain ideas are to be taken in conjunction with certain groups as true 'ideologies' of the latter; i.e., as their function. The seeming contradiction between the views of sociology as specialized science and logic as foundational science can be traced to the fact that the views rest upon altogether different objects: the one on the genuine 'result' and the other on the markedly distinct immanent meaning. We do not need to concern ourselves here with the question whether an epistemological problem results from the nature of the relationship between a specialized and foundational science or whether and which of the two can more adequately grasp the integral phenomenon. We selected this particular example only because the situation which has formed the basis of this entire inquiry can be seen most clearly in the 'personal union' present in the sociologist of thought. In this instance it is possible to see once again the distinction between immanent and genetic attitudes, between result and doctrinal contents. These differences, easily overlooked in a cursory view, become so obvious in the case of the sociologist of thought because the thinker's personal union between the two types of science brings the two attitudes into direct contact with each other. The sociologist of art or of religion also regards the formations under consideration as functions and not immanently; he does not acknowledge the titles to validity which are prescriptive for an immanent attitude. But since here the object belongs not to the theoretical sphere itself but to an extra-theoretical one, he avoids the contradiction we have just described. It will, however, always be repugnant to the feelings of the religious and the ethical person to take part in such investigations, which, as he rightly senses, bring with them a relativization of his commitments. This is the sociological reason why the sociology of cultural formations can arise only in an age in which the immanent attitude of 'belief' has already become unstable and thus permits this non-immanent approach.

We have followed the possibility of a socio-genetic approach to cultural phenomena to its final source and have seen that it arises from the possibility of a dual attitude toward cultural contents, and that this duality of attitude corresponds to a dual stratification in the structure of the cultural contents: on the one hand the functionality stored in it; on the other, the objective meaning-content. If they were nothing but *meaning*, one could only *comprehend* them. That is, a work of art as well as an intellectual construct would present itself to us only as something comprehensible, like numbers or signs: one understands what they mean but they leave one 'cold', one cannot go along with them. But that all these formations can also be *experienced* means that, in addition to their meaning, the experiential contexture from which they arose is more or less given along with them. If they were nothing but experiential contexture, nothing but result (if this is at all conceivable), then the experience of them would just be a sympathetic vibration without tangible content, without objectivity. Something like this does happen when, in a shared experience, we are able to take part in vague nuances of feeling, which are alive but not yet expressible; and we do this without mediation, simply through the rhythm of the shared experience. But just as these shared experiences of a happy moment disappear immediately after the experience dissipates, leaving us with nothing more than the vague recollection that we experienced something in common, so this relationship of functionality would disappear if there were no objective contents to sustain it, nothing to bear its form.

But just as a creative mind can succeed in transforming experiential contents into a work and thus preserve the experiential contexture once and for all in a form in which it is accessible to all, so, once fixed in the form of ideas and meanings, those experiential contextures and functionalities which the interpretative psychologist or sociologist can extract out of the work become available in a form subject to examination together with the meaning-contents. What is miraculous about every cultural·objectification is that while it is beyond experience, it is at the same time experiential, and it is this which makes possible the many kinds of both immanent and genetic approaches.[37]

3 The inner construction of cultural-sociological knowledge

1 Intuition and logical structure

Thus far we have focused on the intuitive component of cultural-sociological experience. As with any cultural science, however, intuition is only one of the preconditions of scientific knowledge in this case. It is a *conditio sine qua non*: only intuition grants us access to the phenomenon. Intuition itself, however, is not yet a scientific achievement. Until now we have emphasized the involvement of intuition in even the most objective formulation; that is, we have shown that the final test of every assertion of cultural sociology consists in 'seeing' the underlying phenomenon and that orientation toward socio-genetic functionality presupposes an intuition of a quite specific kind. It is now our task to show that, on the other hand, the whole theoretical apparatus, which is only brought to full development in a consistently scientific formulation, can already be found in the most primitive 'pre-scientific' formulation of a socio-genetic experience.

The scientist or logician is inclined to forget that his conceptual objectifications can find fullness and fulfilment only in object-giving intuition. We are just as easily inclined to obscure the fact that, no matter how primitive the formulation of a state of affairs, in formulating it we have already dissolved intuition into theoretical elements. The reason why we so easily tend to overlook the theoretical elements contained in pre-scientific experience is that once they have become familiar to us they are employed unreflectively, as though they were completely spontaneous. Our ability to perceive the style of a picture, the intellectual 'tendency' of a train of thought, the Protestant or Catholic quality of a mode of behaviour and life form, the urban or provincial element of conduct, etc.

demonstrates that we readily abandon an exclusively immanent orientation to cultural contents and come directly to discover their relation of functionality to a configuration of socially shared experience. The essential features of sociological 'method' have already been employed in all of these examples of simple, everyday sociological experience. The validity claim of the experience has been bracketed, and orientation to the immanent meaning structure has been abandoned. We must not shy away from the labour of an analysis that attempts to make out the theoretical design of the structure simply because it can show us nothing more than how secondary and even tertiary the relationship between science and the underlying phenomenon may be. And precisely because we want to champion the primacy of object-giving intuition, we must reconcile ourselves to this theoretical, analytical reflection. True methodology is the desperate determination to break through the concepts to the phenomena. A concrete analysis of the concept of style may bring us closer to this.

2 The sociological concept of style

'Style' is at once an aesthetic and a sociological category.[38] Here the same term is employed for two quite different experiences. In the first instance the word derives from the kind of art history which is oriented towards aesthetics. It corresponds to an immanent attitude towards works of art. Here 'style' designates a formal, compositional component which appears repeatedly in many works of the same tendency. In a purely immanent approach to the works of the Gothic period we can grasp the Gothic principles of composition and describe their development. In this instance the term has, in addition, a normative secondary meaning. It contains a principle of selection through which irrelevant characteristics are distinguished from relevant ones; at the same time it is teleological and orients perception. Although it is not an aesthetic principle beyond time, it is nevertheless just as normative within a period as the very concept of aesthetic form itself. But the *sociological-functional use* (involving a 'shift' in the concept) plays a part in even the aesthetic and art-historical conception and application of the concept of style, no matter how rigorously the latter is formulated. We can, of course, begin by classifying formal features appearing in particular works (such as ogives, etc.) and then make these shared characteristics the foundation of a concept of style. We shall soon notice, however, that this classification departs from the level of immanence. We encounter works which do not exhibit any of the external identifying features, or do so only in part, and which nevertheless reveal, as is commonly said, the 'Gothic spirit'. In this case we can see that the functional mode of viewing is already present in the purely aesthetic and art-historical one. Together with the common objective identifying features, we are already bringing into view the relationship of being a function of an experiential contexture of a particular kind. The purely formal characterization of the Gothic style is gradually transposed into the 'Gothic principle' which stands behind it. We recur to that typical contexture of experience whose 'consequence' it is that entire generations could be creative while sharing, as far as form goes, a common definition of visual and representational problems. We should like to call this form of extending the concept's contents, which enriches it not with new characteristics but with the relation of functionality that lies behind these characteristics, a transcendence of the conceptual contents. In other words, where a concept that first constitutes itself as relating to form abandons the level of these formal relationships and signifies the underlying functional relation, we are confronted with a transcendence of the conceptual contents.

Now we have reached a point where we are ready to answer a question that we were at the outset not even in a position to ask. For it should have become obvious that, although we have frequently spoken of an experiential contexture, there has been no specific account of such contexture. Is it at all possible, we ask, to conceptualize and classify experiential contextures? This is a problem that is just as relevant to the foundation of a humanistic psychology, whether it takes the form of individual or social psychology. It is not enough for us to be able to bring certain experiential contextures to mind within ourselves and to become aware of them; it is also necessary to designate them somehow by concepts. But it is known that we have no concepts for inner states and constellations of experience, or that we have at most insufficiently differentiated ones. An experiential contexture can only be characterized by reference to formations produced as results from within. That which pertains to the soul can only be comprehended by means of the spiritual.[39] But there is nothing wrong with our procedure if our naming of the spiritual formation simultaneously designates the experiential contexture pertaining to it, so long as the relevant experiential contexture does actually present itself together with the formation and at the same time, and as long as we clearly distinguish whether the concept is meant to indicate the formation or the pertinent experiential contexture. The same situation arises in the elementary sphere of such phenomena as odours, where due to the lack of suitable expressive possibilites the designation of an olfactory perception is replaced by the designation of the objective cause of the perception (e.g., scent of violets). That it is at all possible to grasp the functionality-factor unequivocally by way of the objective meaning-contents is guaranteed by the facts that the formation is result as well as meaning and that, in so far as the formation is understood, the understanding of its meaning goes together with the corresponding understanding of its character as result. Anyone who adequately takes in an Impressionist work of art as Impressionist has not only recognized the objectively comprehensible Impressionist 'principles of style' but, in keeping with the ambiguity of the word 'Impressionism', has also comprehended the characteristic experiential contexture that lies behind it. In this way he possesses within himself an intuitive test for statements that refer to the structure and distinctive properties of this experience. All functional-genetic interpretation will have to refer back to this point. In order to grasp the functionality of the work with reference to experience, it is necessary to reach back into the structure of the Impressionistic contexture of experience.

Whenever cultural formations and the experiential contextures pertaining to them are designated as belonging to a style, they are comprehended socio-genetically rather than individual-genetically. To comprehend a contexture of form and the corresponding experiential contexture as 'style' is as much as to impute the relevant aspects of the work and the corresponding experiential structures not to the creative individual but to the corresponding group experience. 'Style' is a phenomenon which indicates that certain levels of meaning can be carried forward within works of art. It is only because the pertinent experiential contextures are communal that, in this respect, growth, learning and successive development take place among different individuals. As the example shows, the attitude defining what things are visible must be taken as included in the experiential contexture. An individual work can never be wholly apportioned to its style. It always contains a surplus that must be put to the account of the individual. The deep level to which style can reach marks the common basis which is only made possible by the common experiencing of certain domains within a given age. Style thus designates the predominantly social element in the art object and in the experiential contexture belonging to it.

3 The sociological level of concepts

This detailed analysis of the concept of style demonstrates that an immanent attitude toward an art object automatically turns into a socio-genetic one and that the originally immanent 'aesthetic' concept of style transforms itself into a genetic concept. It no longer designates the work itself but only so much of it as is the result of the communal experiential contexture stored up in it. It is worth while to come down to such conceptual analyses in order to see that a different attitude and a different mode of comprehension assert themselves behind a gradual conceptual shift: the second concept of style is no longer aesthetic, no longer one which grasps the immanence of a work, but one which recurs to functionality.

In the second usage of the concept of style, a socio-genetic experience of the art object is already suggested. We must now emphasize, however, that this is the *loosest formulation of the socio-genetic explanation of culture*. We have already termed 'sociological' an explanation of the cultural object that does nothing more than trace the works to the experiential contexture which stands 'behind' them. An explanation is *sociological in the narrower and more precise sense* only if it is also able to work out a distinctly social characterization of the experiential contexture: thus, for example, when one speaks of Impressionism as a self-dissolution of late bourgeois individualism, of classicism as the style of the rising bourgeoisie, of primitive Christianity as the religiosity of artisans. Only when the sociological conceptual level is brought into play is the complex which has already been withdrawn from immanent consideration made into a genuinely sociological experience. It cannot be our task here to demonstrate the availability of such a distinctly sociological conceptual level by working out all its elements. This would belong in the scope of a systematic sociology, which is available, in a certain sense and in part in Max Weber's treatments.[40] Its most essential part would comprise the elaboration of the types of communalization and association; it would consist, in Max Weber's words, of a determination of 'the general structures of human groups'.[41] Whether these structural forms can be comprehended apart from the contents which serve as community-building factors is a secondary question. It is quite evident that such contents as sexuality, child-rearing, economy, politics, religion – in short, the spiritual as well as natural substrata – influence the 'structural forms of sociation' and must be taken into consideration as substrata. But something novel emerges, in comparison to knowledge of contents alone, precisely in establishing the similarities as well as the differences among the bondings and distancings among men, which come into being by virtue of the diverse contents. It is accordingly not an effective objection to the autonomy of the sociological conceptual level if emphasis is put on a secondary consideration; i.e., if it is asserted that, from a logical point of view, this level can be comprehended only *after* the elaboration of the substantive spheres, such as economy, law, religion, ethics, etc.[42] The relevant question must be whether something new is comprehended at the sociological level. In such concepts as household, clan, sect, etc. we comprehend structural forms of association which, although oriented to contents, nevertheless characterize not these contents but rather the various modes of multi-personal association and activity. If we examine some examples of such structural forms of associative and communal relationships (such as sect, clan, artisans, rising bourgeoisie, medieval feudality, etc.) we shall find two types among them: those which exhibit universal constituents and those which exhibit historical ones. Accordingly cultural sociology arrives at either general or historical-sociological conclusions. While it is the task of sociology as the study of society to elaborate all of these types conceptually and historically, the achievement of cultural sociology consists in bringing the conceptual level so constituted to bear on cultural formations.

The difficulty of our enterprise consists precisely in such application of these concepts. This difficulty appears whenever one attempts to grasp one conceptual level from another. Here, where cognitive understanding attempts to reconstruct the 'undivided unity' of pre-theoretical reality by means of its own conceptual levels, we find ourselves in the paradoxical situation of not being able to put together again what we have broken apart. Similar difficulties occur in attempts to explain the vital in terms of the mechanical, the psychological in terms of the physiological, or the logical in terms of the psychological. How are we to bring together, to 'place in relation' to one another, two worlds which in principle cannot touch: spiritual formations which transcend experience, on the one side, and economic and social reality with its various forms of human aggregation on the other? These two levels are indeed so deeply separated that they could not be related to one another in this way. They must either be somehow brought to bear on one another, or an intermediate level connecting the two must be inserted. As we have seen, an approach has already been made from the cultural side. In place of cultural formations bespeaking validity stands the experiential contexture corresponding to them. And in fact it is the world of the psyche that makes the connection between meaning and 'social reality'. Humanistic psychology bridges the separation between the validity-sphere of cultural formations and the forms of sociation. Thus, the question remaining is how the sociological forms can be raised to the psychological level. Upon closer examination, however, we observe that with most sociological terms, as with the concept of 'style', this shift takes place by itself, without a redefinition of the word. In speaking of the condition of being 'bourgeois', we have come to mean more than the role of a class in the process of producing and distributing the social product. We mean experiential contextures following from this position, whose economic, social, and historical attributes can be more precisely stated. The social categories mentioned above do not denote human groups or concrete individuals but, in the same way, experiential contextures which can be correlated with the 'social relations' indicated by the relevant term. Here, too, it is a matter of starting out from certain objectively comprehensible forms of human association in order to approximate the experiential contextures lying behind them. Uniting two such initially disparate concepts as the conditions of being bourgeois and classicism means that the experiential contexture comprehended once by way of the work can also be circumscribed and comprehended from another side.

4   The concept of world-view

It is humanistic psychology which constructs a world intermediate between the social and spiritual levels, initially so disparate. Psychology creates a common denominator to which we must reduce factors so different as are the social and the spiritual, if we are, in any way, to understand one in terms of the other. The factor which it inserts between these two extreme poles is 'world-view' (*Weltanschauung*).[43]

A world-view (of an era, a group, etc.) is a structurally linked set of experiential contextures which makes up the common footing upon which a multiplicity of individuals together learn from life and enter into it. A world-view is then neither the totality of spiritual formations present in an age nor the sum of individuals then present, but the totality of the structurally interconnected experiential sets which can be derived from either side, from the spiritual creations or from the social group formations.

What is presupposed here throughout is that fundamental experiences and attitudes do not emerge in the substratum of individuals' lives in isolation, but that individuals who are classed together in the same group share a basic stock of experiential contents. A further presupposition is that individual segments of experience are not to be found in isolation alongside one another within these basic forms, but rather that they possess an internal coherence and thereby constitute what may be called a 'life-system'. Since, as noted, this basic form can never be directly described but can only be identified by reference to either the group formation marked by it or the cultural creations pertaining to it, such an expression as 'Christianity as the religiosity of artisans' indicates two aspects of a single life system – as seen from the side of the religion established at the time and then from the side of vocation as social form.

A world-view, then, is by no means a quantity which can be known in itself and on its own, but rather something which can only be formulated in particular cross-sections, so to speak, referring to particular problems. It becomes a theoretical object when it is investigated in relation to particular problems, and this obviously involves a distancing from the underlying experiential foundation. In and of itself this distancing is nothing unusual. For, as we saw above, the objective contents of culture also are grasped theoretically only by means of distancing. The formulation of a 'social relation' is also an abstraction, which only comprehends a portion of its elements, when compared to the relationship as it exists in itself. What distinguishes a world-view (as a 'system' of mutually coherent experiences), however, is that it can be comprehended from any of a variety of the most diverse spheres of objectification and from the problems connected with these spheres. The very same world-view of a given era can be grasped by means of its art, religion, mores, education, politics, economic structure, etc., and it shows us a different aspect, depending on the direction from which we approach it. In this we naturally 'feel' the underlying identicalness of the experiential foundation. We notice that the same 'spirit' expresses itself in these differing cultural objectifications. But the scientist cannot be satisfied with this feeling. His task is to explicate this identicalness to show how the different 'aspects of the same phenomenon' belong together. Since science never deals with the underlying foundation in all its irrationality, but only with the aspects which relate to the various objectifications and the undertakings peculiar to each, the real conceptual work of the sociologist takes shape with the aim of linking these undertakings with one another – but always with the underlying phenomenon in mind, because nothing else can provide the ultimate basis able to test whether his linkages are arbitrary.

If, for example, the sociologist of culture wants to demonstrate that naturalism as a style of drama is an 'efflorescence' of bourgeois individualism, he must first reduce the phenomenon (naturalistic dramatic style) to the problems it undertakes to solve, and then show what sorts of experiential contextures, world-views, are presupposed by this form. On the other hand he must discern, within the historical and social situation of the bourgeoisie, the set of problems to which a world-view, as a coherent system of experiential forms, can be imputed. The imputation of some of the simplest life forms to corresponding social forms is so obvious that it needs no special demonstration. If one asserts that the social forms of the household are the basis for 'loyalty' and 'authority'[44] as experiential forms and that the kin group is the bearer of 'fealty',[45] one is dealing with ultimate correlations that cannot be further analysed. That a 'continuous and intensive social action' like that prescribed to the household by the 'outer structure' of its shared experience draws out, as psychological factor, an authoritative deference for the stronger and more experienced seems so self-evident that it is not thought necessary to subject this relationship to further analysis. At this point the intuitive attitude towards relationships of functionality comes into play. In and of itself, continuous and intensive communal life and action need not warrant authority. Authority contains a qualitatively distinct surplus content, and it is just this which distinguishes external situation from internal psychic elaboration. And yet we 'understand' that these internal and external states belong together, because we can not only attend immanently to the signified contents of 'authority' (knowing what sort of inner and outer demeanour the word signifies) but also grasp it as a 'result'; that is, decipher its functionality within a larger context.

The analysis of such a simple state of affairs serves to show that every socio-genetic investigation ultimately ends in intuitive 'self-evident judgments'. But here it is necessary to point out that while all theoretical work finds its ultimate limit in intuition, it must nevertheless work its way back to these most simple plausibilities. For example, the main flaw of Hausenstein's works[46] is that they misuse the fact that every sociological interpretation must appeal to elements which are ultimately intuitive, inasmuch as they aphoristically list simple correspondences between social situation and artistic style. What is omitted is a showing that the same experiential structure expresses itself in the style and in the social grouping, or, as it may be, in the spirit appropriate to each. That we not only achieve spiritual mastery over spiritual objectifications and social formations but, in fact, have intuitively present before us the life-system to which they are to be imputed cannot be better proved than by the possibility of advancing so far, through precise analysis, as to be able to exhibit verifiably the structural interconnections between the experiential contextures apprehended from the two sides. The impressive rigour of Max Weber's investigations, especially *The Protestant Ethic and the Spirit of Capitalism,* consists in pointing out, step by step, how the very same bearing towards life (or a component of it) that characterizes Protestant religiosity (inner-worldly asceticism) is connected with the spirit of emergent capitalism. In this example as in others, a component feature is crystallized out of the religious objective formation or its ethic and the experiential contexture behind it, is designated by the expression 'other-worldly asceticism', and is displayed; whereupon, starting out from the economic structure, the same experiential contexture is apprehended within its spirit.[47] The theoretical task of the sociologist, in short, consists of attempting a structural penetration of this sphere of experiential contextures, which at first appears to preclude theoretical formulation. Analysis specifically characteristic of cultural sociology is thus not analysis of cultural phenomena or social formations, but rather analysis of the structure of the various world-views in terms of the experiential contextures which may coherently appear together in them. The analysis of cultural phenomena merely serves to comprehend the underlying social experiential contexture, and only so much of the cultural phenomenon is considered as is function of a life context. Sociological analysis of relevant societal forms is also pursued only until certain experiential contextures can be shown to belong to them. This bilateral relation to a unified life-system is precisely what we must understand by the puzzling phrase that particular social situations 'translate' themselves into ideologies.

5 The types of sociological analysis of cultural phenomena

This level of analysis having been reached, it becomes possible to classify in its terms several of the types of cultural-sociological investigation which we can now survey. The lines of investigation which characterize Dilthey's theoretical writings as well as his more specific works on intellectual history can be taken as following *sociological* directions, although only in the broadest sense of that term. Although Dilthey was an opponent of sociology,[48] this opposition can only be related to the sociology with which he was familiar (Condorcet, Saint-Simon, and Spencer). His programme of understanding individual formations by beginning with a collective consciousness, a world-view, falls beyond history or intellectual history in the narrower sense. When individual facts are not explained by other individual facts, or individual sets of events by other individual sets of events, but by some underlying totality which may be called world-view, among other things, it is no longer the history of events that is being written but the sociological-genetic interpretation of meaning.

From this follows a definition of descriptive history that serves to distinguish it from the philosophy of history as well as from sociology. It belongs to the proper order and regulation of such history that it proceeds within the causal nexus of individual events and, wherever possible, traces every occurrence back to immediately operative causes. History deals with individuals and unique entities, whether historical personalities or collective forms.[49] It attempts to discover the lines along which causal connections run: where it is possible to confirm the effects of one individual or work on another. Its processes occur in historical time, which is like a graduator establishing individual segments of causal connections. In contrast, sociology and the philosophy of history share a concept of time characteristic of the latter, an hierarchical one in which a 'before' and 'after' are defined by the height of development attained by an experiential or formative principle. For both the philosophy of history and sociology, 'early Gothic' and 'late Gothic' do not denote a chronological point of origin but rather the developmental stage of an experiential contexture as well as a formative principle that goes with it. Historiography does not become sociological just because it operates with masses. To use a particular action or reaction of human masses, of a nation or class at a given moment, to explain subsequent events is just as much explanation in terms of events as if a specifically nameable, historical individual or personality had been invoked. When this insight, originally coined for political history, is applied to intellectual history, it means that the historiography which is intellectual history in the strict sense (literary history, history of art, etc.) extends only to observing individual sequences of influence and not to explaining things in terms of totalities. The fact, clearly apparent on this occasion, that cultural history tends much more readily to turn into history which is sociological in our sense (i.e., a history explaining in terms of totalities) indicates that it seems to be inherent in spiritual objectifications (in contrast to merely 'political' events) that a socio-genetic approach is better adapted to them than an historical approach linking things in the manner of sequential events. History looks for *causes,* while the approach by way of world-views looks for the *conditions* which make it possible for causes to operate. History works out individual segments; the fundamental category of socio-genetic investigation is 'the constellation'.

When Dilthey explains individual cultural formations ultimately in terms of world-view, we regard this as already a socio-genetic explanation of culture in the broadest sense of the term. It is not sociological in the narrower sense because, in recurring to the totality of the world-view in which the work is anchored, this mode of explanation stops at this totality and does not attempt, as do the approaches still to be mentioned, to relate it to the sociological conceptual level.

The following explanations of cultural forms, which are sociological in the narrower sense, are united in that they not only recur to the totality of a world-view but also consider the sociological conceptual level.[50] Despite this agreement (which expresses similarity in posing the problem for investigation), these explanations can be distinguished according to two criteria of classification, corresponding to differences in the principles governing their solution to these problems: the first classification results from asking about the categories which connect the three levels; the second principle of classification, from asking where they put the most weight, what they identify as primary cause.

Several possibilities can deal with the first of these questions: the category of causality, or the relationship of whole-and-its-parts, functions, or correspondence. Causality is applied either if the social or the cultural is taken as primary cause. Marxism illustrates the first case. Max Weber is an example of either the second or, perhaps, both the first and second, because he wants it to be decided in each individual instance whether the social or the cultural brings the other about. He discerns a pervasive interaction between the two spheres. Sometimes it is, for example, religion which works upon the origins of a socio-economic structure; at other times the socio-economic structure works upon the shaping of a particular religiosity.

Concerning Marxism, it is worth noting that it puts the economic in place of the social in the more general sense, and that it treats the economic as a causal factor, whenever it is a matter of explaining particular segments within historiography. In the passages concerned with philosophy of history, however, Marx works rather with the categories of function. Ideology is then the function of a stage in the development of the process of production. The one-sidedness of Marxism consists in the fact that economic-social forms push aside all other forms of social aggregation, even though it is not at all clear why other socializing factors cannot be co-ordinated with ideologies. The fact of having to function economically is undoubtedly one of the most powerful socializing factors, if for no other reason than that it gives rise to a continuous, persistent, compulsory association among human beings. But it is also the case that this association lies too far from the inner centre of experience to account satisfactorily for the more sublime manifestations of the experiential contextures which are nevertheless shared. It always remains the more or less peripheral limiting framework of world-view systems. If only socio-economically oriented concepts are to be taken as being at the level of social concepts, it is necessary to suppress or neglect a great many experiential contextures, which are nevertheless socially conditioned. The sociologist of culture has one hand tied behind him if he is bound, in his explanations, to trace all cultural formations back to economic causes.

The categories of the whole and the part and of correspondence are being employed when one sees neither the cultural phenomena nor the social but rather the world-view as the ultimate self-developing factor, and when one regards the forms of sociation as well as cultural formations as nothing more than emanations of the same 'substance'. The categories of correspondence and of the whole and the part then signify an ultimate anchoring of the forms of sociation and the forms of culture within the totality that exists through them and in them.

Whichever of the solutions may be attempted, this choice is a secondary matter compared to the homogeneity in posing the fundamental problem, according to which, in all these theories, cultural formations are to be comprehended socio-genetically, i.e., by reference to a totality transcending them.

The concept of world-view made possible a classification of sociologies of culture. But it should be noted that this is not, in our opinion, the most fundamental one, because the point of view from which it faces the various types derives from the categories of possible lines of solution. In our judgment, however, a classification and typical representation of a science only gets to fundamentals when it rests, where possible, upon examination of the total structure of the conceptualized disciplines.[51] Since cultural sociology involves a sociological approach to cultural formations, we must first ask ourselves what types of sociology we can distinguish at all. It is to be expected that cultural sociology will also order itself in the same way, up to a point; i.e., as far as it is concerned with sociology.

Accordingly, we will offer a classification of the ways open to sociology as such before the fundamental classification of cultural sociology.

4 Varieties of sociology

1 Origins of sociology

Glancing back over the diverse ways and means by which sociology has been conducted since its not so distant beginnings gives an impression of motley and unbounded variety and leads to over-hasty doubt that this is a science at all, a science commanding its own distinctive subject matter and investigative method. Looked at more closely, however, the diverse attempts arrange themselves, at least for the most part, into familial groups which can be considered *types of sociology*; that is, they can be considered as implementations of a total plan according to which each group seeks to effect something for which there is no place in the clearly demarcated spheres of the others. We want to try to show that the variety of sociologies did not arise in the course of development in order to displace and destroy one another, but rather that the historical dynamic of thought has here produced, step by step, in temporal sequence the types required to balance one another within a systematic total plan.

Because bearings are taken from the development of the exact natural sciences, it has become customary to consider scientific development as *linear*, and to take it for granted that an earlier phase in a science will be fundamentally superseded by its successor. Where the knowledge of an object may be said to be only loosely connected with the knowing subject's world-view and completely independent of the knowing subject's location in the design comprehended by the philosophy of history, it is possible to accumulate knowledge and discover truths about an object that is at least relatively atemporal (such as nature) without reference to the historical background of the knowing subject. Natural-scientific knowledge is tied to its own history only in so far as later knowledge may be said to presuppose all prior scientific results as necessary premises. Knowledge having to do with historical-cultural reality, in contrast, is connected so closely in its structure to the spiritual standpoint from which it is attained that, for all these sciences, the course and structure of development are altogether different from those of the others. We can observe this lack of linearity in the history of philosophy, where we should speak of a continual rebirth rather than of a linear continuity in the results of this discipline. If we do not want to confine ourselves to the history of philosophy, we find that the histories of art and of literature similarly display a structure of development which we can describe as a continual reconstitution of these sciences. The newly surfacing accumulations of experience and new points of view, derived from the new pivot in the world-view of the observer of history at any given time, bring into prominence new accumulations of subject matter as well as new aspects of subject matter previously observed. In this process, the results of earlier research do not become completely obsolete and older methods, too, are preserved as possible points of view. In this manner, new currents among world-views and in that which is comprehended by the history of ideas form a constitutive factor in the results of the science, as it continues to develop. Just as the modern development of art provided new points of view for considering the historical past of art and was thus fruitful for art history, so it may well be that new ideational and methodological currents offer new entryways into historical reality for the more general forms of historical study as well. The resulting investigations then set themselves off from the original science almost as independent sciences. At least this can be asserted for the development which interests us, that of sociology, which first set itself off from the philosophy of history by applying the natural-scientific, positivist method to the same problems which the latter had treated. But while sociology gave itself form as a positivist philosophy of history, the metaphysical tendency in philosophy of history survived and continued to shape its methods in an immanent development. Thus they co-exist, working up the same substratum from diverse points of view. New spiritual currents, however, which, with the resurgence of Kantianism and then phenomenology, posed the problems of the *a priori* for all disciplines, seemed to construct a new science on the old set of problems. But while pure sociology also attempts to displace the positivist sociology that aims at historical laws,[52] the latter continues in existence as a discipline with its own ongoing immanent development, as does the sociology distinguished by philosophy of history, which was mentioned above. Different spiritual

99

currents thus brought into being different aspects and partial disciplines of the same science. We have now named the three essential tendencies in sociology: philosophy-of-history oriented sociology, which seeks an historical dynamic; general sociology, which seeks general laws and regularities; and pure sociology, which investigates the fundamental forms of the social.

2   The basic phenomenon of the social

All three disciplines have the same fundamental theme, the study of one fundamental phenomenon, that of the social. The many-sidedness of this phenomenon, which appears both in simultaneity and in succession, permits both *static* and *dynamic* as well as *generalizing* and *individualizing* consideration.[53] The very fact that a consideration of the social in its simultaneity only allows investigation of general regularities among these simultaneities, and that this fails to exhaust the historicity of the social and its historical specificity, necessitates an historical individualizing approach as well. That is why both a general and generalizing tendency and a historical or philosophy-of-history tendency, taken up with the individual sequence of happenings, have their determinate place.

The fundamental theme of all these disciplines is, as mentioned, the social; it is a 'dependent object' (in the sense of the phenomenological theory of objects), as colour is a dependent object in relation to surface, or surface in relation to colour. Neither is possible without the other, and yet each is the possible object of a self-contained investigation. The social is similarly an object of many-sided investigation, without its being necessary to consider the substratum of 'multi-personality'[54] in its circumstantial concreteness. What is distinctive is that the social has content beyond multi-personality. While multi-personality is a precondition for the social to emerge, it does not itself contain the social, first, because the mere existence (even the spatial and temporal co-existence) of individuals does not invariably indicate society. Furthermore, not every gathering of the same aggregation of persons takes the same social form. The social is thus something new in relation to the substratum and cannot be deduced without an unwarranted leap from particular qualities and quantities of the individuals.[55] Moreover, the form of the social which happens to exist does not affect the entire compass of the consciousness and physical existence of the aggregate of individuals serving as substratum.[56] Every individual, while sustaining the distinctive social form, is subject to its domain only in part of his consciousness, and certain spheres of consciousness are in principle unaffectable by the social. And mere interaction among individuals does not exhaust the meaning of the social, either, because merely adding the effects of individual group members on one another and the effects of an individual (e.g., of a leader or of a traitor) on the group and, inversely, of the group on the individual do not yield the social form of the specific 'being there' of the group.

Furthermore, the social form is not limited and, in particular, not determined by the multi-personality that supports it at a certain time, for, quite apart from the fact that the individuals can change within time, the form that socializes them has living within it all of the past that has worked toward its crystallization. Accordingly, the social also stands out from its bearers by virtue of its historical character. Only certain group forms can exist at a particular time; and this circumstance is due not so much to the character of the individuals who play a part in them, as it is to the dynamic to which the form in question has been subjected by virtue of its interconnections with the historical change of other social forms.

All this circumscription served merely to indicate that the distinguishing characteristics of the social as a dependent object can be described from several sides. As we shall see, it depends on the level of generality of abstraction, whether the social is viewed in its historical-individual or in its general quality.

3 The problems of pure sociology

Although developmentally the last to emerge,[57] pure sociology is systematically the first, because its constitutive questions about the social have logical priority. Simmel and Tönnies can be considered the founders of pure sociology in Germany; its foremost representatives may be said to be Vierkandt, Leopold von Wiese, and, as we shall see, the representatives of the phenomenological school, in so far as they move toward sociology. There is not even agreement about its name: sometimes it is called pure sociology, sometimes formal sociology, and sometimes general sociology.[58] This diversity of labelling tellingly expresses the central preoccupation as well as the inner confusion which prevail in contemporary thought, where the signs of diverse philosophical standpoints can be traced right into the specialized sciences themselves. A sociology may be called 'pure' only if its method is clearly specified as *a priori* and non-empirical; it can be called 'general', in contrast, only if it is an inductive science about facts; and 'formal' only if it can be established without ambiguity that, putting aside all particular contents, it is the 'forms' of sociation that are to be sought.

Despite all differences in detail, the essential design unifying this

101

orientation can be reduced to a common formula. The most varied forms of human sociation have been brought to light by historical research into the past and by ethnographic and related research into the present. Human beings have lived together, so far as history and exploration extend, everywhere and always. 'Together' has never been the same. It is not only that human groups separated by space and time differ in the forms of their aggregations, but also that the members of one and the same human group constantly enter into new relationships. Some of these persist for a long time, while others are dissolved time and again to make way for new linkages. But it may be asked whether there is not to be found a unity within this multiplicity, an identity within this variety. Could not temporal and spatial differences be so far stripped away as to permit discovery of the inner kernel of human sociation, which always remains the same? Could not archetypes be revealed which first provide the principle underlying the multiplicity? In pure sociology, we meet a tendency of thought which contrives the most varied forms and arguments for its self-justification, but which will in fact always be kept in being as an eternal longing of the human spirit. The pure sociologist belongs to the type of inquirer *a priori*, whose interest is only attracted by unity within diversity. Suppressed by the development of the preceding decades, when historicism and specialized science allowed the spirit of pluralism to reign, these tendencies now rise up everywhere in order to provide a synthesis for the accumulated empirical work. This aprioristic search for the universally human brings the most varied forces into the fray, in order to give its enterprises a theoretical base. All the methodologies and theories of knowledge, ranging from mechanistic naturalism through Kantianism to the Platonism of phenomenology, are employed in laying a foundation for the specialized science seeking the underlying principle, that which remains the same.

Kantianism is represented, in a unique combination with intuitionist insights as well as motifs derived from a view of nature oriented to mechanics, by Simmel, who has surely had the greatest and most lasting impact on the further development of this tendency.[59] In order to ascertain the grounds for the forms of sociation, which are historically-temporally so diverse and complex, he would start out from a vision of a mere sum of human beings living side by side, in a state of reciprocal effects. (This is where atomizing, mechanistically-oriented thought enters.) Next it is a question of working out the forms possible for all these effects of individual upon indivudual – and this, in contrast, is where the Kantian influence comes into play – the forms which first make society possible at all. As Kant had asked 'How is nature possible?', Simmel asks 'How is society possible?'[60] But while the categories, in terms of which nature constitutes itself within an epistemological consciousness, are syntheses of data alien to soul and spirit, the forms according to which society constitutes itself are not merely forms belonging to the knowing subject, but they are also the object itself, which in this case is the substratum possessed of life and soul which shapes society in accord with the very forms known by the knowing subject. (Here intuitionism enters.) These forms can thus be grasped through 'empathy', through an inner connectedness with the 'object'. The great encompassing formations, such as the state, and all organizations which rise above separate individuals, can be analysed into small molecular movements of the soul, whose masterly depiction evinces the impressionistic talent of this philosopher. 'That people look at one another and are jealous of one another; that they exchange letters or dine together; that one asks another man about a certain street, and that people dress and adorn themselves for one another – the whole gamut of relations that play from one person to another and that may be momentary or permanent, conscious or unconscious, ephemeral or of grave consequence (and from which these illustrations are quite casually chosen), all these incessantly tie men together. Here are the interactions among the atoms of society. They account for all the toughness and elasticity, all the colour and consistency of social life, that is so striking and yet so mysterious.'[61]

It is striking how much these passages sound like a translation into the philosophical of the programme of naturalistic-impressionistic literature, which has devoted itself, after the decline of the tragic-dramatic conception of life which comprehends universals, with equal energy to capturing the lyricism and mysteries of everyday and of the moment. In drama, a psychology which was destructive of dramatic form displaced universalistic conceptions of destiny and universalistic images of the world, breaking this conception down into elements and discrete psychic movements. Similarly, for Simmel the 'universals' of societal being dissolve in the sight of this 'psychic microscopy'. Just after the passages cited above, Simmel writes: 'The large systems and the supra-individual organizations that customarily come to mind when we think of society, are nothing but immediate interactions that occur among men constantly, every minute, but that have become crystallized as permanent fields, as autonomous phenomena.'[62] However conditioned by the age and its spirit, these propositions can be tested only from the point of view of a general problem complex; and from such a viewpoint two problems immediately

103

suggest themselves. The theoretical value of these propositions depends on the solution of these problems, and, precisely because of their importance, the further development of this tendency can be characterized by reference to them.

It must *first* be asked whether it is even possible to comprehend in terms of such individual movements the more encompassing social formations, like state, class, family, etc., which rise above the life and activity of separate individuals. And *second*, it must be asked whether these forms of sociation, freed from the condition of temporality, are to be comprehended *a priori* or by induction, and, in either case, what the relevance of the pure sociology which uses them in its construction may be.[63]

To begin with the first question: Simmel is aware of the difficulty. The train of thought interrupted above, which came to speak of the consolidation of these molecular reciprocal effects into a lasting framework, into formations to be understood on their own terms, goes on to say about these more encompassing formations: 'Of course, they thereby attain their own existence and autonomy, by virtue of which they may at times confront and oppose these mutually determining vitalities.'[64] Thus Simmel sees what is at issue here: that the social 'universals', once atomized, are never again fit to be rendered whole, because here the sum of the parts is not the whole. But the problem is not solved with an 'of course'. It is interesting to see that the same problem re-emerges in the work of Leopold von Wiese, who has turned Simmel's beginnings even further in a naturalistic direction, and that he, too, seeks to get rid of it by an act of force. Von Wiese says, in a passage where he comes upon the same problem: 'I can clearly see the way from analysis of the psychic linkages among human beings to society; i.e., to collective societal formations. These formations are nothing but the abstract objectifications of countless effects of people upon one another.'[65] What does 'abstract' mean in this context? Apparently an abstraction on the part of the investigator. But is it possible to speak of abstraction in this instance in a sense *different* from that where the investigator comprehends those molecular relationships which are quite evidently no abstractions for von Wiese? Is there not a reality in the object that corresponds in the same way to each? There is something in the 'object' corresponding to the reciprocal effects moving from individuals to individuals and their forms, and to the more encompassing forms, like family, class and state, in the same manner as there is something corresponding to superordination, subordination and competition.

There can be no objection to someone setting himself the task of investigating the socializing factors which emanate only from individuals. On the contrary: an essential and still unexplored area is opened up for the sociologist. We must, however, guard against limiting pure sociology exclusively to the investigation of these 'molecular movements', and against expecting, out of naturalistic prejudice, to be even able to derive comprehensive forms from these movements. Just as it is possible to ascertain, abstracted from historicity, the archetypes, the sustaining framework of transitory interhuman 'reciprocal effects', so there must be a way of discovering a typology of 'supra-individual' social forms initially construed without reference to time. In the case of Simmel, however, and much more so in the case of von Wiese, the striving for *a priori* factors, referring to that which is human forever, makes its appearance veiled in the prejudices of a mechanistic-nominalist conception. This may be due in no small measure to fear that the concept of society might be confounded with the juristic concept of the state. Since the concept of society was detached from the concept of the state, thereby bringing into view what might be called a substratum proper to sociology, it has become, more or less consciously, the ultimate aspiration of sociologists to uphold this distinction; and it is felt that this distinction is the more safe-guarded the further the social formations are removed from the juristic. And this distance appears best achieved in the atomistic conception. Correspondingly, it is attempted, on the other side, where the orientation is juristic, to invalidate sociology as a distinct science by absorbing the concept of society within the juristic concept of the state. The opposition lives off the remains of this juristic conception and, as is usual in the career of intellectual tendencies, tries to hold its old position by enlisting new philosophical and epistemological justifications. Testifying to this tendency is Hans Kelsen,[66] who plays the juristic concept of the state off against a sociological one, by means of the neo-Kantian apparatus of arguments.

The tendency within pure sociology identified with Simmel supposes that it has arrived at pure factors of the social, which are independent of historical time, when it has found the most elementary relationships, the molecular movements among individuals. But it does not see that these essences, freed from historical time, are not to be attained by dissolving the whole into component parts, by breaking it into pieces, but by abstracting the historically determined moments from it.[67] Just as it is not possible to move from the various concrete actualizations of drama to its timeless concept, by dissolving drama into its most elementary component parts and comprehending it as something like the sum and combination of the most elementary bits of dialogue, but it is possible to move in

105

this way only by removing the accidental from the essential in the *whole* of the individual work, through a distinctive act of abstraction, so it is only possible to attain the timeless existence of the social through a similar sort of abstraction. But, just as it is possible to study the simplest 'elements' of the drama (the dialogue forms) for their most essential component parts and thereby to obtain the pure types of dramatic dialogue (but not of the drama as such), so it is also possible to discover the pure elementary processes of the social simply by detaching them from their historical facticity. With this, however, only the elementary processes of the social have been comprehended and not its higher forms, as yet.

To the second question, whether these forms of sociation are discovered *a priori* by pure sociology or on the basis of inductive methods, Simmel does not give an answer that is altogether unambiguous. He does state quite expressly that pure sociology is to derive the forms of sociation inductively and psychologically from the multiplicity of contents.[68] But his starting point, intensely reminiscent of Kant, as well as the most essential forms which he cites as representative examples (such as the forms of sub- and superordination, competition, etc.), disclose that there is present here a *concealed longing for the a priori*. He pushed the positivist aspect into the foreground only because he did not want to occupy himself with the definitive elucidation of ultimate systematic positions. For him, every posture with regard to system served merely as a means for comprehending the object in the greatest possible detail.[69] With regard to this problem of method, this intellectual tendency comes in consequence to be sharply divided. As we saw above, Leopold von Wiese represents the standpoint of an extreme naturalism on this matter. As auxiliary discipline, he selects empirical psychology, taken as a psychosociology,[70] and he sees it as his task to describe, analyse, classify, measure (!) and systematize social relationships. Vierkandt takes a completely different position on this problem, for he considers the method as an aprioristic one. This tendency is able to penetrate to the ultimate facts mainly because it does not merely generalize from experience but can also establish a set of factual states *a priori*, since it proceeds not just by induction but also, and to a greater extent, phenomenologically.[71] At the same time, Vierkandt attempts to compose a classification of societal conditions by means of 'systematic concepts' and 'historical concepts'. The family, for example, is a historical elaboration of the condition of community as such, and this condition belongs to the systematic categories. It should be noted that Vierkandt takes into account not only the objective basic forms of sociation but also the fundamental acts of consciousness whereby society as such is constituted. This clear distinction between the objective formations, which are to be set forth by the basic types of sociation as such, on the one hand, and acts of consciousness, on the other, was already made by Tönnies, when, in his foundational work, *Community and Society*,[72] he took up the two types of social formations which he discovered and described in the 'First Book', and then, in the 'Second Book' comprehended the two kinds of conscious acts pertaining to them (essential will and unconstrained will)[73] as two forms of the human will as such. It is in the explication of these different acts making society (in the widest sense) possible, that the phenomenological school concentrates its main efforts.[74] The method employed here is already, as Vierkandt correctly discerned, a phenomenological one. The historical material serves merely as illustration and is by no means inductive warrant validating the findings.

If Tönnies's method and findings are to be further developed, however, they must be freed from two features which derive from a specific historical situation. First, one must abstain from the empirical-psychological attitude; i.e., one must gain full awareness that the findings obtained by his method are not attained at all by inductive observation of facts alone, but rather by bringing out the essential states of things which are given with those facts. Second, one must give up the ultimately metaphysical notion (apparently rooted in Schopenhauer) that all the acts worked out in the second part of Tönnies's book are in the final analysis forms of the will. It is also necessary to eliminate at least part of the unwieldy idiosyncratic terminology. However deeply the terminology may be rooted in the pithiness and uniqueness of this work, it is nevertheless only partly capable of transmission and generalization.

As far as its sociological contents are concerned, most of the work of Husserl's phenomenological school goes back to Tönnies's initiatives (Max Scheler,[75] Edith Stein,[76] etc.). Siegfried Kracauer[77] links up the beginnings made by Simmel with a grounding in phenomenology. A logical framework in keeping with the spirit of pure sociology seems far more definitively to have been found in phenomenology. A doctrine which arose from purely philosophical considerations later served to bring into being a concept of the *a priori* for pure sociology differing from that of Kant.

If this method were to be made fruitful for pure sociology, dispensing where possible with the terminology and often exaggerated scholasticism of the phenomenological school while drawing on its insights, it would bring us to the following conclusions concerning the set of problems we have just been pursuing: a pure sociology sets itself the task, on the one hand, of investigating those essential objective conditions which can be distinguished in every social phenomenon and, on the other, of distinguishing the structure of all the acts by means of which the social constitutes itself in consciousness. This assignment is accordingly twofold: first directed towards the objects, the formed things which confront us as social formations, and then directed subjectively towards the consciousness within which the cosmos of society constitutes itself by means of specific and social acts.

Empirical sociology, for its part, investigates the facts of social life in their purely empirical contingency. Pure sociology, in contrast, seeks to lay bare, as essence, the unique, *a priori* kernel amid the spatial and temporal mesh, as it is in fact. This distinction between essence and fact cannot be deductively established although it can be shown to be an ultimate: it is applied in every cognition of an object. If we could not distinguish between the fortuitous elements adhering merely to the object as it happens to exist here and now, and the properties which necessarily pertain to it, in essence, we could never get beyond individual facts. Nor would a comparison of diverse individual facts yield the universal essential to them, since a comparison of facts is possible only on the basis of a point of view. But this point of view (i.e., the universal with reference to which I compare the individual examples of the same species) must be already distinguished as essential in the very first example, if I want to use it as a basis for comparison. Comparative abstraction is not the precondition, logically considered, for comprehending the essence; comprehending the essence is rather the basis which makes comparative abstraction possible.

It is thus upon the instance of an individual, factual social formation that we comprehend its essence, and this directedness towards its essence is altogether different from a directedness towards its actuality. Put up against the fact, the essence is a new object. The individual fact is not a segment of an inductive series leading to empirical generality; it stands, rather, in a relationship of exemplification to essence-generality.

We have already pointed out, in connection with Simmel, that his pure forms of sociation are not obtained by his citing a host of examples of the same species from which he then distils the common element, as pure form. It is rather that he draws that which is general in essence out of the individual case at a single sweep, as it were, by putting its facticity 'in brackets'. It is no objection to this to claim that the other analogous cases are potentially present in us as a result of accumulated experience, and that we are performing, as it were, abbreviated induction. In the first place, no

108

matter how great the number of factualities, it is impossible ever to arrive at more than inductive general validity from them, as long as they are *not* examined with regard to their essential condition. In the second place, it is also incorrect to claim it as psychological fact that we have any great numbers of analogies in mind during such analyses.

The reason why it is hard to attain to this conception of essence is the fear of falling prey to Platonism. It is supposed that this theory would require one to presuppose a metaphysical Beyond for the ideas which are prior to the facts. Facts would then have to be presented as something like a shadowgraph of these ideas. Although the theory easily flows into such a metaphysic, the question of principle can only be whether the state of things important here has been correctly described; i.e., whether it is true that, in every case of a 'this here', we immediately make a distinction between the factors imputable to its contingent existence and the factors which may pertain to it as essential predictables. These latter present themselves to us with the same character of necessity as do the connections between mathematical propositions. A second difficulty in the way of recognizing the intuition, which grasps essences, consists of a misunderstanding of the concept of *a priori* here employed. Apriority in this instance means only that the interconnected factors adhering to the essence cannot be thought to be different; and it cannot be doubted that the non-factual constituents of an object bear this character of necessity. It is a peculiarity of the Kantian concept of the *a priori* that it also possesses the limitation of being formal. For Kant, the material is empirical by chance. But, in contrast to this Kantian contention, a material *a priori* can also be discovered. The dividing line between the *a priori* and the empirical cannot be that between form and content, but only that between essence and fact. In what is contingent 'here and now', the form is as much permeated by contingent form-elements as the content is permeated by contingent content-elements. The essence belonging to it cannot be thought to be different, in its formal or in its material constituents.

Furthermore, all matters of fact (for example, all experiences), notwithstanding their absolute individuality, possess a general essence which is to be drawn out of them and which may recur in large numbers of individual experiences. Within the essence-generality there are, moreover, different levels of generality, a division into species and kinds. Corresponding to the many individual perceptions of a particular thing t, for example, there is an essence – perception of t – to which must also be added, as species of a higher order, 'perception of thing' and perception as such. Just as one can dig out its individual essence and the essence of the drama in general from a particular drama, so with the social. Depending on the level of generality at which one sets the ideational operation, one can attempt to grasp, for example, the essence of community as such, as well as the essence of a particular community.

Within the sphere of facticity only induction, comparison, and trial-and-error are applicable, and findings will possess nothing more than empirical generality and probability. Inquiry that is directed toward the essence of these things will grasp elements which are necessary, so far as essence reaches.

In the case of pure sociology, to the extent that the pure structures of the social are worked out by grasping their essence, the character of necessity in assertions about them will be immediately evident. What is distinguished in community as essential for its characterization will be evident in an individual case, which is only to be taken as an exemplification. The essence of community cannot be inferred from a system. It must be exemplified by illustrative cases. Its presence cannot be 'deduced' *a priori*, without any experience of communities. Once one has grasped the phenomenon of community, however, one will be able to grasp directly what is essential in it by stripping away the features which are merely factual.

What has been said here with regard to objective formations holds also for the acts of consciousness in which these social formations constitute themselves. If I want to know what inner activity of the subject is involved in entering into social relationships – if, for example, I want to understand the act of love – I must and can eliminate all the features which go along with a specific act of love as it is factually contingent, and I must be directed to the essential act of love as such. This stripping away of facticity in order to come upon the supra-empirical properties and constitution of the act of love as such is called the 'phenomenological reduction,' whose essence consists precisely in setting out from empirical-factual consciousness (which is as such the subject matter of empirical psychology) by 'bracketing' the facticity within it, attempting thereby to bring out the essential structure of pure consciousness as such. However unfinished, problematic, and unstable the results of pure phenomenology may be – which is why an unequivocal presentation cannot yet be given – its coupling with pure sociology appears to be in the line of development.

4 General sociology

While pure sociology, in the form we have just described, is always

110

concerned with essence-generalities, general sociology is a science of facts, a discipline proceeding inductively. It grasps the forms of the social not in their essential properties but rather as they have really been formed, existing in just this specific way. But it is possible to carry on the activity of knowing in alternate ways with regard to any facticity and with regard to any sequence of facticities. One can try to comprehend them in their complete uniqueness, in their wholly specific individual make-up, as they have become thus and no other in their historical coming into being. But one can also generalize more or less, and more or less disregard what is entirely individual. One then abstracts from entities distinct in time and space what is common to them in spite of their diversity and one makes this commonality the subject matter of empirical investigation. Modes of examination relating to the world of actualities exist in several varieties, depending on the level of generality. What is factual in the realm of spirit, for example, can always be expressed through its historical location, that is through the general and particular conditions under which an essence particularizes itself as precisely what it is rather than anything else. Generalizing therefore always means some measure of disregarding the historical character of the entity in question. The facticity of a natural object – a stone for example, a 'this here' – cannot be rendered determinate for us by means of the unending sequence of concatenations which allowed the stone to become precisely as we encounter it, with all its specific characteristics of consistency, colour, shape, etc. In characterizing the predominantly unique distinguishing features of spiritual-human formations, it is always possible for us to render determinate this relatively individual thing about them by means of the 'point in time'. (In this context, a point in time does not refer to the chronological location of the entity, but rather to the place assignable to it within a unified developmental sequence: 1850 means something different in the unified developmental sequence of the history of art in France than it does in China.) The problem and the task of dating, which have been developed to such great precision in art history, may be said to reveal in all its purity the fact that the point in time in the realm of spirit calls for an orientation and criterion which involve meaning, and that the concept does not refer directly to chronology, as for example in the sense of astronomical time. The level of generality can thus be expressed by the degree of temporal determinacy. To speak of urban economy as such involves a greater degree of generalization than to speak of the medieval urban economy, or even of the late medieval urban economy.[78] General sociology thus describes in a generalizing perspective the historical realization of the essence-generalities that

111

pure sociology attempted to grasp only in their essential features. It does not merely describe social entities, however, but it also attempts to establish regularities within the patterns that appear in this material. These regularities, too, can be of a more or less general kind, in turn, and, as empirical regularities, they lack the character of absolute necessity. The investigations of Max Weber contained in *Economy and Society* can serve as examples of a generalizing sociology. Here social forms and their reciprocal relations are abstracted from specific historical time (both a 'berserk' and Kurt Eisner count as 'charismatic')[79] and are set side by side and referred to a type, in a manner which may be called 'on the surface'; i.e., in disregard of historical time.

These generalizations, designed to stay on the surface (i.e., abstracted from cultural contexts and their historical stages) serve to master the empirical diversity of social formations in their historically given facticity. They enter into the concrete wealth of individual occurrences only so far as this is important for the point of view governing the inquiry. And the only thing intended, after all, by the regularities that can be grasped in this realm is to establish in the most general terms the patterns which recur in the world of appearances. These patterns, drawn and generalized from the experience of history, not only represent something worth knowing for its own sake, but they can also be employed, as appropriate, in the explanation of quite specific historical cases to assist in correct causal imputation. To the extent that the findings of such a sociology are applied to concrete historical material, the aim is to dissolve as far as possible the many individual causal connections which have generally been already grasped, and to comprehend each individual historical phenomenon as a point of intersection for historical forces generally operative. There is no denying that natural-scientific thinking influences a generalizing sociology to some extent. But this does not mean, as is often assumed, that the justification for investigating such 'historical laws' must be rejected. It is simply necessary never to forget that this mode of explanation can only penetrate to an outer layer of historical events. The characteristics of 'being negatively privileged' enter into the historically unique phenomenon of the 'modern industrial proletariat', for example, only to the extent that these general characteristics correspond to the subject matter to be explained. When it is a matter of explaining the specific structure of the modern proletariat and the always specific structure, the general assertions which apply to 'being negatively privileged as such' can only serve to provide a standard, a guideline for identifying the deviations in this case and the possibilities of accounting for them.

Generalizing sociology thus divides into two disciplines: general sociology as a study of all types of social formation existing in fact and of their regularities; and applied general sociology, a science auxiliary to history. So-called sociological historiography, which aims at comprehending individual connections as well, distinguishes itself from historiography as such only in that it attempts, whenever possible, to explain the concrete course of history in terms of general sociological causes.

General sociology (other than applied) does abandon the plane of temporal essences and orders, and it describes and explains the social types which have arisen in history. But while it incorporates the element of temporality as such, it does not accept historical time as a constituent part. Its basic form is the generation of types, and its types are arranged side by side, on the surface (not hierarchically). Types that are ordered hierarchically in time already bring to the fore the problem of dialectics. With this, however, the limits of this sociological discipline have brought us to sociology as the study of the dynamics of history, which we shall now discuss.

5 Sociology as the study of the dynamics of history

A generalizing (surface) typology of social arrangements would only be adequate, in the final analysis, if the constitution of human social cohabitation, together with the 'arrangements' belonging to it, were not *historical*; in other words, if any social arrangement were possible at any point in time. It is not very difficult to lay out for oneself in imagination a social cohabitation that approximates to the level of abstraction which as a tacit assumption underlies general sociology; that is, one that would correspond to its image of reality. What would be unhistorical about this construction is not that its members would not live in chronological time, nor that they would eternally behave, act, and create in the same way, nor that one generation would follow in the steps of the other and adopt its forms of social association as well as its cultural products. We could easily imagine a race of intelligent living beings in chronological time, which could always choose its forms of social existence as it pleased, which would bring into being first one and then the other of the various types of social forms collected within general sociology. In this world one could think any possible thought at any moment (including those not yet thought by us), and be creative in any species of style, all those that have existed in the past as well as those which may yet be possible for us in the future. This utopia, thought to its conclusion in the spirit of the Enlightenment, would

113

show us the difference which makes up the essence of the historical-social process in contrast to mere temporality. It would show us the factor, in short, which reveals a surface typology of social arrangements as ultimately inadequate. For social as for all the other human spiritual arrangements, their historical location is not irrelevant. It enters into their inner structure, at least as stage, as hierarchical location. What has arisen later contains this 'being later' as an internal feature, even when one abstracts it from historical time in the narrower sense. This idea is not bound to the idea of progress, which contains a valuation, and, unlike that idea, it is indifferent toward the question of approving or disapproving a given historical sequence of arrangements. The processive character of the arrangements displays itself in the fact that earlier arrangements are present in later ones not merely as historical-genetic presuppositions but also as presuppositions in the genealogy of meanings.

This fundamental lesson of experience lay hidden in every philosophy of history, however misleading or premature in its contents. They wanted to comprehend appearances hierarchically, on the basis of the elements defined by the genealogy of meanings, and they took the hierarchy which they discovered in the arrangements, as it was defined by the genealogy of meanings, and projected it directly upon historical time (and in this lies their basic error). This is always a falsification of the facts. But we shall never understand the temporal process, on the other hand, unless we try to grasp it together with the meaning-genetic complex which manifests itself in that process. And general sociology, however useful this may be for its own purpose, destroys this complex by means of its surface typologies. In other words, within the philosophy of history, and even in its forerunners, the theophanies and cosmogonies, there was embedded a valid tendency of thought, a typification of primary human experience, which will always come to the fore, even if also always in altered form. Indeed every past tendency of thought proves to conceal, upon closer examination, a valid scheme of experience.

That such a tendency of thought can disappear for a time from the view of scientific thinking is due to the fact that a different tendency – favoured by causes comprehensible to the sociological history of ideas – gains sole supremacy for a time. The buried tendency returns to life only when there has been a loosening of the more recent one covering it. It goes without saying that the living and still meaningful kernel of a lost type of thinking and experience never returns in its old form, since it has joined itself to new realities and since change on the part of the object has a modifying effect upon the form of thinking which relates to that object.

During the reign of its sole supremacy, which has been only recently broken, positivism signified the repression of all the schemata of thinking fit for comprehending psychic and configurational happenings and previously metaphysically grounded. Detached from their sunken dogmatic foundations, these schemata of thinking rise up again and once more prove themselves fruitful for the comprehension of human-psychic events.

The reception of the lost tendencies already begins in Romanticism, and it is renewed by the neo-Romantic strivings of the present. Among the viable intellectual schemata is to be found the valid kernel of truth which had been embedded in philosophy of history, and which consisted in comprehending the succession of arrangements in the continuity of time as constitutive of the existence of the arrangements which have come to be. A certain cast of things could already be grasped when things were called by name; that is, by the hierarchical designations of philosophy of history.

The essential was destroyed in the realm of spirit, however, by the concept of law which had rendered invaluable service in the comprehension of nature, as apart from meaning. In Comte, this was not yet complete. In his 'law of three stages', a typing is undertaken which still retains the hierarchical character of the temporal element. But it is generalizing in so far as this stadial hierarchy repeats itself in every development. While time is thus acknowledged up to a certain point within the typology, 'historical space' is neglected. That does not refer to 'real' space, to locality, but to that other factor which an adequate typology must also recognize: the 'bodily shape of history' is neglected. In contrast to this, an adequate typology of social formations will be at least nearly complete only when the at least comparatively self-enclosed 'bodily shape of history' is employed as second co-ordinates to fix the hierarchically ordered arrangements. In a word, the most general types of sociological concept (such as family, urban economy, capitalism, etc.) gain pregnant meaning only when they are classified by reference to that unique structure in which each originated. We shall call such typing a dynamic one. What then is the difference between a sociological-dynamic typing of arrangements (whether purely social or cultural) and outright philosophy of history on the one hand, and historiography on the other?

We have already emphasized the inner kinship and the inherited kernel of philosophy of history within this socio-dynamic construction of types: it is the hierarchical element, according to which temporal succession is discovered as determinative of meaning. What distinguishes the one from the other is simply the difference

115

between the two worlds in which the one and the other typology have been undertaken. In the one, typologizing rested on the basis of a metaphysics; in the other, metaphysics – which had prescribed a basic design and ultimate goal for such development – is dispensed with. The foremost consequence of this is that the socio-genetic typology of arrangements is not evaluative. The 'late' does not mean the 'higher' in the sense of the more valuable, but simply a structural constitution in which that which came before (within the same cultural sphere) is taken up in and superseded by that which comes later.

This kind of typing differs from historiography as such, first, in that it does not quite penetrate all the way to historical time but simply reserves to itself the hierarchical component within such time. It should be noted that it is a property of arrangements originating in time that they represent a type of irreversible sequence. But this is only *one* of the elements in the concept of time: historical time contains considerably more; but this element is the only one distinguished by dynamic sociology. Accordingly, we want to distinguish this 'time' as 'time as determined by philosophy of history-sociology'. The second difference between a historical inquiry into a process of happenings and a dynamic-sociological one is that the historian (as ideal type), precisely by virtue of his complete immersion in the historical time continuum, cannot obtain types at all, but only historical individuals (unique particularities). When he studies, for example, the development of the urban economy, the state, or style, there are for him – so long as he remains consistently a historian and steadily progresses from one individual arrangement to the other – only smooth transitions. His motto is: *in historia non datur saltus*. By virtue of the fact that it comprehends the temporal element as hierarchical rather than chronological and that it presents successive stages rather than events in their unique complex of effects, sociology has distance from events; and in that distance, that which has come to be always appears as something which has *abruptly* come to be *different*.

Dynamic sociology, then, can be comprehended as a discipline which is not at all on the surface, but one which constructs types in an individualizing way, a discipline which builds up empirical types in the form of stages, in keeping with the hierarchy of a philosophy of history-sociology. When general sociology contributed its types to historical inquiry, it became one of the auxiliary disciplines of history, and we called this historiography a general-sociological one. In the same way, when sociology's dynamic types are applied in economic or social history, among others, there emerges a dynamic explanation of history, a dynamic historiography. In this case, it is precisely the individual arrangement (a certain urban economy, let us say) which is explained on the basis of the dynamic type corresponding to it. This explanation is teleological in so far as the developmental totality is anticipated by means of the periodizing type-concepts, and the individual arrangement is related to this historical whole. Its historical existence and its distinctiveness of kind are specified in this case in that we plot their hierarchical locus between one developmental type and another. In a certain sense, there is obviously a circle here, because it is clear, for example, that we ultimately extracted the dynamic type of the medieval urban economy from the individual urban economic establishments of the epoch in question, and that we now seek to explain an individual arrangement on the basis of the historical totality. But this circle is present in general-sociological historical explanation as well, although there it is better concealed. Even if we proceed in a thoroughly generalizing way and utilize related phenomena from all epochs and landscapes of the world for the construction of a generalizing concept, the case remains the same. To the extent that we apply this 'general concept' or general regularity to a particular arrangement, we move in a circle by virtue of this application alone or this subsumption alone. This circle is always present, and above all when one writes history setting forth periods. The same state of affairs also presents itself, for example, in the history of styles, which proceeds, when viewed structurally, in just the same way as the dynamic history of purely social formations. Stylistic concepts (such as Renaissance, Baroque, etc.) are nothing but types, constructed in a non-generalizing, non-surface way, and referring to the art-historical manifold. They are auxiliary constructions stemming from a typology possessing dynamic-periodic form. The same circle as that already noted arises whenever these types are applied to individual phenomena in the actual history of styles. As is evident, this periodizing method can be applied in all areas of intellectual history (*Geistesgeschichte*); in the case we have mentioned – that of the urban economy – it was applied to the development of sociological arrangements. This kind of history, which operates with the living remains of the philosophy of history in its concept formation, is not history in the same sense as 'history of events'. But it is not philosophy of history either, because it does not attempt to trace out a *plan* of history wherein it is a matter of a series of events which are hierarchical in their *contents*. Instead it arrives, in the last analysis, at the *structure* of the historical development of individual cultural domains.

The simply hierarchical typology of social formations accordingly expands right away into a doctrine about the structure of this

117

development or of particular developmental sequences. If we leave aside for the present Marx's ideas concerning cultural sociology (the economic interpretation of culture), as we have been doing, we can say that Marx's whole doctrine ultimately tends, in its economic portion, towards a structural history of economic development.

Since the downfall of philosophy of history which was metaphysical in contents, we have ceased to have experiences that are genuinely full of contents. Instead, a terrible acuity of clearsightedness about structures has taken hold of us. All of our sciences are ultimately theories of different structures. This development can be seen most clearly in philosophy, where structural vision has replaced metaphysical-dogmatic contents: philosophy turned into theory of knowledge. One of the culminating points of this development is Kantian philosophy, whose entire force expends itself in the structural analysis of consciousness. And in so far as remnants of a 'prophetic kernel' are still to be found (especially ethical ones), these also assume a structural disguise (e.g., 'primacy of practical reason', 'freedom'). In its subsequent development, philosophy discarded even this last remnant of fullness of contents, and it turned completely into a methodology and a theory of knowledge. We find the same thing in theology or philosophy of religion, so strongly dependent on metaphysics. What has been produced that is new (that is, altogether disregarding mere straggling repetitions of old contents) is either historiography or phenomenologically structural investigations of religious consciousness.[80] A dynamically-typifying sociology, issuing in a theory of 'social movement', corresponds to this sharpened eye for structures.

5   Varieties of cultural sociology

We have been treating the varieties of cultural sociology in a way consistent with our thesis that cultural sociology has set itself a task altogether different from that of sociology as such, and that it has an inner structure of an altogether different kind. That is why we could begin sorting cultural sociology into 'autonomous' groups (i.e., ones that are independent of sociology) according to diverse directions, even before subdividing sociology itself. These directions evinced themselves with regard to the relationship to the concept of world-view. As we showed that any cultural sociology can explain cultural formations socio-genetically only when it relates social arrangements to cultural formations by way of experiential contextures which can be shown to be co-ordinate with them, there emerged various kinds of solution to the problems arising from this. The development of cultural sociology which offers itself at that point is independent of the varieties of sociology.

But there is one tie by which every cultural sociology is attached to sociology as such, and in this respect its conformation depends on sociology. The point of attachment is where sociology projects into cultural sociology as method. We called attention to this incursion of sociology into cultural sociology by speaking of 'bringing the sociological conceptual level up' to cultural formations which had been reduced to world-view. What this bringing up of the sociological conceptual level involves in detail does not need be repeated here, because we have already set it forth at length. But we have seen, in the investigation of various types of sociology, that this sociological conceptual level can take on various shapes, depending on whether it is elaborated as a pure, generalizing, or historical-dynamic one. The varieties of cultural sociology also differentiate themselves from this point of view, so that we shall be able to speak of a pure, a generalizing, or a historical-dynamic one, depending on the corresponding types of sociological concepts employed when relating cultural formations to them by way of world-view. Accordingly we shall subject to separate examination each of the sets of problems which present themselves at this point.

1 Pure cultural sociology

Pure cultural sociology sets itself the task of studying pure cultural formations in a state prior to historical concretization of any kind, in order to determine what it is by virtue of which they are able to become social factors at all, and to what extent they are constituted by the social. The philosophy of culture also sets itself a similar task; which is, to investigate the phenomenon of culture in itself, in its self-possession, in abstraction from historical reality. As might be expected after our earlier account, however, it is directed towards immanence as it does this, as it wholly disregards the community which is behind culture. In their philosophical aspect, cultural formations display themselves as formations of validity,[81] and human existence is allotted no role with reference to them other than that of giving actuality to realms of value. Only by means of an attitude which is not immanent but socio-genetic can it be discerned that these formations not only have a being in themselves but also stand in a functional relationship to the collective existence of individuals. And it must also become evident from this point of view that the completion of cultural formations with regard to their contents is a product of their social environment. We sought to specify, in the first part of this work, the distinctive properties of functionality as a relationship, as well as of the result pertaining to it, precisely in the interest of bringing out the layer in cultural formations which is directly connected to the individual and collective flow of experience (for socio-genetic investigation has no relevance beyond that). But cultural sociology does not seek to dissolve or somehow to reduce to the merely temporal that significant remnant which philosophy encompasses in its sphere of validity, nor is it able to do this.

Before entering upon concrete historical analyses strictly within the domain of cultural sociology, in which one inquires how a specific historical-social environment determines the concrete conformation of the cultural formations to be found there, however, it is both possible and necessary to raise the following fundamental questions: how is it possible that the individual human consciousness produces formations out of itself which do not by any means remain shut up within the monadic closedness of the individual consciousness but become common property of a community, the individual members of which join into a union among themselves and with the generations that go before and after? How is it that historicity is even possible by means of cultural formations on the basis of society? How far does the sphere subject to being socially and culturally affected extend into the existence of the individual human being? What sorts of act of consciousness posit culture as a social phenomenon? Are there spheres within fully human consciousness which are inaccessible to culture (as, for example, pure sensuousness)? What sorts of communication and transmission and what types of understanding, empathy, imitation, and co-operation are there, which make the historical process at all possible within the individual? Such questions and others like them require answering at this point.

This complex of questions may be said to be one extreme of the cultural-social inquiry, the opposite pole to which might be taken to be that most concrete set of questions which address themselves in socio-genetic inquiry to a specific formation, definite in time and place, in its full factuality. What is demanded here is a reaching back to the constitutive structure of consciousness. As one explores the acts by which human consciousness forms culture-society-history, one also discovers, inversely, the socio-cultural and historical determinedness of consciousness.

These theoretical inquiries are actuated by a longing to get to the bottom, in a methodical way, of the question of how far our being a human is in such and such a determinate way determined by the environment: what meaning can some other human being and our culture have for us at all? Is there a way of solitude? Are there spheres within us which must, because of their essential nature, always remain alone? Does the historical-social course of things change anything in the fate of being human?

Historicism had unsettled man's feeling of permanence and set in motion the once stable image of the world, in which every thing and every creature had had its place according to a divine plan. Our sense of life tells us that everything could also be different. Everything has come to be how it happens to be through history, determined to be such by innumerable causes. At the outset, one senses this condition of being historically determined, as we saw, only with regard to 'external formations'; only politics, art, and science seem to be subject to historical transformation. Later, this sense of being historically determined also reaches out to the substance itself: our feelings, our ultimate commitments, and our sensibilities also appear as having become. The ground upon which we had until now considered the world, as from a steady place to stand, is shaken loose; our very self is abandoned; it is as if we are suspended above ourselves. We come to ourselves once more in a thousand guises. The same psychic situation which once drove the sailor to distant places now determines the historian to his wandering and empathizing in the past. In pure cultural sociology, there is a third way of abandoning oneself, of separating the social and historical self from the substantial one, and of experiencing our humanity as such, purely in itself. And just as the homelessness which was empirical-historical at first (and which at first had us roaming through cultural and historical places and times) metamorphosed into the ultimate homelessness of being human, so does the most rigorous structural analysis of social consciousness transcend itself in the direction of new substantive insights, until finally we reach the ultimate point at which it is still possible to stand, a sociological *cogito ergo sum*, something which can no longer be doubted.

The longing of our contemporary consciousness for metaphysical contents cannot be satisfied by resuscitating old contents of belief. We can only follow to the end the way that is left to us.

2 General cultural sociology

While pure cultural sociology sets itself questions, among others, which can be reduced to the type which asks how the group as such stands to ideational contents, how the various fundamental structures of groups (socialization and communalization) relate to the cultural formations corresponding to them, general cultural sociology attempts inductively to order, with reference to their factuality, the most general relationships between historically existent social and cultural structures, and to comprehend them. While the method of pure sociology, *vis-à-vis* cultural contents as well as sociological forms, consisted in bracketing everything belonging merely to historical factuality that there was about the states of affairs serving merely as exemplifications, and in grasping the pure relationships between social and cultural formations as such, general cultural sociology will establish, in the sense already presented, the regular connections, the functional relationships between the two factual spheres, utilizing the method of inductive generalization. If one proceeds at all systematically in this, just as in general sociology, one arrives at surface typologies. But while general sociology limited itself in its typologizing to historically actual social aggregations and sought for regularities among them, general cultural sociology is ready to undertake to constitute re-

lationships between two levels: between the most general sociological formations and the most general cultural types.

Here too, mediation must proceed by way of world-view. And it
is in fact possible to erect a typology of highest generality; Dilthey,
for example, attempted to do this.[82] Considered concretely,
however, a world-view is a concretely completed and unique
whole. The elements which recur in history can only touch upon the
uppermost surface of the phenomena. In consequence, the types of
world-view established by generalization can never reproduce an
image of the world (a closed sequence of experiential contextures
which hangs together), but, at most, it can reproduce its constituent, if also essential, parts: principles which repeat themselves
and remain depictable schematically. And that is also the reason
why a cultural sociology built up in a generalizing way invariably
ends up in the dissolution of the unique complexes of world-views
and in the registering of regularly recurring experiential patterns.
Since the cultural and social elements which can be correlated with
these patterns will have fragmentary character, a general cultural
sociology will be able to bring out relations of functionality only in
a generalizing way. One of the finest examples of such generalizing
comprehension of world-views is Max Weber's essay, 'Religious
Rejections of the World and Their Directions',[83] in which it is a
matter of showing which of the experiential patterns characteriz-
able in a generalizing way (as, for example, asceticism or mysticism), belong to the world religions taken as objective formations.

This sort of socio-genetic explanation is limited by the truth that
situations in history never actually recur in identical form. Asceticism, ethics, etc. always mean something different when placed in a
different system of life and culture. It is only conceptual construction which could create the impression that external, general
features are identical with concrete uniquenesses. The natural-
scientific, generalizing method fails at this point because, consistently applied, it must, if it is to construct its generalizations,
destroy the unique meaning it undertakes to explain. In this respect
too it serves – considered from the overall design of cultural sociology – to provide general concepts, in order to make possible by
this means a further specification of the distinct individual formations.

3 Dynamic cultural sociology[84]

We must now recall that we discerned the essence of cultural-
sociological knowledge in the investigation and theoretical identification of the functionality of cultural formations in relation to a

socially-imputable experiential contexture. With this, however, we cannot but notice that the ultimate meaning of such a functionality-relationship consists precisely in its complete uniqueness in relation to a specific life situation. Something conceptualized as a call for help may well be considered similar to another call for help, thereby schematizing the relationship of functionality. But in the interpretative understanding of this call, we shall always recognize that there is nothing that is genuinely repetitive in this domain. And what has been, to begin with, claimed here with regard to uniqueness in individual-psychological matters, applies equally to the socio-genetic embeddedness of cultural formations. There is no 'asceticism' as such; there is no 'Romantic consciousness' as such. The significance of a formation with regard to its functionality always varies with the world-view totality that underlies it and assigns these phenomena fundamentally different meanings. An imputation which refers particular formations to an uncontextualized, typical experiential pattern (e.g., the bourgeois mode, intimacy in art and life, etc.) is, therefore, only provisional. The bourgeois mode is nothing but a schematic category, so long as its dynamic, unique stage is not specified; and intimacy can assume the most varied forms.

We have seen that within sociology itself, even before it is ready to address itself to synoptical problems of culture, dynamic sociology replaces surface typologies with dynamic ones. This process occurs not only with regard to social forms but also with regard to the dynamic, periodizing examination of individual cultural fields ('cultural systems', in Dilthey's terminology). Style concepts are developed in the history of art and literature; tendencies are discussed in the history of philosophy and religion; individual 'cultural systems' are subjected to periodization along the longitudinal sections of history assigned to them; and the individual work is interpreted in relation to the totality of the style or spiritual tendency of the corresponding epoch. Compared to historical-causal explanations which link matters in a sequence of events, these periodizations, remaining as they do within the history of individual fields – within art history, regarding art; history of philosophy, regarding philosophy; and historically applied sociology, regarding societal forms – already represent a kind of synthesis. It is already a synoptic achievement when the subject matter of historical investigation is not taken to be the individual work of art, but the style, and, in the history of science, the spiritual tendency. The individual work always functions as a point of transit here, representing a phase of this total development. With regard to individual happenings and works, there is a synopsis here which does not confront us as a 'bad

124

infinity' in the form of an unending chain of causes and effects and, equally, which does not merely represent the incoherent onmarch of events. This synopsis represents, to the contrary, an application of the fundamental categories of the comprehension appropriate to interpretative understanding (*verstehendes Erfassen*) of human-spiritual things and happenings, and in this comprehension the forms of 'beginning' and 'end', 'rise' and 'fall' come into use. If this synopsis, which recurred in the periodizing approach of individual disciplines, is already to be taken as a totalizing view, cultural-sociological inquiry is a totalizing view in two directions. One synopsis is the one just discussed, the combination of individual entities within a cultural field or 'cultural system' into units having the character of epochs; which is to say, a synopsis along a longitudinal section of history. This is retained in the sociological examination of culture, but it is complemented by a different examination of a totality, one which considers a cross-sectional view. The various cultural fields (such as art, literature, etc.) present in a unified epoch are not considered in their isolation from one another but as emanations of a unified 'feeling for life', a 'world-view'. This second overview, which comprehends the various fields of culture by taking a unified whole as point of departure, complements the first, which always only combines the entities present within a single field into units having the character of epochs.

This overview is to be called sociological because, as we saw earlier when analysing the concept of style, such terms as 'style' or 'spiritual tendency' inevitably imply experiential contextures which must be imputed to collective rather than individual streams of experience. Every totalizing view of the historical process is sociological in the looser sense, since these totalities contain only those elements of cultural objectifications which correspond to collective experiential contextures. This synoptic view becomes sociological in the narrower sense only when these totalities of objectified cultural formations are related to a typology derived from dynamic sociology (and not from surface-typologizing): in other words, when the epoch or spiritual tendency is characterized not by reference to cultural formations but by reference to social aggregations. The fact that expressions may be employed in this connection which also appear, for instance, in the history of style, alters nothing in the circumstance that they have turned into concepts which relate to socio-genesis. As we have seen, in such a case, the same word denotes different concepts.

A dynamic sociology thus contributes something distinctive to the dynamic-sociological consideration of culture: a typologizing of historical periods which rests upon change immanent within social formations. With the help of such a typology, socio-genetic explanation (whose character we described in the previous chapter) refers the individual cultural formation or unified complex of such formations (e.g., style) to a social subject drawn from historical, dynamic inquiry (such as the proletariat in developed capitalism), and not to an abstract, supra-temporal social referent (such as 'negatively privileged strata' in general).

There is no doubt that historiography – and especially a history of events which offers causal explanations – may also employ such concepts or may even work them out by itself. Its right to do this cannot be disputed and is not in question. Considered from the standpoint of first principles, however – and the classification of the sciences can only be brought about in this manner – the logical location for the origination of these concepts is dynamic sociology, and for their application, dynamic-sociological interpretation of culture. The fact that a historiography focused on events applies such concepts only on occasion (and then in order to organize its materials) and that an interpretation of culture consistently built of such concepts will be something quite different from plain historiography, is already indicated by the circumstance that the professional historian would regard any such interpretation as 'philosophy of history'.

Such attitudes cannot affect the recognition, however, that this kind of explanation for cultural formations and their historical alteration operates with categories that are quite different from the causalities which array individual facts into series of events, and are at least as legitimate. This different way of comprehending individual formations and events – which follow, in relation to the historical, from total situations, total constellations, rather than from complexes of individual causes – rests upon an experiential schematization always employed in the pre-scientific experience of the world, and which consequently imparts astonishing power to the penetration of social-psychic happenings. In everyday experience of life (from which the humanistic sciences can still obtain a good deal of 'method', as has been noted), an action is never considered in isolation within some causal connection or amid the mere interweaving of several causal sequences, but always as function of an 'internal and external general situation'. Such consideration involves reconstruction of a totality, and the action or formation to be interpreted is comprehended as one of its parts.

This category of a 'general situation' which is fixed for an epoch in a relatively stable way, this category of a position which is both social and relative to world-view, on the basis of which individual formations acquire their historical meaning, does not take the place of the search for causal explanations. On the contrary, it actually presupposes such study. But it assigns new meaning to the facts comprehended by it. At this point in the discussion of dynamic-sociological cultural interpretation we must again call attention to something already remarked in the discussion of dynamic sociology as such, and that is that the developmental sequence which appears to a linear historical observation in the form of smoothly gliding transitions, here presents itself, in contrast, as discontinuous, 'dialectical'. While an historically linear consideration of change in art, in its deepest inclination, will be unwilling to admit any actual change of style at all – which is to say that it will prefer to register a continuous, gradually shifting modification rather that abrupt contrasts between styles – an art history focused on differences of styles will speak of the sudden new existence of a new style as of a certain date.[85] Both findings are products of the research methods employed. It will always be possible to prove against an observer directed towards discontinuity that there have already been 'precursors' to the creator of a new style, as it will be possible to point out to a gradualist observer that, from a somewhat more distanced view, two instances which are only slightly apart nevertheless mark something radically new, and that, while motifs have their precursors, a style begins only when artistic system and artistic volition (Riegl's *Kunstwollen*) are both new. This is the other remnant to be salvaged from philosophy of history, and in particular, from that of Hegel. If nothing more is intended by dialectics than that notwithstanding the continuity displayed by spiritual cultural entities in their internal development, such an entity, amid its continuity, abruptly turns into a different one, such a turnabout has a meaning we can also well use. This does not mean, of course, that one must also accept the panlogistical schema of the triad: thesis, antithesis, synthesis. Yet this much truth lies in it: all human spiritual creations have something of the structure most easily traced in the theoretical sphere, in which one confronts the other in their development as a *growing* thing, but only from the outside, while internally it faces it as a new antithetical 'positing'. The word 'antithetical' must naturally be employed with caution here, because it recalls the specific structure of the logical sphere. A style is never the antithetical contrary of another, but it is *another* after a certain stage, for the creative subject as well as for the one observing history. A new world-view is not dialectically distinguishable from its predecessor because it offers completely different fragments of experience, but because, at some point in time, the new aggregation is abruptly differentiated from

127

the other. There is a certain justification, then, for speaking of a new 'life-system' even though the concept 'system' is to be taken here in a figurative sense.

Dynamic cultural sociology takes concepts appropriate to types which are relatively stable for a 'period', and it elaborates them for the explanation and interpretation of cultural formations. These concepts are to be elicited from the valuations and innermost inclinations of the age under study,[86] and they are not to contain wholly alien and 'imported' standards and unifying syntheses, or ones which are only oriented to ourselves. As with dynamic sociology, so we see with dynamic cultural sociology a new problem growing out of this kind of observation of history.

Just as the typology of social arrangements, which was simply hierarchical at first, extended itself into a doctrine of social development in general, and as hierarchical type-construction extended itself in all fields of cultural systems into a historical dynamic of these cultural movements, so there emerge more general problems for cultural sociology, which must achieve dynamic overview here as well. These problems consist in interrelating the immanent structures, the dynamics of several distinct spiritual fields.

So Alfred Weber,[87] for example, sees it as the distinctive task of cultural sociology to come to know the three strata of the total historical process – which he calls the process of society, the process of civilization, and the movement of culture – each in their own dynamic, and to comprehend their mutual interrelationship in a given historical state of things. This brings forth the knowledge that the structure of historical progression is by no means identical within these three factors, each of which is always somehow at hand. While, in his view, the social process (which corresponds on the whole to the dynamic succession of formations which are specifically social in the terminology we have been using) is typical – which is to say that it displays a generalizable typical sequence of developmental stages – this does not by any means apply to the structure of cultural movement. Here there is a different form in every organic unit of history, and typing gets no further than the superficial appearances of the cultural. The process of civilization, which is the third field of the spiritual in general, has quite a different kind of onward movement. It has the structure of 'bad infinity'. It can be transferred from one organic unit of history to another, and it can continue to develop in linear fashion. Technology and science belong here, and their function is not expression of the soul, as in the case of culture, but thoroughgoing intellectualist rationalization of physical and spiritual existence.

Where the older philosophy of history of the past (Hegel)

assumed a unitary dynamic for the development of history as a whole, we see this dynamic monism breached here and a polyphonic explanation of the historical process settling in place. A similar tendency is represented by Scheler in a recently published article,[88] which distinguishes among three kinds of knowing: religion, metaphysics, and positive science, each of which possesses its own distinctive 'form of historical motion'.

With this, the idea of an historical dynamic moves to the fore once again, and it does so precisely in the more recent sociological inquiry;[89] but motives have been altogether changed and reconstructed, in keeping with the overall spiritual state of things from which this idea now springs anew. Poorer in metaphysics, more richly provided with differentiations and structural insights, dynamic sociology assumes the legacy of philosophy of history. It is an attempt to illuminate once again an existence already ordered according to historical causality, from a more sweeping perspective, and to complement purely causal historical inquiry with an investigation of the presuppositions upon which the effectiveness of causes depends.[90]

If the varieties of sociology and cultural sociology complement one another in these ways, fitting together in an overall design, even though they came into being historically one after the other, there remains one issue to explore, one which is to be considered cultural-sociological in any event and which can consequently be readily accommodated within the framework of dynamic sociological explanation.

While sociology operates with the concept of time characteristic of the philosophy of history and therefore takes some one spiritual tendency as representative for each age, within the movement of which the dialectic is to be traced, it must nevertheless recognize, precisely as sociology, that more than one world-view flourishes within one and the same chronological period and even within a single historical entity. Or, as is often said, the men of an age do not live in the same time. It is the time of philosophy of history which is of course intended at the end of that saying. However permissible it may be, in the interests of a unified dynamic, to let the foremost spiritual stratum and its world-view appear as representative for a whole epoch and society, it is necessary to counterbalance this conscious exaggeration, made in the interests of the dynamic, with the insight that there are present in every age several simultaneous world-views, distributed among several social strata. A thoroughgoing sociological dynamic investigation will not content itself with asking about the development and transformation undergone by the preponderant world-view, but it will also ask about the dispo-

129

sition of world-views which have become irrelevant from the standpoint of the total movement but which nevertheless transform themselves during their continued existence and which live on in these altered forms. Although the nobility, for example, has been deprived of its primacy, and the bourgeoisie has taken over the role of culture-bearer, the world-views imputable to the nobility continue to exist and the nobility's forms of life and cultural formations remain rooted in these primary cultural elements, which have lost relevance. What changes of form do their creations undergo and what kinds of inner dialectic is followed by such a secondary, contrapuntally interplaying spiritual development? Are there not moments when it asserts itself once more within the dominant dynamic? Another developmental problem concerns what happens to world-views and the cultural formations belonging to them when they are taken over by alien culture-bearers. What transformation is typically to be observed in such cases?

All these problems, which are designed to broaden the straightforward structure of philosophy of history into a complex network of socially dynamic developmental tendencies, constitute a plan of study which is fit to discern within history a character of necessity in keeping with its essence, and thus not in the sense of laws transferred from nature but in the sense appropriate to the structural vision emanating from its own spirit.

Notes

1 An example of a description of the cultural spheres' struggle for autonomy can be found in Ernst Cassirer, *Freiheit und Form: Studien zur
deutschen Geistesgeschichte* (Freedom and Form: Studies in German
Intellectual History), Berlin: Bruno Cassirer, 1916.
2 On the history of the concept of culture see Rudolf Eucken, *Geschichte
und Kritik der Grundbegriffe der Gegenwart* (History and Critique of
Fundamental Concepts of the Present), 1st edn, Leipzig: Veit & Co.,
1878, pp. 185–94; Rudolf Eucken, *Geschichte der philosophischen Ter-
minologie. Im Umriß dargestellt* (Outline of the History of Philosophical Terminology), Leipzig: Veit & Co., 1879; and Paul Barth, *Die
Philosophie der Geschichte als Soziologie* (The Philosophy of History
as Sociology), 3rd and 4th edns, Leipzig: O. R. Reisland, 1922, Part 1.
3 See, for example, Meister Eckhart's sermon 'Mary and Martha,
Sermon on Luke 10:38' in *Meister Eckhart's Schriften und Predigten*
(Meister Eckhart's Writings and Sermons), trans. and ed. Herman
Büttner, Jena: Diederichs, 1921.
4 See Friedrich Gundolf, *Goethe*, 10th ed, Berlin: G. Boni, 1922, p. 27.
5 Ferdinand Tönnies, *Gemeinschaft und Gesellschaft: Grundbegriffe
der reinen Soziologie,* 3rd rev. edn, Berlin: K. Curtius, 1920. [Com-
munity and Society, trans. and ed. Charles P. Loomis, New York:
Harper & Row, 1957.]
6 Otto von Gierke, *Johannes Althusius und die Entwicklung der natur-
rechtlichen Staatstheorien,* 3rd edn with supplements, Breslau: M. & H.
Marcus, 1913, pp. 338f, 56ff. (*The Development of Political Theory,*
trans. Bernard Freyd, London: Allen & Unwin, 1939); Wilhelm
Dilthey, *Einleitung in die Geisteswissenschaften: Versuch einer Grundlegung für das Studium der Gesellschaft und der Geschichte* (Introduction to the Humanistic Sciences: Essay Towards a Foundation for the
Study of Society and of History), Leipzig: Duncker & Humblot, 1883,
vol. 1, pp. 418ff; and Adolf Menzel, *Naturrecht und Soziologie*
(Natural Law and Sociology), Vienna and Leipzig: C. Fromme, 1912.
7 See Georg Simmel, *Grundfragen der Soziologie (Individuum und Ge-*

sellschaft); 2nd edn, Berlin-Leipzig: Walter de Gruyter, 1920, p. 21. [Fundamental Problems of Sociology (Individual and Society), part one of Kurt H. Wolff (ed.), *The Sociology of Georg Simmel*, Chicago: The Free Press, 1950.]

8 Theodor Kistiakowski, *Gesellschaft und Einzelwesen* (Society and the Individual), Berlin: O. Liebmann, 1899, pp. 56–87.

9 Max Weber, *Wirtschaft und Gesellschaft*, Tübingen: J. C. B. Mohr, 1922. [*Economy and Society: An Outline of Interpretive Sociology*, ed. Guenther Roth and Claus Wittich; trans. Ephraim Fischoff *et al.*, New York: Bedminster Press, 1968.]

10 Ernst Bernheim, *Lehrbuch der historischen Methode und der Geschichtsphilosophie* (Manual of Historical Method and Philosophy of History), 5th & 6th edns, Leipzig: Duncker & Humblot, 1908, pp. 22ff.

11 There are several points of departure in recent scholarship for the theory of the different 'attitudes' which is taking form. Among others, see Edmund Husserl, *Ideen zu einer reinen Phänomenologie und phänomenologischen Philosophie*, Erstes Buch, Halle a.d.S.: M. Niemeyer, 1913, pp. 48ff. [*Ideas: General Introduction to Pure Phenomenology*, trans. W. R. Boyce, London: Allen & Unwin, 1931]. Husserl distinguishes here between a natural and a phenomenological attitude. Max Scheler speaks of 'spiritual postures' (*Geisteshaltungen*). See 'Vom Wesen der Philosophie and der moralischen Bedingung des philosophischen Erkennens', in *Vom Ewigen im Menschen*, vol. I, Leipzig: Der Neue Geist Verlag, 1921, pp. 65ff. ['The Nature of Philosophy and of the Moral Precondition of Philosophical Knowledge' in *On the Eternal in Man*, trans. Bernhard Noble, London: SCM Press, 1954]. See also Martin Heidegger (in lectures); and Karl Jaspers, *Psychologie der Weltanschauungen* (Psychology of World-Views), Berlin: J. Springer, 1919, pp. 48ff. With regard to a natural object, there is the possibility of different points of view, and it can correspondingly become relevant to theory at several conceptual levels. In the case of spiritual creations, there is added to this the variety of 'attitudes', and, as we shall see, to this corresponds a variety in the constitution of concepts.

12 Georg Lukács, *Ästhetik* (Manuscript). [Here Mannheim is referring to Lukács's first version of a systematic aesthetics, which was first published in 1974 as *Heidelberger Ästhetik (1916–1918)* (Heidelberg Aesthetics, 1916–1918), ed. György Markus and Frank Benseler from Lukács's literary estate. See Lukács, *Werke*, vol. 17, Darmstadt and Neuwied: Luchterhand, 1974.]

13 Fausto Squillace, *Die soziologischen Theorien* (Sociological Theories), translated from the Italian [*Le dottrine sociologiche*, Rome: Columbo, 1902] by Rudolf Eisler, Philosophische-soziologische Bücherei, vol. 23. Leipzig: W. Klinghardt, 1911.

14 Paul Barth, *op. cit.*

15 Cultural sociology is opposed on principle by those who consider a 'normative approach' the only one appropriate for cultural phenomena. They consider a valid sociological approach to phenomena as

either completely impossible or justified only with regard to the 'originating causes' and 'functional character' of such phenomena. As an example of the first position we cite Franz Oppenheimer, *System der Soziologie* (System of Sociology), Jena: Fischer, 1922, vol. 1, p. 440ff. Oppenheimer upholds the Hegelian distinction between 'objective' and 'absolute' spirit; and the things included in the latter (religion, art, and philosophy) fall into the area of the non-social. An example of the second position is Othmar Spann, *Kurzgefaßtes System der Gesellschaftslehre* (Brief System of the Science of Society), Berlin: Quelle & Meyer, 1914, pp. 57ff. and pp. 535f. At the opposite extreme are the purely pragmatic doctrines, such as vulgar Marxism, which claim that the higher forms can be completely explained in terms of causes which are not meaningful. One of our tasks is to determine the reach of the sociological approach to 'valid' phenomena without overlooking the fact of 'validity', and to proceed instead by determining the relevance of cultural-sociological knowledge through incorporating 'validity' into the inquiry.

16 Max Weber, *Wirtschaft und Gesellschaft*, p. 368. [We have preferred to retranslate this and some subsequent quotes from Max Weber's *Wirtschaft und Gesellschaft* rather than to follow the otherwise excellent translation by Guenther Roth and Claus Wittich (*Economy and Society*, New York: Bedminster Press, 1968) and have rendered *Handlung* as 'transaction' rather than 'action'. We think it important that Weber chose a term so closely linked to economic activity and so far from the world of actions and deeds. The 'commercial' connotation of *handeln*, furthermore, links to Weber's conception of the relationship between sociology and political economy *and* to Mannheim's differences with him.]

17 Max Weber, *Wirtschaft und Gesellschaft,* p. 1.

18 Max Weber, *op.cit.*, p. 369.

19 A phenomenon of consciousness in the sense of the conscious focus of attention upon it.

20 'Needing to be apprehended' (*Vernehmungsbedürftigkeit*) is an expression of Adolf Reinach's. See his 'Die apriorischen Grundlagen des bürgerlichen Rechtes' (The *a priori* Foundations of Bourgeois Law) in *Jahrbuch für Philosophie und phänomenologische Forschung*, I, 2 (1913), p. 707.

21 Max Scheler, *Zur Phänomenologie und Theorie der Sympathiegefühle und von Liebe und Haß*, Halle a.d.S., M. Niemeyer, 1913), pp. 118ff. [*The Nature of Sympathy*, trans. Peter Heath, London: Routledge & Kegan Paul, 1954.]

22 Here we are employing that meaning of the word 'intuitive' according to which it signifies any act of apprehension that is completely independent of meaning, not only of theoretical meaning but equally of aesthetic, religious, or other relations of meaning.

23 The following example can be used to illustrate clearly the difference between objective meaning and functional relation. A proposition can be true or false. This alternative refers to its objective theoretical

content. Both a theoretically true, correct proposition or a false one can be a 'lie'. This expresses a functional relationship, in this case with reference to ethical categories.

24 On this subject see Edith Stein, 'Beiträge zur philosophischen Begründung der Psychologie und der Geisteswissenschaften, Zweite Abhandlung: Individuum und Gemeinschaft' (Contributions to the Philosophical Foundation of Psychology and the Humanistic Sciences. Second part: Individual and Community), in *Jahrbuch für Philosophie und phänomenologische Forschung*, 5 (1922), pp. 116–283.

25 See Siegfried Kracauer, 'Die Gruppe als Ideenträger' (The Group as Bearer of Ideas), *Archiv für Sozialwissenschaft und Sozialpolitik*, 3 (1922), p. 602.

26 Karl Marx, *Die Neue Zeit*, 21, 1 (1903). [This quotation occurs in the introduction to the *Grundrisse: Foundation of the Critique of Political Economy*, trans. Martin Nicolaus, New York: Random House, 1979, p. 84. The introduction was discovered in Marx's papers in 1902 and first published in 1903 in the newspaper *Die Neue Zeit*.]

27 Dilthey had made everyday experience or 'general experience of the world' a problem of philosophy. We consider it to be one of the most important problems of cultural sociology. To explain its structure and location in the movement of culture is one of the most important projects one could adopt. See Wilhelm Dilthey, *Der Aufbau der geschichtlichen Welt in den Geisteswissenschaften* (The Structure of the Historical World in the Humanistic Sciences), Berlin: Verlag der Königlichen Akademie der Wissenschaften, 1910, pp. 3–123.

28 Comte had expected his positivistic method to bring about this regeneration of the social sciences. See Auguste Comte, *Soziologie*, translated [from the last three volumes of the *Cours de philosophie positive*] by Valentine Dorn, Jena: G. Fischer, 1907; see especially p. 213. [*The Positive Philosophy of Auguste Comte*, freely translated and condensed by Harriet Martineau, New York: AMS Press, 1974.] Among more recent works is Emile Durkheim, *Die Methode der Soziologie* [*Les règles de la méthode sociologique*, Paris: F. Alcan, 1895.] Philosophische-soziologische Bücherei, vol. 5, Leipzig: A. Kröner, 1908. [*The Rules of Sociological Method*, 8th edn, trans. Sarah A. Solovay and John H. Miller; ed. George E. G. Catlin, Chicago: University of Chicago Press, 1938.]

29 Benedetto Croce, 'Geschichte und Chronik' (History and Chronicle), in his *Zur Theorie und Geschichte der Historiographie*, trans. from the Italian [*Teoria e storia della storiografia*. Bari: G. Laterza, 1917] by Enrico Pizzo, Tübingen: J. C. B. Mohr, 1915. [First appeared in Italian in the form of articles in proceedings of Italian accademies and Italian reviews 1912–13. First publication in book form in German.]

30 Here history of style is meant in the sense of the history of *motifs*.

31 We have attempted elsewhere to provide a typology of epistemology. See Karl Mannheim, 'Die Strukturanalyse der Erkenntnistheorie', Supplement 57 to *Kant-Studien* (1922). ['Structural Analysis of Epistemology', in Karl Mannheim, *Essays on Sociology and Social Psycho-*

logy, ed. Paul Kecskemeti, London: Routledge & Kegan Paul, 1953.]
In our opinion, a typology of this sort can and must be established as a
prelude to the sociological study of cultural formations.

32 On the difference between 'explanation' and 'understanding', which
was originally formulated without reference to differentiation, see
Max Weber, *Wirtschaft und Gesellschaft*, p. 5; and 'Über einige Kategorien der verstehenden Soziologie' (On Some Categories of Interpretative Sociology) in *Gesammelte Aufsätze zur Wissenschaftslehre*
(Collected Essays on the Theory of Science), Tübingen: J. C. B.
Mohr, 1922.

33 See, for example, Sigmund Freud's recent *Massenpsychologie und Ich-
Analyse*, Leipzig-Vienna-Zurich: Internationaler Psychoanalytischer
Verlag, 1921. [*Group Psychology and the Analysis of the Ego*, trans.
James Strachey, International Psycho-Analytical Library No. 6,
London: Boni & Liveright, 1922.]

34 See Karl Jaspers, *op. cit.*, p. 190ff.; and Eduard Spranger, *Lebensfor-
men: geisteswissenschaftliche Psychologie und Ethik der Persönlich-
keit* (Forms of Life: Humanistic Psychology and the Ethics of
Personality), 2nd revised and expanded edition, Halle a.d.S.: Niemeyer, 1921, p. 107ff.

35 Karl Marx, *Das Elend der Philosophie*, 9th ed, Stuttgart: J. H. W.
Dietz, 1921, p. 101. [Here quoted from 'The Poverty of Philosophy', in
Marx/Engels, *Collected Works*, vol. 6, New York: International Publi-
shers, 1976, p. 166.]

36 Wilhelm Jerusalem, 'Soziologie des Erkennens' (Sociology of Cognition), *Kölner Vierteljahreshefte für Sozialwissenschaften*, 1, 3,
(1921).

37 A charming description of this ascent of cultural entities from 'life' into
self-subsistence can be found in Georg Simmel's 'Die Wendung zur
Idee' (The Tropism Toward the Idea), in his last work, *Lebensan-
schauung: Vier metaphysische Kapital* (A View of Life: Four Metaphysical Chapters), Munich-Leipzig: Duncker & Humblot, 1918.

38 This double existence of style was first seen by Lukács. See Georg
Lukács, 'Bemerkungen zur Theorie der Literaturgeschichte'
(Remarks on the Theory of Literary History), which has appeared only
in Hungarian.

39 See Eduard Spranger's important essay, 'Zur Theorie des Verstehens
und zur geisteswissenschaftlichen Psychologie' (On the Theory of
Interpretative Understanding and on Humanistic Psychology), in the
Festschrift Johannes Volkelt zum 70. Geburtstag dargebracht, Munich:
Beck, 1918, pp. 371ff.

40 Max Weber, *Wirtschaft und Gesellschaft*, vol. 1

41 *Ibid.*, p. 194. [Here quoted from *Economy and Society*, p. 356.]

42 In the last analysis this is Hans Kelsen's criticism in his *Der soziologische und juristische Staatsbegriff: kritische Untersuchung des Verhält-
nisses von Staat und Recht* (The Sociological and the Juristic Concept
of the State: Critical Investigation of the Relationship between State
and Law), Tübingen: J. C. B. Mohr, 1922, p. 1970.

43 On this problem see my forthcoming essay, 'Beiträge zur Theorie der Weltanschauungs-Interpretation', *Jahrbuch für Kunstgeschichte*, I(XV), 4 (1921–2), pp. 298–302, from which some of this discussion is taken. ['The Interpretation of "Weltanschauung"', in Karl Mannheim, *Essays on the Sociology of Knowledge*, ed. Paul Kecskemeti, London: Routledge & Kegan Paul, 1952.] In the essay I have sought to work out one specific sort of meaning in cultural formations: the 'documentary'. The relationship of social functionality, which is related to it, must nevertheless be distinguished from it in spite of this inner connection. We must reserve a complete discussion of this distinction for a later systematic treatment of the problems of interpretation.

44 See Max Weber, *Wirtschaft und Gesellschaft*, p. 196. [*Economy and Society*, p. 359.]

45 *Ibid.*, p. 201ff. [*Economy and Society*, pp. 365f.]

46 See among others Wilhelm Hausestein, *Der nackte Mensch in der Kunst aller Zeiten und Völker* (The Nude in the Art of All Times and Nations), 2nd edn, (Munich: Piper, 1913), and *Bild und Gemeinschaft: Entwurf einer Soziologie der Kunst* (Image and Community: Toward a Sociology of Art), Munich: K. Wolff, 1920.

47 Max Weber, *Gesammelte Aufsätze zur Religionssoziologie* (Collected Essays on the Sociology of Religion), Tübingen: J. C. B. Mohr, 1920–1, vol. I.

48 Wilhelm Dilthey, *Einleitung in die Geisteswissenschaften*.

49 Heinrich Rickert, *Die Grenzen der naturwissenschaftlichen Begriffsbildung* (The Limits of Concept Formation in the Natural Sciences), 3rd and 4th revised and expanded editions, Tübingen: J. C. B. Mohr, 1921, p. 122.

50 The specific working out of the sociological conceptual level distinguishes the various types of sociology.

51 I have dealt with this at greater length in my 'Zum Problem einer Klassifikation der Wissenschaften' (On the Problem of the Classification of the Sciences), *Archiv für Sozialwissenschaft und Sozialpolitik*, 50, 1 (1922).

52 See Paul Barth, *op. cit.*

53 Heinrich Rickert, *op. cit.*, p. 200.

54 The expression is used by Adolf Reinach in 'Die apriorischen Grundlagen des bürgerlichen Rechtes'.

55 Cf. Emile Durkheim, *op. cit.*, p. 13.

56 Cf. Georg Simmel, *Soziologie: Untersuchungen über die Formen der Vergesellschaftung*, Leipzig: Duncker & Humblot, 1908, p. 35. [Most of this book is contained, as parts two to five, in Kurt H. Wolff (ed.), *The Sociology of Georg Simmel*.]

57 We are treating 'pure sociology' in greater detail, with reference to individual authors, since, as a still emerging discipline, it does not yet allow of a summary exposition.

58 Alfred Vierkandt also calls it 'general sociology', and Leopold von Wiese refers to it as 'science of relations' (*Beziehungslehre*). See Alfred Vierkandt, 'Programm einer formalen Gesellschaftslehre'

(Programme of a Formal Science of Society) and Leopold von Wiese, 'Zur Methodologie der Beziehungslehre' (On the Methodology of the Science of Relations), both of which appear in *Kölner Vierteljahreshefte für Sozialwissenschaften*, 1, 1 (1921).

59 Georg Simmel, *Soziologie*, as well as *Grundfragen der Soziologie (Individuum und Gesellschaft)*.

60 *Soziologie*, p. 27ff.

61 Georg Simmel, *Grundfragen der Soziologie*, p. 13f. [Kurt H. Wolff (ed.), *The Sociology of Georg Simmel*, p. 10.]

62 *Ibid.*, p. 14. [*The Sociology of Georg Simmel*, p. 10.]

63 The problem of what Simmel means by form, important as it may be in general, is not relevant in this context.

64 *Ibid.*, p. 14.

65 Leopold von Wiese, *op. cit.*, p. 52.

66 Hans Kelsen, *op. cit.*

67 Spann's universalism can be considered as the opposite pole of this nominalistic and atomizing way of thought. See Othmar Spann, *op. cit.*

68 See Georg Simmel, *Grundfragen der Soziologie*, p. 29.

69 How little it is really a question of induction here is shown by an observation of Simmel's about the nature of examples: 'The investigation could be carried out even on the basis of fictitious examples, whose importance for the interpretation of reality could be left to the reader's accidental knowledge of fact' (Simmel, *Soziologie*, p. 49). [*The Sociology of Georg Simmel*, p. 89.] In other words, the concrete individual case appears as an exemplification and not as part of an infinite inductive series such that the individual case would only be complemented and corroborated through this series.

70 This term is used by Hans Lorenz Stoltenberg in his *Sozialpsychologie*, 2 vols, Berlin: K. Curtius, 1914–22.

71 Cf. Alfred Vierkandt, *op. cit.*, p. 65.

72 Ferdinand Tönnies, *op. cit.*

73 [In translating *Kürwille*, the editors and translators have not followed Werner J. Cahnmann and Rudolf Heberle who, justifiably abandoning the earlier translation of this term as 'rational will', render it as 'arbitrary will' (*Ferdinand Tönnies on Sociology: Pure, Applied, and Empirical*, ed. Werner J. Cahnmann and Rudolf Heberle, Chicago and London: University of Chicago Press, 1971). Since 'arbitrary will' has pejorative connotations in English which *Kürwille* lacks, and which we have therefore wanted to avoid, we have preferred 'unconstrained will' instead.]

74 Hans Lorenz Stoltenberg's *Sozialpsychologie* represents a purely classificatory approach to community-forming actions.

75 Max Scheler, *Der Formalismus in der Ethik und die materielle Wertethik*, 2nd edn, Halle a.d.S.: M. Niemeyer, 1921. [*Formalism in Ethics and Non-formal Ethics of Values*, trans. Manfred S. Frings and Roger L. Funk, Evanston: Northwestern University Press, 1973.]

76 Edith Stein, *op. cit.*

77 Siegfried Kracauer, *op. cit.*, and his *Soziologie als Wissenschaft*

137

(Sociology as Science), Dresden: Sibyllenverlag, 1922.

78 Alexander von Schelting, 'Die logische Theorie der historischen Kulturwissenschaft von Max Weber und im besonderen sein Begriff des Idealtypus' (The Logical Theory of Max Weber's Historical Science of Culture and in Particular his Concept of Ideal Type), in *Archiv für Sozialwissenschaft und Sozialpolitik*, 49, 3 (1922), pp. 746ff. We have not discussed the problem of ideal types because it is not relevant at this stage of our argument.

79 Max Weber, *Wirtschaft und Gesellschaft*, p. 140. [*Economy and Society*, p. 242.]

80 We should like to cite, for example, Rudolf Otto's *Das Heilige: Über das Irrationale in der Idee des Göttlichen und sein Verhältnis zum Rationalen*, Breslau: Trewendt und Granier, 1917. [*The Idea of the Holy: An Inquiry into the Non-Rational Factor in the Idea of the Divine and its Relation to the Rational*, trans. John W. Harvey, London: Humphrey Milford, Oxford University Press, 1923.] See also Friedrich Heiler's *Das Gebet: Eine religionsgeschichtliche und religionspsychologische Untersuchung*, 3rd edn, Munich: E. Reinhardt, 1921. [*Prayer: a Study in the History and Psychology of Religion*, trans. Samuel McComb, London; New York, etc.: Oxford University Press, 1932.]

81 See J. Eichner, 'Das Problem des Gegebenen in der Kunstgeschichte' (The Problem of the Given in Art History), *Festschrift für Alois Riehl: Von Freunden und Schülern zu seinem siebzigsten Geburtstage dargebracht* (*Festschrift* for Alois Riehl on his 70th birthday from friends and students), Halle a.d.S.: M. Niemeyer, 1914, p. 203.

82 Wilhelm Dilthey, 'Die Typen der Weltanschauung und ihre Ausbildung in den metaphysischen Systemen' (The Types of World-view and their Elaboration in Metaphysical Systems), in Max Frischeisen-Köhler ed., *Weltanschauung*, Berlin: Reichl & Co., 1911.

83 Max Weber, 'Zwischenbetrachtung: Theorie der Stufen und Richtungen religiöser Weltablehnung', *Gesammelte Aufsätze zur Religionssoziologie*, pp. 536–73. [Hans Gerth and C. Wright Mills, eds, *From Max Weber*, New York: Oxford University Press, 1946, chapter 8.]

84 The following remarks originated in part under the influence of Professor Alfred Weber's sociological seminars.

85 These two viewpoints can be clearly distinguished within art history. Wickhoff, for example, sees the development as a whole as consisting of only three periods, while the Riegl school, which contributes the concept of 'artistic volition' (*Kunstwollen*), opens the way to a much more differentiated periodization. See Franz Wickhoff, 'Über die Einteilung der Kunstgeschichte in Hauptperioden' (Division of Art History into Major Periods), in Max Dvořák (ed.), *Die Schriften Franz Wickhoffs* (Franz Wickhoff's Writings), Berlin: Meyer & Jessen, 1912–13, pp. 446ff.

86 See Ernst Troeltsch, 'Über Maßstäbe zur Beurteilung historischer Dinge' (On Standards for the Judgment of Historical Things), *Historische Zeitschrift*, vol. 116 (1916), third series, 20, 1, p. 116.

87 Alfred Weber, 'Prinzipielles zur Kultursoziologie', (Fundamental Considerations on Cultural Sociology), *Archiv für Sozialwissenschaft und Sozialpolitik*, 47, 1 (1920).

88 Max Scheler, 'Die positivistische Geschichtsphilosophie des Wissens und die Aufgaben einer Soziologie der Erkenntnis', *Kölner Vierteljahreshefte für Sozialwissenschaften*, 1, (1921). [Scheler's essay appeared in revised form under the title 'Die positivistische Geschichtsphilosophie des Wissens (Dreistadiegesetz)' in *Moralia* (1924). English translation by Rainer Koehne, 'On the positivistic philosophy of the history of knowledge and its law of three stages', in *The Sociology of Knowledge: A Reader*, ed. James E. Curtis and John W. Petras, New York: Praeger, London: Duckworth, 1970, pp. 161–9].

89 See Ernst Troeltsch, 'Über den Begriff einer historischen Dialektik' (On the Concept of an Historical Dialect), *Historische Zeitschrift*, vol. 119 (1919), Third Series, 23, 3, and 24, 3.

90 See Heinrich Cunow, *Die Marxsche Geschichts-, Gesellschafts- und Staatstheorie; Grundzüge der Marxschen Soziologie* (Marxian Theory of History, Society, and the State: Elements of Marxian Sociology), Berlin: J. H. W. Dietz, 1921, vol. II, pp. 265ff.

Part two

A sociological theory of culture and its knowability
(Conjunctive and communicative thinking)

Contents

nomous and appear as such with the growth of class society. The historical, philosophical, and sociological conditions of purposive-rational interpretation. Generalizing sociology as a trans-conjunctive discipline. The problem of everyday thinking. The phenomenon of cultivation.

The task of a cultural sociology. The ideological superstructure. Immediate interest and mediated involvement. Essential perspectivity and propagandistic science. Linkage between natural-scientific and humanistic methods in cultural sociology. The emergence of the problem of culture.

Preface

At work on the problems of a methodology for the humanistic sciences, we became convinced, after much reflection, that not even purely methodological problems of thinking can be solved without sociological orientation. As a rule, the methodology and logic of thought proceed in a strictly immanent way when they formulate their inquiries; that is, they exclude all historical, sociological, or other 'genetic' inquiries and expect to gain methodological insight from nothing but absorption in the structural problems of scientific thought as they find it. In this, however, such inquiry takes as starting point a fiction of which it remains altogether unaware: that thinking in the manner which a given logician or methodologist finds established is not a historically determined form of thinking, but that thinking in this form can be equated with thinking 'as such'; and that methodology above all, which pronounces judgment, as it were, upon this thinking is itself without presuppositions and elevated above all standpoints limited by time. While it is readily admitted in all other areas of cultural development that there are several styles in art, in the history of literature (even more than one existing at the same time), that there are clashing political tendencies, and while the possible sociological imputability of each of these to some social stratum as its bearer is at least considered as a problem, there is resistance among most against drawing the logical conclusions from the fact that is especially clear in the history of thought, the fact that here too there are several mutually incompatible tendencies and methods, which might be similarly imputable to more general sociological currents, and that there could well be correspondingly many standpoints for formulating methodological inquiries.

The plurality of methodological standpoints and their inner connectedness with specific currents in the history of thought became apparent to us as we were endeavouring to solve the methodological problems of the humanistic sciences, and especially the problem of interpretative understanding (*Verstehen*). We could not avoid seeing that these problems were altogether differently approached from the one side, oriented to the natural sciences, than from the other, oriented to the cultural. We could not avoid seeing that there are at least two standpoints for defining methodological inquiry, and that they, deriving from different traditions, pose the problem quite differently and consequently also deal differently with it. This opened our eyes to something which the dogma of a timeless reason usually obscures. We saw that the logician or methodologist, like every systematic thinker, is located within a specific tendency, a specific style of thinking. And this awoke in us the need to make clear to ourselves, if only in outline, the current of thinking within which our own definition of the inquiry and our manner of handling questions have their place, how such questions could, from a sociological point of view, arise at all, and how the most important clashing currents of thought relate to the most important clashing social currents which bear the social process as a whole. No small part in attracting us to these questions was played by the aspiration to extend the study of ideology, as it is called, to even so remote a field in the intellectual world as that exemplified by methodology, a field in which a direct connection in the form of interestedness does not occur, but where it may nevertheless be correct to speak of sociological determination, in the sense of imputing certain tendencies of thought to specific world-views of specific social classes.

The first chapter in this part deals with problems of this sort, and can be considered as introduction, in the manner of historical sociology, to the systematic approach of the second chapter. The second chapter represents a systematic contribution to the methodology of the humanistic sciences, and especially an analysis of interpretative understanding, and, as such, it attempts to solve a methodological problem of that interpretative sociology which depends on such understanding.

But even in this systematic inquiry we could not dispense with the sociological point of view. For here within systematic inquiry, we see a second possibility for utilizing a sociological point of view in a science of knowing. If the first use of the sociological approach consisted in the self-orientation of the thinker concerning his own standpoint within the social process as a whole, the use of the sociological approach in the systematic inquiry which is now to be discussed consists in doing justice at last, within a theory of thinking and especially of interpretative understanding, to the fact that all thinking is social and that, by virtue of this social connectedness and this characteristic of being a social achievement, more than one type of thinking as well as interpreting is possible The methodology of thought and interpretation must draw out the lessons and consequences of the fact that thinking and interpreting are an always vital function of the social community, and that one sees only one side of the matter when one takes as point of departure in methodology and epistemology some abstract consciousness as such or results of thinking, complete and detached.

Enriched by the sociological point of view, this second chapter of a theory of interpretative understanding had to be expanded into a more comprehensive sociological theory of culture, because we could not forgo projecting an overview where the problems constantly point from one to the other. Despite this striving for an overview, we intend these two studies to stand as individual investigations and to lay claim to all the excuses which are due when one feels one's way into new domains.

1 The sociological determination of methodology

For some time now, there has been a recurrent demand for a *novum organon* in the humanistic sciences. Even a cursory glance at the humanistic sciences, as they have actually developed and continue to unfold, and at the methodological and logical knowledge *about* these fields reveals a discrepancy between science and logic, a discrepancy which fully justifies the demand for a new methodology.

Researches in the histories of literature and philosophy along the lines of the history of ideas, the approach to the history of art by way of the history of styles, the analyses of world-views in all fields of the humanistic sciences, the cultural-sociological pattern of inquiry among sociologists and researchers into specialized topics, systematic research into ideology in Marxist sociology: all seem to aspire toward a similar goal and to work, despite many presuppositions differing in contents, with similar, as yet barely analysed methods. Corresponding to this process in the *historical* disciplines is a similar turn in the *systematic* disciplines related to the humanistic sciences and more or less fundamental to them. Psychology's turn from the method of experimenting and explaining to that of describing and interpreting, and the powerful current of the phenomenological tendency in philosophy: both bring to the fore the universally applicable method of description. And when one also considers that cultural philosophy is taking the place of systematic philosophy as the structural theory of historical world-views, one realizes that the systematic disciplines are taking a direction similar to the change under way in the historical disciplines.

In all these disciplines, new (or, at least, relatively new) sets of questions are emerging; they pursue a new kind of goal and employ new methods of thinking in this pursuit. Working out these methods represents an assignment yet to be fulfilled, for these disciplines as well as for the history of thought.

That methodological theory has failed to comprehend these fields altogether, or has grasped them only inadequately, is primarily due to the circumstance that the new disciplines of human-scientific research have grown out of a philosophy different from that in which the still dominant methodological theory originated. For it is most essential to pay attention to something which one generally tends to pass over, viz., that methodologies also possess perspectival and philosophical presuppositions. And their range and fruitfulness initially extend only as far as the things which have grown up out of the same world-view and its appropriate manner of life. Just as classical aesthetics, for example, could grasp the principles of classical art only, which was akin to it in spirit, so there are – *mutatis mutandis* – methods and tendencies of thought in the history of thought which variously bring out only one mode, one side of the knowledge possible, a side which stands in intimate relationship to the overall perspectival and philosophical position of the time. The distinctive properties, the methodological construction of such a tendency of thought will be most accessible, moreover, to the tendency in methodological theory which has grown up out of the same (or at least related) presuppositions as the thinking it seeks to investigate.

To apply these general assertions directly to the problem with which we are concerned, it is only necessary to call to mind that modern natural science arose out of a spirit and philosophical attitude completely different from the tendency in historiography becoming relevant at the present time. While modern natural science first found the codification of the philosophy and methodology corresponding to it in Cartesian principles, and while the methodology and the practice of this science are emanations of one and the same style of thought, contemporary historical research, striving for analyses of world-views, received its scientific fecundation from the Romantic consciousness. Two philosophies, thoroughly different in their foundations, thus stand at the place of origin of these two complexes of scientific knowledge, and their distinctive methodological properties as well as their being sociologically grounded can only be grasped by reaching back to these spiritually different origins. To see clearly in these matters, one must not forget that philosophy, life, and scientific knowledge never go along side by side in isolation. Philosophy, in its various tendencies, always rises, rather, out of a current of life (and usually one that is socially conditioned), and serves as pioneer for it, first formulating, in premonitory anticipation and programmatically,

151

the new 'will to the world' (*Weltwollen*), only to return in the sequel and penetrate life and science itself. It then pervades these, advances its own development within them, and achieves genuine concreteness only at the end. It attains its highest stage, however, only when it is once again released, at a subsequent stage, from its embedment in realities, by means of reflection, and systematized. Applying this insight, then, to the first current mentioned above, to philosophy oriented to natural science, the Cartesian teachings concerning first principles can be considered as the earliest reflective clarification of the intellectual project (*Denkwollen*) which was striving, together with the natural sciences developing themselves at the same time, to form the world throughout. How this new cosmic and cognitive project (*Welt-und Erkenntniswollen*) of which methodology is only a part, came to be, can best be traced in its practice, that is, in the coming into being of the exact natural sciences, which began in the intellectual work of a Kepler and a Galileo but acquired its human ideal-typical representative rather in Leonardo da Vinci.[1]

The entire process going on in all this gains its character from the determination to put another world-view in the place of one which has become faded and no longer credible, to establish new intellectual methods in place of those which have long been employed. It is on this occasion that there can be heard, perhaps for the first time in modern thought, the call of 'back to nature!' which is later repeatedly sounded (whenever it is a question of putting through a new representation of the world). That this return to nature was always bound to prove a self-deception can be no surprise, since mankind never meets bare nature, unendowed with meanings, but puts a new-formed representation of the totality in place of a decadent old one.

'The struggle was for the right of perception, but the outcome is at once a new idea and a new systematization of the concept.'[2] To the historian of this process, accordingly, with this development already behind him, the slogan of a return to nature discloses itself as a means for overcoming an antiquated method of thought, which is to be got out of the way in order to make room for a creative, new world-design. But it is also to be deceived to believe that the new forms of thought have been conjured up out of the void or that some form of thought, once overcome, could have been consigned to oblivion once and for all. Intellectual tendencies battle and conquer one another, but every possibility remains stored up for experience. It is always only a matter of victory for the time being, and of the unfolding of one of the tendencies: the other one, the one defeated, does come back at a later stage of development, if also in altered form. The intellectual project of naturalistic rationalism thus simply picked up threads which had been left hanging in the history of thought, and the type of thought which it conquered continued to live, even if only as a cultural current, to become the foundation for oppositional tendencies of thought.

Tracing the first tendency, it appears that the emerging, mathematically grounded mechanistic representation of the world, toward which the early modern intellectual tendency aspired, begins, as already noted, by taking up threads and directions already brought out in the philosophy and natural science of antiquity, in order to bring these to full development, now under more favourable conditions. The mathematical system of Euclid and Archimedes preserved insights in which the mathematical rudiments of Democritus, Archytas and Eudoxus were refined. In particular, Plato's *Timaeus*, newly interpreted, was played off against Aristotle.[3] Galileo, Kepler, Giordano Bruno, as well as Leibniz[4] read Plato again and again, but now he was interpreted from the point of view of the new intellectual and cosmic project, in that the mathematical, natural-scientific elements going back to Archytas and preserved in his work received emphasis. One sees most clearly what made up this new intellectual project if one asks oneself, what were they struggling against? And one finds a battle on two lines, the first an attack, bringing Plato into play, against Aristotelian scholastic philosophy of nature. That the latter front involved an internal struggle as well derives from the circumstance that modern natural science arose out of modern philosophy of nature. A process is re-enacted here which has had its parallels in antiquity, where an interest in nature directed by magic also turned into an interest in nature oriented to technique. The magical mastery of nature metamorphosed into a technical mastery of nature. But what was it, then, that was to be combated in the Aristotelian scholastic method of thought, and what was it in the Renaissance philosophy of nature?

The proponents of the new natural-scientific tendency struggled against the Aristotelian representation of the world because it was qualitatively directed[5] and concerned to comprehend everything as founded upon itself, in terms of an inherent final cause and an in-dwelling determinacy of form. But the new intellectual project was after a representation of the world that undertook to explain the individual object in terms of general causes and laws, and sought to represent the world as a sum of masses and powers. Precisely in order to vanquish this qualitatively conditioned thinking, they had recourse to mathematics, so as to make it the foundation for knowledge of nature.

153

In the Renaissance philosophy of nature, however, which had been taken up and from which it was now necessary to be extricated, they struggled primarily against the element of anthropomorphism.[6] This is a process by stages, in which the anthropomorphic, pantheistic, nature-philosophical element is progressively eradicated from knowledge. We know, after all, that Kepler was still led to astronomical researches by the astrological idea of cosmic harmony and its investigation, and we know that the fundamental concepts of natural science (law, number, power [*Kraft*]) have anthropomorphic, nature-philosophical origins. The internal struggle to overcome these originally anthropomorphic conceptions discovers its symbolic career in the gradual overthrow of the concept of power in physics. The concept of power, which originally derives from an 'inner experience', is transformed from its animistic meaning into one of mathematical function.[7] The inner make-up of this style of thought is suggested by the dominant themes of these two struggles: first, the fundamental tendency to eradicate everything qualitative; and second, mistrust towards any source of knowledge with anthropomorphic connections. It is necessary to do more than to note that the ultimate ground for this mistrust of bases of experience associated with the human body appears under the auspices of a decline of pantheistic feelings for the world.

If we look more closely, this design of transforming, wherever possible, everything qualitative into quantity cannot, obviously, be set up as more than a utopian ideal of knowledge at the pinnacle of this tendency of thought. But it is important to have the ideal of an intellectual tendency in view, because the dominant themes are most readily apparent within it. The ideal presents the goal that is sought and that is made into an absolute. Theoretical physics performs the miracle of resolving the wealth and variety of the world into a conceptual system, whose every part adheres to all the others, thereby rendering this variety ultimately translatable into a system of mathematical relationships. This quantification of the qualitative also derives from the tendency to de-anthropomorphize knowledge, involving the rationalistic prejudice, of course, that everything anthropomorphic is rooted in sensuous and inner apprehension, while the rational contains a guarantee for the objectivity of knowledge, which cannot be challenged on such grounds. Only where one can hope that one is learning something that is not humanly limited is truth to be found, and only pure reason is, so to speak, the superhuman in man. Another motif clearly enters into this direction of intellectual aspiration opposing anthropomorphism and resorting to the level of pure reason: an aspiration to render knowledge social, i.e., the tendency to drop out of the known all elements bound to the personal or to a specific community, and to cling only to determinations which are universally communicable.

The certainties to be discovered are those demonstrable to anyone and not those evidential only for a believing community; and since it is precisely reason, and especially the arithmetical which appears to be of this sort, the intellectual objective of transposing the qualitative into the quantitative follows of its own accord.

What Descartes had inaugurated in methodology has remained the inescapable basis for the entire rationalistic development in philosophy (in Kant as in Leibniz), and this fundamental tendency continues to survive in most themes within German idealism: a certain conception of the concept and of cognition governs methodology and lets it appear as the self-justification of a certain intellectual project. This basis indicates to us, in so far as it gradually brings into being a unique coupling of general validity with truth, that it approaches the analysis of cognition with the completely unproven prejudice that man has knowledge only in so far as what he learns can be demonstrated to everyone. It is a matter, then, of that depersonalizing and decommunalizing of knowledge to which we alluded above, where the known is to be detached from any particular and communally-rooted subject in order to locate it on a conceptual level accessible to any conceivable subject. In this mathematization occurs in exemplary fashion the process of putting down the group-connected subject, the concrete historical subject, in order to resort to what is abstractly and universally human. And here there is indeed a correlation between subject and object: the more abstract the elements of the object which are comprehended and emphasized (hence the recourse to *res extensa* and universal laws of nature), the more abstract the knowledge obtained and hence the greater the number of subjects for whom it has validity. Universal knowledge is general in both senses of the word: it is valid for many objects and many subjects.

By virtue of the productive one-sidedness characteristic of every theory, this school of thought overlooked the fact that it had hypostatized itself, in its methodological doctrine, as thought as such, that from the very outset it had set about, in attempting to render the world calculable, to know only so much about the world as might be so rendered. It was not noticed then, that there are also other ways of experiencing and knowing, arising out of an altogether different kind of relationship between subject and object; that these continue to function although they are despised by the dominant methodology; that as soon as a new intellectual project

155

emerged which wanted to comprehend as well the knowledge neglected by the natural scientific style of thought, it would reach back to these ways of knowing; and that new methodological insights would be attainable by starting out from this new intention. But just as modern natural-scientific knowledge, when it reached back to the mathematical natural-scientific elements in antiquity, refined them and let them develop, so it is to be expected that the methods of thinking repressed by the natural-scientific mode of thought will not experience their revitalization in the form of a mere reproduction of pre-scientific modes of learning, but that it can only be a question of seeing how many legitimate and developable beginnings may be present in those repressed methods.

But before we turn our attention to the continued existence of these elements repressed by natural-scientific thinking, we must first elucidate the sociological function of the style of thought we have been treating.

When one has traced the strands of the ultimate motives of thought of natural-scientific rationalism back to this point, a sociological imputability to the spirit of capitalism – and particularly to the spiritual tendencies that first created this capitalism, which is to say to the spirit of the aspiring bourgeoisie – is irresistible. It has often been pointed out that the same (bourgeois) rationalism manifests itself in the new economic systems as in early modern natural science.[8] When the qualitative is reduced to the quantitative in the observation of nature, it is the same structural change in attitude toward things as when commodity production takes the place of production of goods for one's own needs. Just as the world of goods, which still comprises in the natural economy all sorts of qualitatively distinct goods, qualitatively distinguished as use values, is seen in the capitalist system from its commodity-aspect alone, which is to say as merely an equivalent for a numerically specifiable amount of money, so do, for this inclination of consciousness, all things and later also all human beings appear ever more and in growing measure transformed: they appear only in so far as they can be taken into account by a rationalistic calculability. Within the possibility and capability of seeing a qualitatively distinct good as nothing more than the expression of a quantum of money, then, there is implicitly contained a manner of relating to the world as such, which simply manifests itself especially palpably in the quantifying traced in the natural-scientific mode of thought.

But the same change in attitude also occurs with regard to human beings: while the Other is, in a patriarchally or feudally organized world, somehow a totality or at least a part of an hierarchically ordered community,[9] he is, in a commodity-producing society, nothing but himself a commodity, his labour-power a magnitude specifiable in numbers, which one takes into account just as one does other quantities.

It is not as if the psychological possibility of relating to other human beings and to objects as to other than equivalents for money were henceforth eliminated, or as if any individual member of the aspiring bourgeoisie always found himself only on this level of world experience. But from now on the possibility exists of entering into the world from this direction, consistently and in principle. That the calculating attitude is to be sociologically imputed to the aspiring bourgeoisie does not amount at all to a notion of reality (which would be incorrect as such) according to which every individual bourgeois always maintains this attitude toward his environment, but it amounts simply to the claim that a systematically consistent and fundamentally novel inclination towards quantifying everything in the world was brought into the realm of possibility out of the will brought to the world by this new stratum, which had borne the rise of capitalism. Other strata can also share this attitude and increasingly adopt this way of relating to the world; but it will be ever more dominant, steadily repressing all other tendencies, specifically in that stratum which is placed directly amid relationships of this kind by the life's work which occupies its everyday existence, the stratum for which this world, which it created, becomes immediate environment. But the more spheres of life are drawn into this attitude, the more does this existential and cognitive frame of reference repress the remaining, time-honoured modes of relating to the world; so that, in the end, when philosophical reflection turns to the relationship between man and environment, this reflection bases itself on this ground, hypostatizes this calculating-rational way of relating as the only relationship, and in so far as other relationships remain visible to it at all, denies them their worth. To this doctrine of knowledge then, any way of learning about the world that does not proceed analogously to quantification appears inferior, pre-scientific, subjective, or restricted to the external appearance of things.

But the other factor we have singled out also has its sociologically determined background. We designated this factor as the coupling of universal validity with the criterion of truth, and it rested upon presupposition that man really knows only in so far as what he learns is demonstrable to all: in sum, the movement from personal and communally-bound certainties to truths valid for all men. What is going on here is the process from the state of community to the state of society, which also expresses itself in the concept of truth.[10] The steady expansion in the organization of communications technique, the democratization accompanying the newly rising capitalism here become manifest in the conception of knowledge. The appearance of saving certainties bound to personal life, the phenomenon of revealed truth bound to communities, are still known to religious consciousness. For the capitalist world the collective subject falls away and there remains, on the one hand, the isolated individual, and, on the other, the 'consciousness as such' that dwells within him. For this reason, from now on we also find as starting point for epistemological construction the ego, as given immediately and in isolation (the ego, but not the personal 'I'), and we find the ascent from here to 'consciousness as such', whereby this type of thought skips various concrete stages of collective consciousness ('We'-consciousness).

The aspiring bourgeoisie thus turned one sphere of knowledge into the paradigm for knowledge as such, and they elaborated this tendency in their logical reflections to the exaggerated exclusion of any other. In this rationalizing fervour, it was not seen that there are spheres of knowledge which could not be adapted to this manner of thinking, so sharply pointed toward quantification, that there are methods of thinking and modes of knowing that differ from this structural model, and which are bound to elude methodological reflections if assessed by the criteria of the exact sciences. But it is naturally only reflective methodology that these methods of thinking elude; real life naively continued to employ methods of knowing incomprehensible to the official logic. In everyday life, men continued to have *physiognomic* knowledge; that is, learning that does not emerge on grounds of dissection and analysis but owes its assurance precisely to a holistic apprehension which first makes analysis possible; in political dealings, men continued to act on the basis of renderings of situations and to accumulate sociological impressions rooted in them. This last is a mode of learning too, which gains its distinctiveness from being rooted in situations. While natural-scientific knowledge abstracts completely from the specific situation of the knowing subject, practical-political knowledge gains its distinctive character precisely from the fact that it gains knowledge from within situations and acts with situations in view. Where theory lacks general rules and lawful regularities, the practical actor knows enough to act on the basis of the situation; and while general rules could teach anything except in what concrete situation one happens to be placed at the moment, the special capacity of the concrete, pre-scientific practical actor consists in perspectivistically bringing the facts given into an order relevant to himself and to his own situation, by means of the category 'situation'. What kind of thinking is at work here? Is it the thinking we have been discussing? Is it altogether identical in structure with natural-scientific thinking? This is just where the problem lies. This species of neglected forms and methods of knowing has re-emerged as a problem for us just at this time, and our foremost preoccupation consists in somehow comprehending the methodological problems as well as the sociologically determined fate of this style of thought, only now becoming truly visible, on the basis of this recognition. This step must be ventured, even though, since the preparatory work could not yet be done, mistakes must occur.

It also cannot escape notice that natural-scientific psychology, which was to have become as such the basic science for all the humanistic sciences, however precise it may be becoming, offers nothing to the historian or literary historian engaged in concrete work, while the so-called vulgar psychology has enabled him to undertake, with its unmeditated methods, the most sensitive psychological descriptions and analyses. What methods is life employing here? Again we must ask: is the thinking in use the same as that which we portrayed methodologically on the model of the exact natural sciences?

Where fixed prejudices about the meaning of knowledge are loosened, and knowledge is no longer presumed to be present only where knowledge of laws can be had, the revision of the concept of knowledge moves even further afield and more than one type of concept is also found. It is not only the concept established by definition which secures knowledge; there are also 'naming' and 'describing' concepts which secure learning by means of their interrelationships and must be understood in contrast to the defined concept.

Once entered upon this path, we are bound also to recognize that the individual can be grasped in its individuality and that it can even be articulated, and not only so far as it partakes of universal concepts and subjection to universal laws; that a living Other belongs to us not only so far as it can be dissolved into relations; that we partake of spiritual and sensual learning whose substance we grasp directly and allow to affect us at a single contact. It is bound to come to our attention, in other words, that there is a wide undercurrent of knowledge about whose methods we are not as yet able to give ourselves an accounting.

Rationalism, in essence oriented to quantification, shrugged these problems off with a summary gesture of contempt by terming this species of knowledge 'pre-scientific'. But it failed to remark that this is exactly where the problem lies. How does one proceed in these pre-scientific methods of knowledge? How do insights come about, able to provide at least an orientation for action?

159

How is this 'pre-scientific way of knowing' distinguished from the allegedly 'only scientific way'? In time the call must arise for a methodological doctrine, a theory of knowing the qualitative. By 'qualitative thinking' we mean at this point to designate, as with a slogan, everything in the complex of that alternate style of thought we have just characterized, just as the expression 'quantitative natural-scientific thought' served us as an abbreviated, summary designation which we could fix more exactly only in the course of our presentation. This problem of qualitative and situation-bound thinking could not but become ever more urgent since history, a field ever more taking the shape of a science, employed just these methods in all its parts; and indeed the problem of the left-over, hidden species of knowledge became unavoidable for methodology, which is primarily directed to the exploration of scientific thought, in contrast between natural and humanistic sciences. We believe that we can discern an even more far-reaching difference among possible 'styles of thought' in this contest over method (*Methodenstreit*) and dualism. This is not to dispute the ultimate unity of consciousness or even of thought. In our present context and in the light of the present-day task, however, it is not as important for us to go in search of this unity as it is to see, first of all, the hidden differences within this unity.

As is well known, it was for Vico that the problem of history first became visible in a striking way; but because of their rationalism neither he nor the Enlightenment – whose accomplishments in the study of history have also been recognized by the late Dilthey – could bring the whole problem complex into view. Even the Kantian system, the most all-encompassing philosophical system in the line of enlightened rationalism, was oriented to the exact natural sciences, as is now well enough acknowledged, in an altogether one-sided way; and little could be drawn from it for a theory of history and historical knowing. When the methodological problems of history first came up for solution, attempts were made to answer the questions within the framework of Kantian philosophy. It was asked whether it would not be possible to design, through additions and corrections, a methodology and logic of history which would on the whole uphold the Kantian scheme and formulation of the questions.

This experiment was performed by Windelband and then especially by Rickert, but much as the contrast between two types of knowledge (universalizing natural sciences and individualizing history) was made the axis around which their studies turned, the problem cannot be seen in its full breadth in this way because the philosophical background, the specification, and the characterization of intellectual attainment are still attempted on the basis of a philosophical position which has taken up into the philosophy of thought the very presuppositions it would have been its first task to overcome, if it were really to uncover the distinctive properties of the methods of thinking which are distinctively *not* like the natural-scientific knowledge.

The starting point alone, from which the problem is approached, closes off, in our opinion, the possibility of a fundamental solution to the questions relevant here. Methodology is assigned the task of showing the difference between the two sciences strictly on the level of the known, that which knowledge produces, on the level of concept formation. It cannot be surprising, then, that the whole difference was seen in the fact that the one intellectual tendency (designated as natural-scientific) proceeds in a generalizing, and the other (the historical) in an individualizing way. Is this powerful distinction really to consist in nothing but the employment of different types of concept in the one and the other? The way to a substantial methodology is barred also because ontological inquiry is brought in belatedly, and then only very inadequately; that is, the inquiry whether the object of the natural sciences differs from that of history in its mode of being. Although the still useful ontological distinction between the world of nature bare of meaning and the world of meaningful forms (culture) is actually seen, instead of allowing this distinction to subsist as an ontological one, it is too emphatically attached to the subjective activity of the knower. Another ontological pre-methodological question is not touched: whether it is not the case that the knowing subject stands in an altogether different relationship to the object in the cultural sciences than he does in the natural sciences, where laws are sought. In addition, a whole series of other assumptions, to be discussed later, make this way to a solution appear unsatisfactory to us.[11]

The error of this line of investigation does not lie, in our judgment, in the individual argumentations, but in the starting points, the rationalistic premises and prejudices which had come into it out of the rationalistic tradition of the Enlightenment, even before the initiation of methodological inquiry. The methodological elucidation of the methods of knowing which are distinctly *not* like the exact natural sciences can come only out of a tradition which derives its philosophical and experiential foundations from the tendency which is preserved in the historical disciplines, as well as living in the 'pre-scientific modes of knowing' which continue to assert themselves in everyday life.

Despite the relative paucity of their findings, the great significance of Dilthey's methodological writings consists in the fact that

they attempt to grasp this same problem of the distinctive properties of knowledge in the humanistic sciences upon philosophical
grounds more congenial to those disciplines. Dilthey is borne by,
and may be the most important exponent of, that irrationalistic
undercurrent which first became self-aware in Romanticism, and
which, in the neo-Romanticism of the present, is on the way, in
altered form, to effecting its counter-attack against bourgeois
rationalism. In order fully to appreciate the methodological
achievement and especially in order to see the wider sociological
and philosophy-of-history ground from which these ways of setting
questions arise, it is as necessary in this case as it was with rationalism to widen our field of vision with regard to the history of the
problem.

We have already seen how modern rationalism, which hypostatized one of the possible modes of attending and knowing as the
paradigm of all knowledge, by refining and rendering absolute one
type of knowledge (that of the so-called exact natural sciences),
constructed its theory of knowledge, its philosophy as a whole,
from this starting point. But it is always important to keep in mind
that modern natural-scientific knowledge was not the 'first cause'
of this process of transformation, which went so far as to determine
the new shape of philosophy, but that the new scientific orientation
and the new philosophy ultimately represent aspects of the redirection in psychology and world-view with regard to man, things, and
world which marked a new type of man. The distinctive attitude
towards nature, where every personal and immediate relationship
to her is to be given up, so that she can be ultimately transmuted
into quantities or at least into a nexus of objective concepts,
deprived of every subjectively present and concretely communal
association, is a redirection which gradually took effect in all the
modes of conduct of capitalist man. If one man was at one time, as
long as the feeling of community analysed by Tönnies was still sufficiently vital, a concrete individual for another, and a unified totality in a certain situation, a striving becomes ever more evident now,
to regard him as abstract individual or to comprehend him merely
in his function in a universal process, by depersonalizing him altogether, as a conductor, say, or mailman, or party to a contract. The
possibilities for reducing all organic relationships to contractual
form depersonalized property and capital, and enterprises in the
form of joint stock companies, can only be come upon by way of
this new manner of relating, which eliminates everything that is
qualitatively distinctive.[12]

In this abstract relationship to the Other, however, the abstract,
so-called epistemological subject is already present in essence. The

point of departure for the natural law doctrine of the time, which aimed at formal democracy, also employs this 'man as such' within us, who is removed from every concrete situation of rank or family or anything else. That the same impersonal relationship increasingly emerged with regard to the world of things as well, in contrast to an earlier world where property was something personal and, accordingly, integrated into the existential domain, so to speak, of each individual, had been already observed by the Romantics and played off by them against the present, to the advantage of earlier times.

The change in the cognitive relationship of men can only be explained on the basis of this general change in the existential relationship among these same men, and in the relationship between men and things. For it is commonly overlooked – and this will later be taken as the crux of our study – that while every instance of knowing is simply knowledge when viewed form the 'inside', it simultaneously refers, when viewed from the 'outside,' to a specific existential relationship between the knowing subject and the object known.[13] It is only when one has grasped this fact of inner connection between thinking and existence that one has cleared one's way to the questions posed by the sociology of thought, because it is only from this vantage point that one can see how new existential relationships among men and between men and things make possible and underlie cognitive relationships of a type which is correspondingly new.

Now that we have seen by these means that a certain rationalism, as a form of thought, belongs to capitalism's 'reifying' manner of living, as a form of existence, and that the methodological doctrine which is part of this style of thought shares in the existential presuppositions it contains, it is time to ask what happened, in the course of history, to the existential relationships and to the cognitive relationships corresponding to them, which were repressed by the style of thought we have been considering.

They still endured, as is to be expected; but, as is often the case in history, their existence became latent and asserted itself, at most, in counter-currents complementary to the main stream. The counter-currents were at first assumed and transmitted by the spiritual and social strata which were not drawn into the capitalist rationalization process, or, at least, were not its carriers. The earlier, personal, concrete human relationships remained alive in the peasant ranks, in the ranks of the lower middle class which stayed in historical continuity with artisan experience, and in the traditions of the nobility (in different forms and levels of intensity, which could, in each case, be made phenomenologically more precise). The largely implicit and unbroken tradition of the religious sects (like those of pietism[14]), notably retained a bearing towards life, an attitude to life, and methods for taking things in, with regard to the inner life, above all, which was bound to disappear from the style of life of the bourgeoisie, the more it was drawn into the capitalist process, but also from the life of the industrial workers.

But not even the latter two strata, in the foremost rank of those committed to the capitalistically rationalized process, have altogether abandoned the original bearing towards life; this bearing simply disappeared from the foreground, so to speak, of public and official life. Intimate relationships, so far as they are untouched by the capitalist process, continue to run their course in a manner which is not calculating or rationalist. Just this phenomenon of such spheres (suffused with personal and religious feeling) which had earlier (as Max Weber has already pointed out) been matters of public concern, becoming intimate, is a development complementary to the thoroughgoing rationalization of public life, the work place, the market, politics, etc.

In this way, the 'irrational' (which is closer to the original relationship of man to man and man to thing) henceforth limits itself to the 'periphery' of individual life in a double sense: first, inasmuch as that which is alive vibrates only in the intimate relationships of human beings, while experiences having public standing are ever more rationally structured; and second in the strict sociological sense, as the strata upon which the new world rests (the bourgeoisie and the proletariat) immerse themselves, with an ever wider proportion of their consciousness, in the new style of thinking and being, and as life is lived on the strength of the old seminal elements and traditions only on the periphery of the new world – in peasant life, in the life of the nobility, and in that of the petty bourgeoisie.

Here, on the periphery in two senses, slumber the seeds of a style of living and thinking that once constituted the world. These seeds were long latent, and they only became a 'tendency', something 'to be noticed' later, when they were fostered in the social struggle, when the forces of counter-revolution resurrected these repressed elements of experiencing and thinking and fastened them to their standards.

It is the sociological significance of Romanticism that, as a reaction against the thinking of the Enlightenment (against this philosophical proponent of capitalism) at the level of experience, it took up the decaying earlier substantive themes, consciously spelled them out, and opposed them to the rationalistic style of thought.

Romanticism took up the very spheres of life and bearing towards life which still survived as nothing more than residual counter-currents, and over which bourgeois rationalism was threatening to trample. Romanticism set itself the task of rescuing precisely these, bestowing a new dignity on them, and preventing their demise. The experiences bound to community were invoked, in various forms, against the manifestations of society (to characterize the state of things in Tönnies's terminology): family against contract, emotional certainties against rationality, inner modes of knowing against mechanistic ones. All the substances and contents which had hitherto invisibly given shape to the substratum of life suddenly come into view for reflexive scrutiny. And they are fought for.

Since, as is well known, Romanticism grew out of the Enlightenment as antithesis to a thesis,[15] and is conditioned by its thesis, like every antithesis, it is the paradoxical fate of Romanticism that even as counter-current it is conditioned structurally in its foundations by the attitudes and methods of the Enlightenment, which occasioned it.

Romanticism sought to rescue these repressed irrational forces of life by fostering them, but failed to realize that paying them conscious attention at the same time rationalized them. It accomplished a feat of rationalization which the bourgeois-rationalist Enlightenment could never have carried out, not only because its methods were inadequate for this, but also because the contents themselves were not active enough to hold their attention. It is simply the fate of even the irrational that it could only be grasped from the level forming the element basic to the age.

Romanticism is thus a capturing and collecting of the elements of life and the bearing towards life which ultimately derived from the religious consciousness and were pushed aside by the capitalist-rationalist onmarch; but it is a seizing and a collecting and taking in of these elements at the level of reflection. What Romanticism accomplishes is by no means a belated reconstitution of the Middle Ages, religion, and the irrational as foundation and bedrock of life, but rather a comprehension of these contents by reflection, rendering them visible, securing knowledge of them. But Romanticism thereby accomplishes something that was not at all its aim: it developed methods, modes of knowing, conceptual possibilities, and language adapted to rendering into theory all the forces of life which would always elude the Enlightenment. Here, then, all the elements, bearing towards life, and attitudes towards man, things and world which had been eclipsed for a whole epoch were once again conjured up; but they were not conjured up in their quality as an under-earthly creator of existence, as *humus*, but rather as a task, as content of a resolution.

After all these contents had materialized at the level of reflection and had been rendered visible, they entered, as is known, into alliances, viewed sociologically, with anti-capitalist social currents.[16]

All the social strata without interest in the capitalist process or even threatened with ruin, which were also traditionally associated with the submerged world-forms of various medieval phases – in short, living in a greater proximity, determined by tradition, to these contents – used the discovery of these contents against the bourgeoisie and the industrial world. Entrepreneurship and enlightened monarchy had, by virtue of their historical interconnectedness, if for no other reason, an interest in rationalism; feudal forces, as well as small peasant proprietorship and petty bourgeois layers arising out of the traditions of artisanship and guild, possessed, in differing degrees, a sense for and interest in the Romantic (cf. Salomon). These strata already do their part in the emergence of these contents as matter for reflective knowledge; but it is especially during the socially conditioned struggle over culture, where it is a matter of applying these contents, that the proponents of these strata carry their takings from Romanticism into their ideologies. It is well known, for instance, that the coming to awareness of national feeling was nourished by such Romantic elements.

After the diffusion of the Romantic offensive, which was at the same time its self-dissolution, the second half of the nineteenth century brings a renewed sweep by the rationalism oriented to natural science, and it draws ever broader social strata within its orbit, just as mature capitalism has engaged ever broader strata in its world-forming structure. In this flood-tide of rationalism, Romantic experience and thought had once again to sink under. But its dissolution was not complete: in the succession of historiography and in the traditions and methods of historicism, which grew out of the Romantic inheritance, the repressed elements survived. They re-emerged in irrationalist currents within philosophy, and today offer the breeding ground and starting point for the new counterthrust being launched by the neo-Romanticism which forms the atmosphere within which we now find ourselves.

This anti-rationalist interest, nourished by Romantic stuff, which cultivates a way of being attuned to things, world and knowledge which is different from rationalism, can increasingly be seen today in diverse tendencies. It survives in anti-Kantian philosophy, in the line of succession from Schopenhauer, Nietzsche, Bergson, Dilthey, to Simmel, as well as in the historicism of a Troeltsch; but beyond that it has come altogether to be the philosophical bedrock of the phenomenological school.[17]

It should be noted, however, that this reappearance of Romantic irrationalist elements, as we have them today, is once more co-determined by the state of rationalism itself, as counter-current to which it once more appears today. If the irrational, the reviving religious consciousness, presented itself at the stage of reflection under the conditions of Romanticism, and if therefore the special achievement of Romanticism consisted in having discovered and rationalized contents overlooked in the Enlightenment, unconsciously having applied new methods in this rationalization, then the creativeness of the present epoch does not by any means consist in taking up the old posture once more, making newly accessible for our age contents additional to those already grasped by Romanticism but once again submerged during the naturalistic epoch of the second half of the nineteenth century. On closer inspection, all the discoveries of neo-Romanticism appear as rediscoveries. They are for the most part contents which Romanticism had already grasped and which are novel only for our generation, a generation which grew up in the period of positivism. It is upon quite a different level that present-day neo-Romanticism achieves something new: in its methodological reflections, which address the knowability of these irrational elements. Romanticism had discovered the methods by means of which one can know the irrational, but it possessed an interest in its own methods only in rudimentary form. It was still more or less naive in this respect. Now we possess the irrational elements not only upon one reflective level, but upon the stage of a double reflection. This is the place of our productivity; this is where our genuine accomplishments get under way.

The fact that we possess the irrational elements, the contents of the religious and, later, of the Romantic consciousness, at the stage of methodological reflection is also due to the fact that the rational-Enlightenment line of succession in our philosophy has run out of its system-building power, so to speak, within the revitalized German idealism of our time, and that this philosophy has turned into a methodology. In the age of Romanticism, the critical philosophy, as well as the idealism which carried it forward, were productive, if only along rationalist lines, in creating a depiction of the world. The new forward movement of idealist philosophy into neo-Kantianism, neo-Fichteanism, and neo-Hegelianism approached the philosophies of their models from the very outset impelled by methodological interests. Neither Kantianism nor Hegelianism is useful to us in its substantive affirmations. No neo-Kantian or neo-Hegelian intends to revive Kant or Hegel word for word; i.e., no

167

one wants to make the positive contents of these philosophies credible once again. It is always rather a matter of rediscovering the fruitfulness of systematic points of departure, the fruitfulness of the methods of these philosophies. But that means that the newly reconstituted idealism, heir to the rationalist line took up only that which had relevance to method: and even though the idealists of our time did begin to philosophize anew from these points of departure, all will have to admit that the material, substantial filling out of the systematic frameworks gained in this way displays no genuinely productive power of creating anew, and that they have not succeeded at all in figuring out, in terms of their systems, the world which has since come into being.[18]

In this respect as well, it is new that our creativity resides in skill and clearsightedness with regard to logical structures. That is to say that our poverty in lacking a substantive philosophy of our own has its positive side in that we are in a position to see, to an unprecedented degree, the systematic framework, the logical structure of all systematizations. We can penetrate to the way in which – from a purely logical point of view – the philosophical systems are built up, where the ultimate points of departure for philosophies are to be found, what types of systematizations may have been possible at all, etc. We see connections which ages more substantively productive and philosophically creative could not see, in part because they were too much caught up in their own philosophy to look beyond its contours (and so could at most try to assimilate or to controvert the other standpoints from their own), and in part because they could not reflexively seize hold of the system itself because they had their life within its structures, within the process of systematizing. The relationships obtaining here are similar to those in our dealings with art: we have become productive in the history of styles only because we similarly do not possess in art a style of our own, dominating the epoch to the exclusion of others. We see stylistic connections, lines of development, and the like, because we lack a distinctive style of our own and because there occur, in our time, stylistic changes at a remarkable rate of succession, although they are, for the most part, simply stylistic repetitions. This also makes it possible to explain how it is that the creative artist of our time sets about his work with an attitude different from that of the artist of past epochs. The artist of our time has already absorbed much of the attitude of the critic and historian of style. It is not only that he is knowledgeable about styles, but also that he actually creates with certain styles in view, instead of living spontaneously within one of them. A shift in the creative power and creative centre of an epoch comes together with such a shift in the total basis. Creative productivity wanders, from age to age, among the various cultural domains, and, as long as there does not set in among us a naive affirmation of philosophical substance similar to religious affirmation, the creative field of endeavour in philosophy (the demand of the hour) will be found only in the spheres of methodological theory and logic and, ultimately, in structural analysis.

If then our philosophy as a whole moves on a level of double reflection, on the level of methodology, and if, in accord with this there is, as we saw, a clearsightedness regarding structures of objective formations in the rationalistic line of development, there is correspondingly, in the line of the irrationalist tendency, a comparable clearsightedness regarding subjective irrational elements, the modalities of subjective consciousness, from which the various objective formations have sprung. Phenomenology, as the study of attitudes of consciousness, a study of the typical modalities of the subject as a whole, is simply an extended rationalizing of all the factors which precede objectification and out of which objectification first emerges. Phenomenology, directed towards total consciousness and towards the attitude of subjects, is in this manner the counterpart to that structural analysis which has developed in the rationalistic line of succession as a sort of logic of objective cultural formations. As long as these two types of inquiry are carried on in isolation and are not set into a broader framework, they remain individual specialized studies. They turn into a new type of philosophical regarding of the world, however, as soon as they are employed as parts of a striving for a totality to comprehend the world.

It is, however, questionable nowadays whether there exist any starting points in our consciousness which give promise of a positive affirmation of our own, able to give shape to the world. (And we must pursue these questions about the spiritual condition of the age, since we have already gone so far in raising the question of 'where we stand'.) Many will deny that there are such points and will insist that we have our existence in an age of complete relativity, and that what we have said so far would have to confirm this, unless there were something to be added. We had ourselves insisted, after all, that our entire productivity resides in the formal; that we can see structures and phenomenological modalities only because we have no contents to hold us: that we have history of art because we have no art; and phenomenology of religion because we have no religion – or, at most, an unfulfilled intention to have them. Others will, in contrast, take precisely the presence of such intentions regarding religion, metaphysics, and, indeed, positive affirmations in general as point of departure for their interpretation of the age, and they will insist that this intention is already half a fulfilment, and they will promulgate 'the leap' and strike a prophetic pose to stand for some positive affirmation to transcend the present state. But this manner of overcoming the situation is, in our judgment, a false and inauthentic one; and there is a criterion for making this judgment. It always turns out on closer inspection of these affirmations (be they Catholic or humanist), that there is a mere reassertion of obsolete positions, or that there is only talk about them, but that the actual presentation of the affirmations demanded in abstraction is simply not there.

The whole broad spectrum of essayistic literature that puts itself forward as unrelativistic because 'religious' and 'affirmative' can only be understood by reference to this unfulfilled intention towards affirmation; and its 'leap' is the 'quick heroic deed' (of which Dostoyevsky speaks) through which some individual may comfort himself amid the discomfort of his seeking for a worldview. But these slogans have no significance for the age, because they are not capable of overcoming organically the stage of contemporary consciousness, from which these thinkers themselves have suffered as much as anyone.

As far as this first manner of overcoming the present situation is concerned – that is, the unaltered acceptance of past affirmations, as neo-Catholicism, for instance, seeks to do – this movement is not to be thought inauthentic simply because it attempts a recapturing of past contents. Most cultural innovations began as reinterpretations of past contents: thus, the Reformation was a reinterpretation of the Bible, and classicism a reinterpretation of classical antiquity. But there is also a criterion for judging whether such a reinterpretation is essentially creative or in fact merely imitative. While it turns out in the case of every creative reinterpretation that the 'return to the old' was merely a cloak, the productive self-deception of a consciousness seeking the new, the return which amounts to mere repetition is characterized by the absence of genuinely new contents. Creative epochs were naive, especially in what they were about. That is why they could become productive: the return to the Bible became a new religion only because the tensions of the time were taken up in the reinterpretation; and classicism became a new art, a new style, manifestation of a distinctive artistic volition (*Kunstwollen*) because the reinterpretation was not a philological but a newly creative one. With our reinterpreters, however, the acceptance of the old actually takes place at the level of interpretative historical research, and they falsify too little to get something really new under way, taking up the tensions of the present, and they falsify too much to be at least fruitful as historians. The same applies to the other type of overcomers of the present, who merely talk about the religious and do not so much propagate religious contents as they do, in the last analysis, offer contributions to religious phenomenology as a science. They could become good scientists, because their and our link to religion would be sufficient to understand the historical forms of religious consciousness 'from the inside out', but they are poorly equipped for this phenomenological work, because their scientific disinterestedness is constantly marred by dogmatic contents which insinuate themselves.

Shall we then remain in this state of suspension, in a state where relativity is already in principle overcome and made untenable, and where the intention towards positive affirmation is already present, without, however, finding fulfilment? That would not be the worst thing. One could accept this as fated and at least give recognition to the authenticity of such a way of bearing oneself (the solution of Max Weber and Karl Jaspers). But there is a way out, even here. And the real way out of a situation for consciousness always arises by virtue of the fact that one has followed the designated road completely to its end, that one does not consciously make leaps but instead has confidence that the matter will in the end transcend itself on its own. And it does in fact transcend itself.

The primary source of our relativism is our historicism, which has taught us to see all positive affirmations as historically conditioned, and to comprehend and interpret all contents – religious, artistic, or philosophical – as parts of a total situation, and, ultimately, of a total movement. It is a fact that historicism, this mightiest heir of Romantic consciousness, is on the one hand the cause of our utter dissolution, our relativism, but, on the other hand, also the only means capable of extricating us from this state.

First of all, historicism is the positive framework which provides a home and a context of meaning for our methodological analyses (be they structural analyses of objectivized formations or phenomenological analyses of the modes of subjective bearing which pertain to them). It is only thanks to historicism that at least the part of the world which we master in the study of our history does not appear to us as a senseless succession of events and forms, but that the positive penetration of the world can get under way for us spontaneously and naively at this place at least. Here, within methodological analysis, philosophy and depiction of the world emerge unforced, albeit at first as historical depiction of the world. Philosophy lives at first within specialized studies; it is not programmatic any more, but actualizes itself without being intended, spontaneously, in the form of a world-view which fulfils us.

What must be seen next is that one cannot pursue methodology or the analysis of world-views at length without aspiring, at the same time or in the end, towards a totality, without arriving in the vicinity of a metaphysics of history – but this time one which is not contrived, but follows as spontaneous result of our critical consideration of the world. By this turn of things, historicism, which had begun by relativizing everything, becomes, behind our backs, a philosophy of history: not one thought up by some individual, but one which emerges out of the historical-sociological researches of generations. Since historicism offers a formal framework for all the investigations which at first come out isolated and scattered, occurring as analyses of world-views, structural analyses of cultural formations, phenomenological analyses of the various psychological types and modes of subjective bearing which are possible, it unites these dispersed efforts into planful work, in which they mutually complement one another and finally metamorphose, within this consolidated casing, into a content-rich philosophy of history. That is to say that they become the means for genuine philosophical penetration of the world.

Dilthey took the decisive step in this direction, in our view, perhaps without recognizing the wider ramifications of his conduct. All the spiritual-philosophical energies generated by contemporary forces come together in him into a productive synthesis. A sense for the irrational is transmitted to him from the taking up of Romantic strands, and the authenticity of his existential contemporaneity is reflected in the effort to find methods by means of which irrational forces can be made accessible to knowledge. During this effort to comprehend the irrational within historical consciousness, the central problem for any methodology of the human sciences, the problem of interpretative understanding first becomes visible to Dilthey. The problem of interpretative understanding was subsequently also given recognition, as to its importance, by the methodology of the rationalist tradition (by Rickert), but the attempt to master the problem from there must be considered a failure. For the problem of interpretative understanding is the *experimentum crucis* in which ultimate premises must be revealed. Here it becomes evident how much Rickert's philosophy is oriented, in the final analysis, to natural-scientific thinking and its premises, despite the merit of having treated the problem of history for the first time on a grand scale; and it becomes equally evident that precisely the phenomenon of interpretative understanding cannot be comprehended until all premises derived from non-historical thinking, from thinking outside the human sciences, have been abandoned. Here too, Dilthey saw the most essential: the problem of interpretative understanding cannot be solved as long as methodology builds on the epistemological subject and does not also take the 'whole man' into consideration. Interpretative understanding, as a foreign body in rationalistically-oriented methodology must, if it is really to be comprehended, bring to light the philosophical pre-methodological premises which have been carried over from the structure of exact knowledge of nature into knowledge of history and into the theory of such knowledge. From this endeavour to make the whole man the basis of analysis arose, during his later years, Dilthey's interest in phenomenology. But while phenomenology continued to operate with a timeless consciousness, in this respect resembling Kantianism, Dilthey put forward the extremely important requirement that consciousness be seen historically, a thought transmitted to him out of the Hegelian philosophy. In addition to Dilthey, it was probably Troeltsch who most nearly saw the whole set of problems connected with the historicity of consciousness, with structures of values, and so on. Despite its lack of plan, his posthumous work placed these elements clearly enough into the foreground. Dilthey's anticipations are also important in other respects to the set of problems to be found here. In historical investigations as well as methodological essays he had earlier set about bringing into being a comprehensive inquiry into the historical world of ideas and structures of consciousness.

His endeavour to attempt analysis of world-views as a theoretical task, and in this to include within his sphere of concern more than the rational domains, remains the most important point of departure for any succeeding endeavour with similar aims. In this respect too, he made Hegel essentially accessible to us; but he let the dialectical framework fall – Hegel's formal triad of thesis, antithesis, and synthesis – in order to assure a free hand to the work of historical research, which is no longer, in tracing the development of spirit, to restrict itself to filling out a framework derived from elsewhere, from logic, but is rather, through its own penetration of the materials, to follow after the course of development of consciousness. He doubtless went too far in this loosening of the framework; his studies in the history of ideas do not have a plan delineated sharply enough; and, even though sociologically subtle observations are interwoven throughout, the new framework of philosophy of history is not yet present, or, at least, it is not graspable with any precision. The error must doubtless lie in a self-misunderstanding. His prescriptive fight against Western European sociology, waged from the ground and traditions of German philosophy of spirit, did not let him recognize what Marx had seen: that there is a fruitful kernel in positivism, the anchoring of free-

173

floating spirit in the social economic level discovered by positivism.

The history of ideology, in the sense of the totality of spiritual formations, is no free-floating evolution of spiritual spheres deducible from a purely immanent dialectic. It is, rather, carried by the social process, which does not, indeed, determine it completely, as if it simply issues it forth, but which stands in a determinate relationship to this unfolding of ideas. Marx saw that the Hegelian philosophy has to be put on its feet so that it does not proceed on its head, and thereby he provided at least the beginning of a positivist framework for the historical development of ideas. Dilthey saw only that it is impossible to make a methodology for the human sciences out of positivist – and thus also out of natural-scientific – beginnings. But he did not see that the amalgamation between Hegel (German philosophy of spirit) and Western European positivism that Marx undertook was a most fortunate one. The methodological, the dialectical apprehension of totality, was taken over by Marx from Hegel, and it serves as a framework for the philosophy of history; the substantive content, the social process in its economic class-conditioned dependency, is borrowed from Western European sociology. Dilthey was also shot through with positivist elements, but just at points at which the elements could not become fruitful. That he remained a psychologist despite his insight into the need for a psychology appropriate to the human sciences, that he learned to appreciate that meaningful entities exist in a mode beyond the psychological only at the very end of his development, stemmed from the lingering effects of his positivist environment.

It is interesting to recall in this connection that Troeltsch, who also comes out of a philosophy-of-history orientation and is by and large in tune with the world of ideas and has a sense for the independent contents of the ideological, after a long search for a framework to provide a firm support to the construction of history, finds such a framework, despite an attitude which is otherwise not socialist, in Marx, in the change of the economic substratum.[19] This only goes to show the extent to which, at least for those of us who have passed through positivism and may be said to have a fair measure of it in our blood, it is precisely the economic social determination of history which has become something immediately given and which is alone capable of providing a framework for considering the historical process adequate to *our* bearing with regard to world-view.

With this, however, a further historical concatenation not yet done justice by us enters into the basis of our observations, a concatenation not yet analysed in this introduction, which had set itself the task of self-orientation with regard to our place as defined by a sociology linked to philosophy of history. We have in mind the ideas and insights that stem from the newly ascending 'fourth estate'. In characterizing the oppositional forces environing capitalism as it came into being and unfolded, we have called attention only to the tendencies stemming from pre-capitalist social forms and seeking in some manner to conserve these, those which associated themselves more or less (although not without exception) with the irrational life-components assembled and brought to consciousness by Romanticism. We have not yet spoken of that opponent of capitalism which emerged from capitalism itself and not from the conservative side, which owed its existence to capitalism only to turn against it. We are thinking of the complex of ideas known as 'the proletarian idea'. Inasmuch as the proletariat grew out of capitalism, it also incorporates its rationalistic inclination, but in a unique form. That is to say that proletarian rationalism cannot be simply considered as a new variety of bourgeois rationalism.

Proletarian thought has a marked affinity with conservative thought in many respects, an affinity which, though it flows from positions which are poles apart, represents, in common with conservatism and reaction, an opposition to the bourgeois capitalist cosmic project and its abstractness.[20] If we wanted to pursue the relationship of the 'proletarian' to the 'irrational' – and the detailed elucidation of this cannot be our task here – we would have to begin by tracing the fate of irrationalist chiliastic elements which ultimately originate in 'ecstatic consciousness', which have formed the nucleus of all revolutions since the Peasant Wars, and which have, in the course of time, entered into the proletarian world-view, however rationalistic it may have become. Here a connection between the most extreme rationalism and the most extreme irrationalist elements is brought about, and this indicates that the 'irrational', when it is more closely examined, proves to be more variegated than could have been first supposed. Through detailed analysis, it could be demonstrated that the irrationalist elements which constitute ecstatic consciousness are fundamentally different from the irrationalist elements which we have hitherto briefly designated as remnants of religious consciousness and towards which Romantic consciousness subsequently directed itself.

But proletarian revolutionary consciousness also has its connection with the conservative line at another point, on the subject of dialectics, where Marx, out of inner necessity, could link up with the conservative Hegel.

The idea of the dialectic – of the logical triad of thesis, antithesis, synthesis – is, on a superficial view, an extremely rationalistic idea, since it is, after all, a question of attempting to force all development into a logical formula and generally to present all historical reality as subject to rational deduction. And yet this rationalism is completely different from that which, in the line of succession of the bourgeois spirit, found its expression within the natural sciences, in the search for universal regularities. Accordingly, all natural-scientific thinking is hostile to dialectic; and the most recent generation, oriented to natural science, was quite consistent, from its point of view, when it tried to eliminate the dialectic element in Marx.

Looking more closely, then, it becomes necessary to distinguish among different types of rationalization, just as we have just had occasion to distinguish within the domain of the irrational between the chiliastic element and the contemplative mystical element with which the Romantic consciousness aligned itself. The fact is that already in Hegel the dialectic was there to solve problems that are actually Romantic problems which later live on in the 'Historical School'.

The primary function of the dialectic is, first of all, the rational comprehension of the historical individual. While the historical in its uniqueness disappears in any view which generalizes and explores laws, it appears here as part of a unique historical growing. Dialectic is designed to bring forth out of itself a kind of rationalization in which rationalism will, so to speak, transcend itself.

The second thing, which does not lie so much in the outer schema as in the inner meaning of every dialectic, is the desire to trace the internal developmental line of a cultural domain: here too, in other words, a kind of rationalizing of an irrational element whose comprehension lies far from naturalistic thought.

Third, every dialectical scrutiny is a scrutiny which attempts to extract meaning from a process, it is a rationalizing in the sense of philosophy of history, and, as such, a kind of rationality not so easily brought into accord with the spirit of natural-scientific positivism, value-free and a stranger to metaphysics.

Taking these points into account, all must admit that bourgeois rationalism had already reversed itself here in Hegel and created a form of thought which is anything but expression of a naturalistic rationalization which calculates and is determined to calculate all things.[21] That Marxism can run parallel to historicism for so long a stretch, that Marxism, although approaching from a different direction, represented as great an opposition to bourgeois consciousness oriented to natural law and rights as did the Historical School itself, points to common features which must not be overlooked. And yet, despite all the affinities with the irrational repressed by bourgeois consciousness which are common to 'proletarian' and 'conservative' thinking, the fundamental attitude of the 'proletarian' is strictly rationalistic, consonant in basic tone with the positivist tendency of bourgeois philosophy. This positivist kernel can be made apparent, above all, by noticing the circumstance that within the proletarian philosophy of history the focal point around which world events are constructed has been transferred into the social sphere, and that the movement of ideas is to be understood by reference to the economically centred movement of society. The hierarchy of spheres which had gradually become reality for bourgeois consciousness is thus taken up into proletarian thinking, at least in regard to this focal point for construction. Proletarian thinking is thus rationalistic to the extent that it must pass through capitalism; it is in a certain sense even more rationalistic, since it must not merely acknowledge but actually accelerate the tempo of capitalist development. But it turns irrational to the extent that it counts on a 'reversal' of this capitalism, where this 'reversal' itself already signifies something irrational, something supra-rational, when measured by the readily traceable individual causalities of bourgeois rationality.

The whole set of problems associated with base and superstructure originates here; and, whatever reservations one may have about certain kinds of applications of 'historical materialism', it is just this correlation between base and superstructure which has become the inescapable foundation of every modern sociology of culture.[22]

So far we have depicted separately in their social connectedness each of the currents of thought which appear fruitful to us and susceptible to further development. Our solution is meant to represent a synthesis of these tendencies, which we have seen until now embedded in part in quite different directions of thought, and which will attain to complete development only when they are raised above their one-sidedness and mutually complement one another.

If we have thus far sought to show that the history of thought by no means reveals a single current of thought unified in content or method of thought, but that it far rather points to a 'marching in single file' of the distinctive tendencies of thought, and if we are endeavouring to lay down in what is to follow the theoretical basis for a perspectivism in essentials with regard to the knowability of the historical, it must at first seem odd that nevertheless we are attempting to bring about a *synthesis* of earlier tendencies of thought, by preserving what appears fruitful to us out of the irrational as well as out of the rational lines of succession. This attempt at synthesis obviously requires justification.

Combining a doctrine of perspectivism (i.e., the presence of several standpoints for regarding history and thinking it through) with an attempt at synthesis appears paradoxical only to thought which has not yet realized that solutions by way of synthesis can succeed only after radical sharpening of antinomies. If one starts out from a monism according to which there can only be *one* truth, such a theory of historical cognition must neglect the most essential fact about the history of thought – that there simply are diverse tendencies and viewpoints, and that the theorist who wants to achieve synthesis cannot avoid placement within one of these tendencies – because such a monist must always be afraid that he is bound to lower himself to being a mere 'partisan' among the 'parties' were he to acknowledge that fact. But such forcible suppression of undeniable fact and, what is more, disregard for the relevance of such a fact must always revenge itself upon the systematizer. The revenge of facts upon a system always consists in their not going into the system and in opposing it from the outside. This kind of opposition is the most devastating, because a system is never so decisively refuted as when facts which have become visible to the age and which are relevant to the system remain unmastered. In our view, the value of a system is not to be primarily measured by the absence of contradictions in it but by its breadth and inclusiveness. Inner contradictions can be later overcome by thought; but a starting point too narrowly selected ends all hope for the system's capacity for thinking. The problem of relativism, as it has become the question of our life, can only be mastered if we make it into the axis, the starting point for theory, and only afterwards ask how it could be overcome at the stage at which it confronts us. Applied to our problem-setting, this means that the fact of the existence of diverse tendencies of thought, of diverse standpoints for viewing history, each of which dynamically changes itself, can be mastered only if one does not only avoid neglecting this fact, but if one actually makes it one's starting point, asking oneself only afterwards: how is it now with truth about history? Does it too resolve itself into these standpoints, and is truth itself dependent on standpoint? And here we must say no. There is a truth about every epoch; the epoch did exist in some certain way; its structure of meaning actually and truly has being in some certain way. But no one comes into possession of this truth at a bound, as if by inspired revelation, because, in so far as this truth can be seen by us at all, this is possible only from standpoints that have formed themselves in history and arise as a function of history. Since every tendency of thought is thus partial (as are the social currents bearing it, together with their fundamental designs) totality can be comprehended only in a synthesis.

Just as we have observed it as a fact of history that there are tendencies of thought that 'march in single file' and that even separately these have significance for the comprehensive understanding of the social process, by virtue of the fact that each makes something visible (and precisely that which would not otherwise have become so, because of the inevitable one-sidedness of the remaining standpoints) so there are also as a matter of fact always attempts at synthesis, which are undertaken now from one and now from another standpoint, and which attempt to bring into their own encompassing order the contents newly made visible as well as the new methods.

The existence of attempts at synthesis is correlative to the fact that tendencies of thought 'march in single file'. One of the most powerful of these syntheses was the Hegelian attempt, which sought to combine the methods and the contents of constructive types of bourgeois rationalism with the problem-set of the romantic-religious consciousness. His attempt emerges as culmination of a period of bourgeois development, and Hegel's understandable self-deception consisted in viewing himself or (in other contexts) his philosophy as the pinnacle, as it were, of the world-process and as the ultimate synthesis.

His self-deception consisted, in other words, in believing himself to have reached the state where *the* world had become transparent, when, in fact, it was simply a matter of *a* world becoming visible to itself. This deception is easily understood and is made up, considered sociologically, of the fact that every social stratum identifies its world with the world as such. Hegel, who was the most radical in rendering the conception of thought dynamic, became altogether unfaithful to this dynamicization when it came to his own thinking, inasmuch as he pushed, so to speak, his own location and epoch out of the stream of time. Since it took up within itself all the fundamental tensions on the total horizon of its time, his synthesis was a genuine synthesis, seeking to unify what had until then developed apart, but able to attempt this unification only from a standpoint of its own. Even at this time, we can already specify the place where Hegel stood sociologically: it was the place of that conservative thinking which saw in the Prussian state the *telos* of world events; and we can trace history's revenge upon this absolutization when we observe how this synthesis dissolves once more into tendencies, one of which happens to constitute the place where Marxism stands and thus helps to build up the starting point for the ascending proletariat.

179

Syntheses are therefore possible and necessary, and they attempt to achieve the highest which is given to historically limited human consciousness: to see the body of history itself from within the underlying currents of time. But syntheses are relative, since they cannot transcend the limitation imposed by existence. And this limitation is twofold. It consists first of all in the circumstance that even synthesizing thought can only take into account the life-elements and tendencies which have become visible to the epoch, and it can manage these only with the methods of thinking, view-points, and concepts which have manifested themselves in thought up to then. Syntheses are furthermore relative, despite the most upright intention of doing justice to all tendencies, because they can undertake their function (ascertaining the structure internal to world events in terms of philosophy of history) only from a place where they themselves stand, a place which is historically determinate; and this circumstance inevitably makes one-sided their assignment of roles to meaningful formations within the depiction of history. Syntheses are ultimately relative because they will unavoidably be transcended by the process within which cognition itself is implicated.

But this self-relativization carries with it no self-denigration of thinker and synthesizer. That will be seen in it only by those who take their departure from a scheme for portraying thinking which has to be overcome in knowing history. Over against this false or one-sided type of thinking, there has to be counterposed another, which may be briefly designated as 'thinking linked to existence'. In the theory of historical thinking, it is a matter of working out this type of thinking, whose fortunes we have sketchily traced in this chapter, so far as it is comprehensible to us at this time, a type of thinking which is expressly not knowledge of things, but knowledge of meaningful life, life which does not stand outside thinking, in contrast to it, but which forms a unity of being with it, always in a state of becoming.

If this type of thinking is to be correctly described and assessed, it is first necessary to give up all the presuppositions built up out of a type of thinking that arose from an altogether different attitude toward things. It is above all essential to abandon the conception of truth which sets it above existence as something altogether detached from it and pre-existent, a conception for which the truth derived from the finite, the historical, can be reached, if at all, only by a leap.

History cannot be found to be penetrable by a 'leap' out of history, but only by an ever deeper engagement in it.

In the next chapter, we shall attempt to provide a systematic foundation for the thinking and knowing linked to existence whose historical-sociological career we have sketched.

2 Toward a sociological theory of culture and interpretative understanding

Introduction: the fundamental theme of a sociology of thinking

The leitmotiv of our previous reflections, which attempted to connect the development of methodology and logic with the social process, was the observation that this total process in its modern development had produced two currents in epistemology. The first was oriented toward knowledge of the exact natural sciences, which saw the ideal of knowledge, to phrase this sharply, in the quantification of everything qualitative or at least in de-anthropomorphizing what is known[23] (which in the final analysis amounts to socializing it). The second found the basis for another form of knowledge primarily in the model of religious experience and later in the example of historical knowledge, and selected completely different points of departure for a methodology. It is actually not surprising that the polarity of the two existing modes of experience is crystallized for us with greatest clarity in the duality of the natural sciences and the historical sciences of culture, and that in this form it found its way into methodological inquiry. For it is precisely these two classes of science which are the most powerful creations of the modern spirit.

We have already emphasized that the methodology and epistemology proceeding from the paradigm of natural-scientific knowledge make and must make completely different ontological, logical, and methodological assumptions than a philosophy whose focus is historical knowledge. In our historical-sociological sketch we attempted to show that the way in which the subject of knowledge of natural laws relates to its object is completely different from that of the subject of historical knowledge. The former grew out of the spiritual current of bourgeois rationalism, whereas the latter only constituted itself in the spiritual counter-movement of conservative Romanticism, which preserved older attitudes and behaviour of the subject that had been repressed by the bourgeois Enlightenment and raised them to the level of awareness.

We observe here a distinctive feature of intellectual history. Consciousness, which at first appears to be unitary, splits, and certain of its possible directions are borne at a given point by specific social groups, whose world project elaborates these directions and makes them into absolutes. The opposing groups for their part take up the remaining tendencies of thought. This is one of the most important facts in the sociology of thinking, but it has not been sufficiently acknowledged until now because the abstract dogma of the philosophy of reason (which sees reason as something beyond time that remains identical with itself) has been accepted without revision and the concrete shaping of this unitary reason in history and the social process has not been investigated. At the same time we should also like to point out that it is not at all our view that the division of roles among social groups described in the previous chapter must always remain the same, that rationalism (or its heirs) is always connected with a progressive cosmic project and irrationalism with the opposing tendencies. Indeed, we have already seen that this schematic opposition is inadequate and that the analysis of the composition of the intellectual methods of the 'fourth estate' (including socialist thought as it occurs in Marxism) must further differentiate this provisional opposition between rationalism and irrationalism. We also saw that this progressive opposition of socialism to capitalism already contained an unusual combination of the irrational and the rational. But even if this were not the case, if the division of roles had taken a completely simple form up to now, with rationalization showing itself to be thoroughly progressive and attachment to the irrational always conservative, the possibility of a change of function would still be more nearly probable than impossible. Everything depends on the direction of the process as a whole; capitalism, for example, after reaching its apogee, could give way to a different economic and social structure, in which strata which previously promoted social development would become conservative and the intellectual trend connected with them – rationalism – would suddenly present itself as conservative. Only as a possible construction let us point out that – aside from the fact that capitalism could overturn – there is also the possibility that a planned economy occurring through the formation of trusts could take the place of liberal-democratic capitalism. This change alone, which would still take place within capitalism, would give rise to a new division and a change in function of the existing and additional social strata whose interestedness in and commitment to the thus evolving new world would be different from that of the present. Groups which today are still progressive (the rising bourgeoisie, for example, which would be pushed into the background in a stabilized world directed by trust magnates) would become conservative groups and their historical conjunction with Enlightenment thought would transform that thought into a conservative intellectual tendency. This is meant only as a thought experiment to point out that these things too must be seen dynamically and that analysing a historical period in terms of the sociological structure of its thought forms does not lead to general laws valid for all periods. In such cases it must always be remembered that a social stratum, even one which suddenly becomes dominant, does not conjure its style of thought up out of nothing. It grows into an already existing world-view and system of thought by appropriating a particular intellectual tendency which may have existed only in an undeveloped form, subjecting it to a change of function, and only in this way letting it become, objectively impelled by the times, something which is new in substance too.[24] ,

To return to our primary theme, we shall now develop in detail the distinction which we suggested in the previous chapter, but did not render precise, between the two types of knowledge and their respective methodologies, between 'natural-scientific' and 'historical' thought.

To prevent possible misunderstandings we must point out that the characterization of historical knowledge we shall offer for purposes of a theory of method does not refer to the entire range of knowledge of the historical. Not everything which history registers and treats in a cognitive way receives this treatment by means of the historical method. Only the spheres of contents which are only grasped by means of interpretative understanding and only to the extent that they are grasped by this means, are subject to the problematic to be discussed. To be more precise: in our opinion, the theory of interpretation must undergo a revision which begins with methodology. In any case, despite this qualification, our focus, on closer examination, includes most of the matters which occupy historians, for what is essential in the historical is indeed conveyed by means of interpretative understanding.

In any case, we do *not* at all believe that, for example, the chronological dating of a historical fact (whether an event took place in this year or that; the determination of a connection between two external events) is subject to the problems in which we are interested. The complex of problems which cannot be mastered by the frame of reference of the natural sciences first sets in when the historian or sociologist of culture attempts to understand concrete cultural objectifications or individual characters; where he tries to fix complexes of understandable relationships between individual objectifications and the world-view totalities appropriate to them, between social strata and their ideologies; where he is concerned with working out continuities of ideas and their changes in function; in sum, when the vehicle is interpretative understanding in its various forms and it is not a question of simply ascertaining the facts and their lawlike regularities.[25]

Only because this mode of thought, which precedes and transcends that of the natural sciences, does not arise as a problem before this point, is it possible that even sociology, in so far as it is restricted to the social process, could work successfully with the natural-scientific method. For it, too, the problems with which we are concerned first become relevant at the point where concrete interpretation in a certain form begins, as the study of ideology or cultural sociology. In fact, this is true historically as well. The new problematic arose only at this point. It was only the new assignment of inquiring into ideology which awoke a need within sociology to join those confronting the problem of interpretative understanding.

In the following remarks we shall get down to the actual theme of this chapter and work out the presuppositions of a methodology of interpretative understanding.

1 The subject-object relation in interpretative understanding

We have already pointed out that one of the unjustified assumptions of every natural-scientific conception of thinking consists of hypostasizing one form of knowledge as knowledge *per se,* and that it is neither capable nor willing to become aware that every kind of knowing signifies a distinct kind of existential relationship *per se.* To put this in another way: by setting up as the ideal model of all knowledge the distinct kind of comprehension of the object that occurs in the 'calculating experience' of what confronts the subject, natural-scientific methodology not only constitutes an overly narrow concept of knowledge but also, even where it has given up quantification as such, incorporates the assumptions of a quantifying knowledge into its design of thought. For quantification, as the most extreme form of a certain type of knowledge, represents in fact not only a specific way of de-personalizing and de-humanizing knowledge, and as such undertakes an alienation of the object, but also presupposes just such 'estrangement'. We have seen that for this kind of knowledge (which we designated as 'calculating', in short) to have become dominant presupposed a change in the way people related to one another and to things, and that this change lay in the direction of a capitalistic will to the world. *If* in quantification every existential relation to the object is eradicated, one could at most distinguish this as a characteristic of *this* mode of knowing. But it would be altogether wrong, proceeding from this one-sided example, either to deny such an existential feature to knowledge in general or to treat it as a vestige to be eliminated and, still more, to make its exclusion the very principle of all thought. And yet this is precisely the programme of this kind of methodology. Isolating and abstracting as it is, it sets the act of thinking, thought, theoretical activity, apart from the other existential relations of the subject ('loving', 'acting', 'wanting to change') in which it is always embedded, and it will not see the totality of the whole existential relationship of which 'knowing' is only one side. The sharp separation between theoretical and practical activity in transcendental philosophy is the most pregnant formulation of this mode of thought. Through this procedure of absolute separation an abstract distillate of thought as such comes into being, 'pure thought', and this stands up to an analysis which establishes its object phenomenologically just as poorly as does a similar abstraction belonging to this mode of thought; namely, the theory of the existence of 'sense data'. It is alleged that, as 'simplest elements', these are primary building blocks of every experience, but they can be as little established in an immediate phenomenological way as the pure thought just described. (We do not experience a sense datum 'green' but only 'green trees'. The so-called sense element is not the simplest and primary but rather a very late abstraction and construction.) In the same sense there is an artificial abstraction in the hypothetical construction of a pure thinking. One can undo it by confronting it with the fact that every act of knowledge is only a dependent part of an existential relation between subject and object, an existential relation which in every distinct instance founds a different kind of communion and a specific kind of unity between the two.

In the characterization of natural-scientific methodology this moment of existential relatedness could be neglected without harm (in so far as 'nature' meant only, as with Kant, reality in so far as it is thought in accordance with laws) but it becomes relevant again when one tries to characterize the experiences transmitted by interpretative understanding. If one wants to penetrate the mystery of how we learn from experience in daily life, how it is that in this sphere we have strikingly obvious robust knowledge of things and people, only an extended concept[26] of knowledge and a more wide-ranging analysis of the matter at hand will help us.

To come back to the principal idea: we said that every act of knowledge is a specific kind of existential relation to the object and founds a specific communion, a specific unity between subject and object. And further: every existential relation to the object takes it up into consciousness and in this 'taking up into consciousness' the object's being known is only one aspect. By this we mean the following: knowledge does not begin with conceptualization, which is only a late, mostly analytic phase with reference to a condition where one already *has* that which is 'to be known'. This *having* is thus the extended concept of knowledge in relation to which conceptual determination is only something secondary and not at all the place of origin for the constitution of the object. The extended concept of knowledge includes every existential reception of something out there into consciousness, whereas the narrower concept of knowledge means conceptual objectification. 'Knowing in the extended sense' is thus a total process of taking up the object into the subject and into its total consciousness (thus not only into 'theoretical consciousness'). What is usually called knowledge can only be understood from this point of view, as a part or phase of this total relation between subject and object, as a phase of objectification that is not even always the goal. And yet, what is experienced in this way and not reduced to concepts serves as the basis which makes up our image of the world, which forms, in turn, the most important part of our experience as a whole. In this sense, however, touching and feeling a thing is already practically knowing it. Just as what is formulated here as knowledge is only one side of a more far-reaching existential relationship; namely, that of contagion as such (in which the thing is drawn into my sphere of existence – even if fleetingly – through its hardness, through its being felt), so, too, is this incorporation into my subjective sphere present in every form of knowledge, including the higher ones.

At the moment of touching or bumping up against a stone, for example, I form a unity with it, which then immediately or simultaneously splits up into a duality of the self and the *vis-à-vis* (*Gegenüber*). But our duality is possible only on the ground of this existential contact and the unity which occurs in it. I become conscious of myself always and ever again in the course of being directed towards a *vis-à-vis,* which is not always necessarily something spatial and material, and I make the *vis-à-vis* into a *vis-à-vis* by projecting it outward after this prior reception into my subject.

But objectification as such, which alone is what one tends to call

187

knowledge, may have quite varied directions and stages; and, for its part, the existential relationship out of which the objectification emerges may vary in kind, a circumstance which is not without effect upon the character of the objectifications emerging from it.

We spoke of 'contagion' with the stone, thus with a thing without self or soul, which is given to us through tactile perception. We might at this point trace the entire range of apprehensions of the world of things by the other senses, if that would not lead us too far from the actual goal of our reflection, the apprehension of the *vis-à-vis* through interpretative understanding. It is enough to note that sensory perceptions (hearing, smelling, seeing, and so forth) mediate the apprehension of the *vis-à-vis* in a very different sense and that it is worth remarking how the sense-physiological ground-ing of epistemology was oriented to the analysis of visual percep-tion, and how the theory of the 'impressions' and 'symbols' was derived from this starting point, the theory which rendered the 'im-mediate contagion' of existential relation unnoticeable. What is still palpable in tactile communication can be more easily lost to view in the much more rarefied reception of the *vis-à-vis* in 'sight', namely the fact that here too it is a matter of a 'taking-up', a 'touch-ing' of the *vis-à-vis,* a union with it. This can be disguised only by the third dimension of visual space, by the circumstance that we see objects at a distance from our body. But it is surely not necessary to emphasize that this optical and spatial distance has nothing what-ever to do with the contagion, the taking-in of the seen into the self-sphere, which nevertheless occurs. Things may well remain 'out there'; but what we take of them into ourselves is a fusion between them and our self, and our knowledge of them is not a distancing, but rather their reception into our existential repository.

We deliberately started out from tactile experience in this de-monstration of the fact that all conceptually fixed knowledge is pre-ceded by a touching borne by our bodily being, a taking-in of the *vis-à-vis,* because here the existential relation cannot be denied or doubted. We believe, however, that this phenomenon of direct touching and reception of the *vis-à-vis* into the sphere of our self is not limited to the domain of tactile experience, but simply presents itself most precisely there. We touch with our body. But bodies also have the ability to grasp in their immediacy, quite in the manner of contagion, things of the spirit through the spirit, and things of the soul through the soul. To be sure, the expression 'con-tagion' contact – as already mentioned – refers to tactile sensation, but we believe that we are on the right track when we say that the specific phenomenon of direct contact (which at the same time sig-nifies our being touched) simply specifies a general form of subject-object relationship in the sphere of the sensory. Contagion is a kind of existential relatedness, a specific union with the object. We believe that the same phenomenon of contagion is before us when, for example, there walks into our room a strange person whom we have never seen before, who has not yet spoken a word but from whose physiognomy and bearing, from whose gestures and movements we nevertheless take in his whole being in a distinct way and all at once. In the true sense of the word we 'taste' the distinctive properties of his soul. We think that we can rightly speak of 'contagion' here, tasting, etc., because the essential structure of contagion – the total immediacy of the reception of something qualitative, which is unique – simply reproduces itself here at a level higher than in sensibility restricted to the body. Although such sensibility mediates in this instance too, since we must hear the sound of his voice and see the pattern of his movements, the immediate experience of the *vis-à-vis* is not reducible to these sensory contagions. We do not *have* him in these sensory 'touchings' alone – because on their basis alone we would be able to establish only the colour of his hair, the pitch of his speech, etc. – but it is that which pertains to the soul and is given with him and in him that immediately touches our soul at the same time. We are not of the opinion that it is empathy or analogical inferences which mediate in these cases,[27] but rather that our soul is affected along with the external senses. That which pertains to the alien soul, in so far as it is immediately present in physiognomy, movement, etc., is able to affect our soul quite in the sense of contagion.

In our opinion, however, this kind of contagion (in which, so to speak, we taste the other human being, we palpate him with our soul in his inimitable psychic uniqueness) does *not* contain that other kind of knowledge of human beings which constructs an image of the person's character with the help of meaningful forms (through the other's expressive movements, speech, actions, proving himself).

We shall speak later of this other kind of interpretative understanding, which rests on mediating forms; but at this point we must already point out that psychic contagion is a precondition of this understanding mediated through forms as well, and that it possesses a certain independence in relation to the understanding that rests on mediations. There is already a significant experiential basis contained within the immediate psychic contagion, and the immediate psychic contact that arises in the first moment of encounter suffices to found an existential relationship, an ontological relation to the Other, which will become the groundwork for every subsequent communication and every experience of him. Already at the first meeting there arises an existential relation, which recreates itself in its distinctive quality every time we meet the person in question. There arises a relationship having its own history, a relationship which is added as a new existence to the world of the existent, and which is graspable not only by us but also by the Other to whom it is directed, who grasps it also and immediately reacts meaningfully to it. Here the phenomenon decisive for us comes fully in view: since it arises in a specific existential relationship to the Other or, as the case may be, is one side of this existential relationship, every act of knowing establishes a specific communion with the Other. This phenomenon can be seen most clearly in our relationship with the 'other human being', because the other human being is a 'responding' object in the broadest sense of the word, while things to which we can also have such a relationship cannot in this manner take in the intention we direct at them and consequently cannot reflect anything either.

With regard to our relation to the 'other human being', moreover, it is demonstrable beyond challenge that our knowledge of him does not occur in the vacuum of events, but that our experience subsequent to the first contagion is always grounded upon that specific existential relation to the Other which is immediately rekindled and reconstitutes itself as soon as we focus ourselves upon him again with our whole existence, whether it is the case that we encounter him once more or that we think of him in his absence, in the form of longing and recollection. This existential relationship, through which I form a unity with the Other by virtue of the fact that I draw him into the sphere of myself,[28] is always different in its particular quality and is different with regard to every person. It always possesses its own distinctive 'coloration', 'atmosphere', in which I live as soon as and every time that my *vis-à-vis* approaches me or every time I think of him. This existential relationship is steadily transformed and revised as matters proceed. It also has a destiny as such, since it is after all something alive; and it is as well something which can be abstracted in itself, deliberately attended as a separate object, and known – but only by those who participate in it. To every human being who comes within my ken, accordingly, I stand in an existential relationship, within which all experiential learning concerning us and for us takes place, a relationship which is, as a living relationship, itself knowable – but only for those who exist within it. And, beside myself, it is above all my *vis-à-vis* who participates in this existential relationship, who approaches me with an intention of contagion similar in kind to mine, whose relatedness to me I am able to grasp in its specific 'coloration'. This knowing one another, and the immediately ensuing onset of change in the 'feelings' of the other toward me, which repeatedly brings about a self-correction in my own attitude of intention, has no small part to play in this common destiny of our common relationship. Is there not here in this first contagion, where there has not yet been a talk or any avowals – this contagion which radiates at the same time from both of us, which is received at the same time on both sides, and which aims at fusing itself into a unified relationship – is there not already in this knowing a knowledge of the other that is sufficiently concrete and definite to enable us to orient ourselves by it right away and to react adequately every time? It cannot be doubted that we have before us, prior to any conceptual formulation, a certain kind of knowledge, a knowing common to both of us, that *we* can grasp in a way subject to controls, even though there are as yet no objectifications in evidence. It is knowledge, but not knowledge for everyone, only for the two of us. This is a kind of knowledge for which the best designation has been offered, on the basis of a related point of departure, though in another context, by Victor von Weizsäcker, working on the physiology of sensation, who coined the term 'conjunctive knowledge'.[29]

2 Conjunctive knowledge

This conjunctive experience is materially characterized first of all by the fact that it captures only one aspect, one perspective of the *vis-à-vis*. To these dispositions belong both the facts that I am a human being who experiences through sense organs and also much more personal particularities, as, for example, that I am here and now, so and so, and that the souls or humans with which we are face to face mean this and nothing else to me, to my interests, and to my desires. This knowledge is thus completely one-sided. But does that mean that it is not knowledge? We called this knowledge 'a perspective'. Although this is expressed in a metaphor derived from the field of optical perception, this field has many essential things in common with the type of experiencing which is to be elucidated.

We shall next inquire how the distinctive perspectivistic attributes of optical perception can be characterized. In the optical consideration of a thing or a landscape, one gets a different picture of the object from every point in space. But is not each of these pictures an experience of *this* landscape, even if each 'foreshortening' or 'displacement' is oriented towards the standpoint from which one is looking? For the material contents of this optical image, my location in space as well as the properties of the object being looked at are constitutive. And notwithstanding, or precisely by virtue of the fact that it is perspectivistic, this location-bound image has its truth. For landscape is an object which can in principle only be grasped perspectivistically. If perspectivity disappears, the landscape disappears. If someone wants to experience a landscape, he does not set about making a map, which is an artificial projection, a fiction of an objectivity beyond location, since it fixes objective conditions. Instead he himself must unavoidably take up a location in space. Were he not to do so, and sought to see in the manner of the map, the landscape would disappear for him, and that is the very object with which alone everything is at this time concerned. But in just the same way, someone who is trying to learn about things, persons, and the relationships that obtain between them will not see a sacrifice of learning in the anthropomorphic and still more in the altogether personal bondedness of every such experience of the world, but will rather seek the only possible way, in essence, in this conjunctive manner of knowing, which is perspectivistic in this higher sense. For the same reason, the basic form for conveying things that have happened is narration, behind which the narrator stands. This primal form of perspectivity remains right up to the most rigorously conducted history. This is a distinction which will not be relevant until later but which here is to be taken as an example. So much for the material characterization of conjunctive knowledge.

As far as the range of validity of conjunctive learning is concerned, such knowledge is at first valid only for me, when I come to know a thing. If the object of my knowledge is a person, then – as becomes clear in the example just analysed – the perspectivistic image (the side of his psychic self that is turned toward me) – is transferable from my knowledge to his on the basis of the existential relationship in which we stand, just as conversely he can convey to me his knowledge of me. This happens very often even without words; but even when words are used, they never exhaust the contents actually conveyed, which largely spare us the work of formulation by virtue of the living relationship in which we exist together. But however rich this cognition of the Other may be, neither of us knows the Other as he may hypothetically be 'in himself'. What each of us knows about the Other is limited by the extent and manner of his entering into our common relationship, his existing in it, explicating himself in it.

We go further: we can know *ourselves* only to the extent that we enter into existential relationships to others. The precondition of self-knowledge is social existence: first, because we can put ourselves into human existential relationships only in this way; second, because every person actualizes a different aspect of our self; third, because it is easier for us to see ourselves through the eyes and in the perspective of another than by taking ourselves as point of departure.[30] Let all this illustrate that this kind of knowledge is always anchored in far-reaching existential foundations, and that products of knowledge of this kind are valid only for the circles whose existential attachments they express and in the form in which they present themselves. This kind of knowledge, then, has conjunctive validity only, not objective validity.[31] In our example it is valid only for the two of us, for those initiated into this existential bond and taking part in it.

But there is more to be said. It is not only the items of knowledge relating to the two of us and therefore belonging to the domain of mutual knowledge which take on the conjunctive character of 'being valid only for us', 'being verifiable only by us', and the perspectivistic character of being one-sidedly turned towards a specific 'experiential space',[32] grown up between us in the course of a common 'existence-for-one-another'. All shared experiences relating to things in the external world (landscapes, people, politics, etc.) are equally brought into relationship to this shared 'experiential space' and are given an orientation directed towards this place. It follows that it is the case not only that the individual person shares a specific conjunctivity with his *vis-à-vis,* but also that as few as two persons can bring into being, by means of 'third persons' (things as well as men) an 'experiential space' possessing conjunctive validity, in which and by reference to which experiential knowledge gains a validity which is conjunctive rather than objective. But this restriction of objectivity does not at all mean that what is going on in this most personal way or within the more extended conjunctive community is not knowing. It is just that the range of communicability of these pieces of knowledge is restricted to those who participate in the total existential relationship within which and out of which this knowledge arises. We have already indicated that this existential relationship, which forms itself at the time of the initial psychic contagion between one human being and another, has its course of development as well, and that it is something alive and caught up in a process of becoming, so that what we have before us is a dynamic basis for knowledge. *I* become different and the *Other* becomes different, at every moment; and our conjunction becomes different thereby, since it is constantly being created anew by means of self-correction and mutual orientation. One state of affairs naturally does not spring abruptly out of the other; nor can the Other become at any moment anything at all which might be abstractly possible. This guarantees that the conjunction too (that third thing in which we come together) will be

193

something we are able to follow in its transformations. It is a dynamic nexus connecting us. The things which are drawn into our relationship and known from there also change their appearances, in themselves and for us. We visit a natural setting, we capture one of its aspects, which now belongs to us alone and is accessible to us in a way which is determined by the specific unique constellation of illumination, sun, and atmosphere, as well as by the state of our mutuality, into which it enters.

The living relationship is the basis of every subsequent conjunctive experience. It is the background for anything new that may be added, the fundamental temper within which all knowledge of man dwells. But temper is something much more complex than a cloud of feeling surrounding objectivities; at this level of experience, it is constitutive of the object. We seek to repeat an experience; we return to the 'same' landscape. But it has changed completely in the meantime. And this is not only because the sun no longer shines as it did, the wind no longer blows as it did, but also – and above all – our existential relationship has in the meantime been running its course, and has undergone change along with us and within us. We recognize the experience of the landscape as a repetition, because we remain in continuity with ourselves, with the Other, and with our mutual relationship (which supplies the basis for recognition), even if everything else has changed. The relationship stays with us. But it can also break off. A long separation denies us continuity with regard to the Other and to mutual relationships. And if the relationship is truly broken off, there is no more *common* knowing, either regarding ourselves or regarding the phenomena we meet together – unless it is possible once more to break through to the Other.

3 The extension of the conjunctive experiential community

This conjunctive knowledge, limited to two people and their mutuality, is bound to the continuability of direct contact. What is learned is thoroughly personal, even when, as in our case, it is bipersonally anchored;[33] it is not simply transmittable to 'third parties', unless these bind themselves to us by an 'initiation' into our relationship, through reception of our existence into their own. And this occurs in the following way: The third party enters into a specific existential relationship to me and to the other, and in this living together takes up into himself, so far as possible, the relationship between the two of us. Through living together with us, through stretches of life now lived jointly among three, he learns to know our way of seeing things and to join in it. He shares our experiential space and thus gradually builds up for himself a more expanded experiential space, based on the three of us. This experiential space is already closed off against the outside, accessible to others, to strangers, only in its superficial manifestations, and not in the concreteness with which it exists for us and about which we can come to an understanding because *we* are connected with one another through it.

The third party, who was at first a 'he' for us, becomes a 'you' by sharing in our we-experience. Many have remarked on the subtlety of language which is expressed in the use of personal pronouns. It would easily be possible to replace the personal pronouns by a depersonalizing series (such as the numerical series), and once one leaves the level of experience at which personal pronouns really apply, that of conjunctive experiential community, one man is indeed interchangeable with another. At this other level it is not comprehensible why the third person should receive the special designation of 'he' while the fourth and fifth persons in the series are not accorded any special personal pronouns. From this point of view it is also not clear why everyone beyond the third person is a 'he', but everyone can also suddenly become a 'you', and why, moreover, one group is taken up into the 'we', another strange group is addressed as 'you' and why all the remaining ones can be juxtaposed to us in sum as 'they'. All this derives from the fact that every direct address signifies a reception of the *vis-à-vis* within us – at least in so far as we speak with this Other, and to the extent of the ensuing connection.

Thus this 'we-sphere' can be extended, as ever more third parties become 'you' and come to take part in the common experiential space. But to trace this expansion more concretely, we must discuss something that we had earlier put aside: the role of language and conceptual specification, which alone permits a long-term unification and expansion of the experiential space. The continuity of the existential relationships between two subjects could not be upheld by mere contagion, by the soul being touched, even though what is most essential in the existential relationship rests on this level of direct contagion which we have been treating, and even though we only grasp the conjunctive significance of concepts on the basis of this existential attachment.

4 The role of concept and language in conjunctive knowledge

As described in the preceding chapter, natural-scientifically oriented methodology hypostatizes one type of knowledge as knowledge *per se*. A second essential prejudice of this methodology consists in the fact that it correspondingly hypostatizes one type of concept – the so-called exact concepts, which have their origin, according to their essence, in definitions – as the only type. To this corresponds still another one-sidedness on the part of this methodology. Just as it saw thinking only from the conceptual level and abstracted what is thought from the existential relation, so it investigated concepts only in their immanent context and refused to see that concepts are a partial function of a total process of existentially anchored thinking as well, and that there is at least one type of concept whose significance can only be understood when one also takes into consideration this functional anchoring. The utopian ideal of the mode of concept-formation having the character of natural-scientific universal validity would be the creation of a timeless conceptual level upon which every concept which occurs would have its place, would secure its unambiguous meaning and its contents from the other components, and would be defined once and for all through its relationship to these others.[34]

Everything subject to assertion is to be identical for everyone in every assertion of it; and the concept thus universally valid in two ways: referable to all objects of the same kind (the concept 'table' is thus applicable to all tables that have ever existed or ever will exist), and valid for all subjects who ever will utter it, and who accordingly always understand the same thing by 'table'. That this tendency inheres in every concept-formation cannot be doubted; and the creation of such a conceptual plane upon which one concept can be defined by others, with all concepts thereby forming an objective self-contained system, should not be denied. This systematization succeeded most thoroughly in theoretical physics, where everything conceptual could be expressed through relations of the system of numbers and where even the original concepts with their anthropomorphic cast (as, for example, the concept of power) were subjected to a reshaping in this direction. This ideal of reducing every qualitative specificity to quantities could be realized only in physics, of course; but even in the remaining sciences, which do without quantification, a rationalization by means of definitions aspiring to precision also moves in the direction of a timeless, supra-conjunctive conceptual system.

In contrast to this, there is also an altogether different tendency in concept-formation, long in existence and rooted in a different movement, and this alternative must not be neglected. It rests on the possibility of using every concept, including the most general, as a *name*; and what is to be understood by name in this case is the specific property of words whereby they designate a specific thing in a specific function in its unique relationship to us and to our specific conjunctive community. It is a common observation that the language of a community which knows conjunctively becomes ever more sectarian as the community becomes more close-knit. Within this community, a distinctive terminology takes shape, in which the words of the wider linguistic community become ever less comprehensible, not only because terms of art grow up peculiar to the narrower group, but also because the same complex of sounds, which is a familiar general concept for the rest, acquires a distinctive conjunctively determined meaning for the narrower community, and this meaning is understood only by those who have taken part in the pattern of experience in which the word in question suddenly springs forth as designation. In this case, the word does not register a general relationship to a thing or an event, but only the event that is turned toward the cognitive community. The most pregnant types of such concepts are terms of endearment or the distorted word-formations that occur in the speech of children and that of lovers and friends. But it is not only these most striking examples of verbal types that have such a stamp of being conjunctively anchored; in living speech, all working concepts acquire this capacity for individualization.

That is precisely the miracle of living speech: that it always places each word in a unique context and that it can bestow an individual meaning to each word from the specific totality of the sentence and, even more, from the undercurrent of the communication flowing from its rhythm and the stream of association.[35]

Whereas a scientific essay of utopian perfection would have to consist, at least in tendency, of nothing but rigorously defined conceptual mosaics capable of being separately grasped as well (for which a unique supra-conjunctive, timeless conceptual system would provide the building blocks), utopian speech would be a complete retraction of all intrinsic meanings of words, so that everything would secure its meaning from the totality of a context of meaning, which would have its real basis, in turn, in the nexus of experience.

It is well known that especially important revolutionary speeches, when they are merely read in printed form, often appear trivial and insignificant, while they were experienced as measuring up in the assembly, where the conjunctive experiential space was still present and the function of the speech was, so to speak, nothing more than pointing toward the common experience. In such cases the speech is no longer really understood when it is read, for we are scarcely able, after the fact, to penetrate fully into the conjunctive experiential community, and can no longer adequately grasp the specific functional references of the verbal complexes.

We grasp the words more or less exclusively in their general meanings, which are all that is accessible to us, and not in their unique reference to the experiential complex which was experienced in common and which continues to vibrate in all of the listeners at the time of the living address.

This already reveals something that would be certain to be overlooked, as a rule, if one were exclusively attuned to the other type of verbal meanings: here is a type that cannot be grasped on the analogy of strictly defined concepts, as within a model of a uniquely abstractable conceptual plane, and whose ultimate meaning discloses itself only when one reconnects the verbal meaning and the speech as a whole with the existential referent out of which and for the sake of which it arose.

Methodology can therefore do justice to conjunctive learning only if it always takes the recourse to concepts, which occurs here as well, as part of an existential general process in which the conceptual represents only one side. Viewed from this existential relationship, words which seemingly remain unaltered can have very different functions; and it is important to consider these, if for no other reason, because the change of function in each case influences the objective substantive contents of these units of meaning. It is naturally impossible for us to trace all the functional relationships which are possible between words and existential complex. We only want to point out the difference already developed, that a word displays an altogether different meaning in a naming function than it does as general concept in a state of having been characterized by definition. While the former signification of the word has meaning only when the word is restored to its intuitive, experiential foundations, the latter possesses at least a relative separability from the complex of experience and experiential learning; and this latter circumstance gives rise to the misperception that knowing as such, that knowing of every kind, takes place upon this plane of separability and that what is thought can always be separated from the existential undercurrent and rendered independent and self-explanatory (*verselbständigt*).

But we must not be satisfied to bring out the functional rootedness of concepts and thinking in the existential dimension only with regard to the fact that they constantly draw their contentual substance from a background which is alive (naming concepts always meaning only as much as is understood by them). We also want to emphasize an easily overlooked additional characteristic functional relationship they exemplify. Thought is not only linked to function prior to and in its genesis, but it is also so linked with regard to the objects for the sake of which concepts arise: in their purposiveness they are not so much rooted in existence as they are themselves living existence. Conventional methodology is in the habit of playing all thinking off against life as something dead. This succeeds to the extent that such methodology artificially cuts away the functional relatedness of concepts. But life – and especially life in conjunctive experiential space – does not create concepts for the sake of theoretical contemplation, in order to rest in them, but rather in order to pursue life in and through them. They are at the same time an organ of life in its flow and a living activity. To put this another way: concepts in conjunctive experiential space are not only functionally determined in their genesis, in that they manifest what they have taken up into themselves in the course of existence in order to fix the contents which thus arise upon a theoretical plane that is outside of life, but these concepts are also subsequently retrieved into life. They have a function as concepts for the furtherance of life, and this signifies not only an apprehension of reality but also its transformation. Marx formulated this antithesis in a magnificent way when he said, 'Philosophers have only interpreted the world in different ways; the point is to change it' ('Theses on Feuerbach'). Every concept possesses this transformative impulse at all times in the conjunctive space of life and experience. Even when concepts have no function other than naming, they already contain a distinctive supra-theoretical capacity, and that is the capacity to fix. It is well known that already in the ages of magic naming did not have primarily a communicative significance (to render someone or something recognizable) but rather had the function of gaining power over men and things.[36]

We do not actually have to return to this magical function of the word, for our need in the conjunctive experiential community to name shared experiences does not correspond to a longing for scientific classification but to the need to hold on to experience for our particular experiential community, to fix it, in the specific way in which it was experienced. We do this not in a manner that could make the contents universally communicable, but only so that it becomes meaningful for us who are part of the experiential community.[37] Apart from this sort of functionality (which, as has now become clear, represents a completely different kind of retention and fixation of an experience from the definitional establishment of general determinations), concept and thinking can also have the distinct function of changing the world. All sociological thought is originally embedded in a drive for change. That namings alone already possess such a capacity to transform being, at least for the psychic domain, is proved by psychoanalysis, in which the working out of a 'repression' or a 'complex' not only aims at determining

199

that this or that was the cause of the malady, but also to free the patient of this malady by means of this knowledge; i.e., to bring about a change in his psychic being. If psychoanalytic practical knowledge inclines toward general theory, in a different projection it is at one and the same time activity, desire to transform, and power to transform.[38]

If there is thus a pull towards fixation even within conjunctive knowing and naming, which is to say an effort to raise certain components of flowing life above change and becoming, there is also at the same time the other tendency, to take the word, speech, naming, back into life and to reinvolve them as a living element in the rest of what is living. But even the removal from existence that takes place in the course of conjunctive knowledge with the help of the naming process differs completely from the one that takes place in objectification through definition. We have already pointed out, but must stay with the problem, that even if it is the case that something is removed from the stream of experience in conjunctive experiential knowledge, this kind of objectification does not occur in the interest of de-personalization or a de-perspectivization. Quite the opposite; the relatedness between the contents to be objectified and the particular experiential space in which they have arisen remains constitutive for this kind of knowledge, and what is retained and how it is retained is determined by the fact that it is being fixed for a particular experiential community (even if that community consists of only two members.)

Having cleared up some questions about the role of the concept and of language in the conjunctive experiential community, we are now in a position to answer the question which we put aside earlier, concerning the extent to which language is important in maintaining an experiential community.

If only the purely existential relations between the individuals taking part in an experiential community existed, without language and conceptualization, a lasting relationship between the individuals could hardly come into being. It would be conditioned upon an uninterrupted existential being-together and upon purely instinctual relationships. In this sense lasting association, common experiential space, must also exist among animals. What is added to all this in man through language, which he alone possesses? Language brings articulation and fixation into the stream of conjunctive experience. It brings commonly experienced stretches into relief, fixes them, and suspends the universal flow. It can even go so far as to stereotype that which has been learned in common. But this stereotyping is not the same as that of universal concepts which, while they also name things, extract that which is to be designated out of its specific experiential space. The type of stereotyping with which we are concerned, however, is distinguished by the fact that it does not generalize, does not move in the direction of an arrangement into genus and species (which attempts to abstract from every particular experiential space). Instead it leaves the relatedness to a specific experiential space and perspectivity untouched and strips from experience only the momentary and idiosyncratic.

Knowledge remains perspectivistic, bound to a particular experiential space. It is only that this experiential space is already filled with repeatable elements which, however, could only occur as such in this experiential space. This is obviously abstraction in a direction different from generalizing abstraction. The conjunctive concept which arises in this process of abstraction is abstract in relation to the unique fullness of each experience, but, despite its abstractness, it is not free of perspectivity, of rootedness in the specific experiential space. It is probably already evident here that ultimately this entire discussion aims at understanding historical concept-formation and now, since it is a question of finding a proper example of concepts structured in this way, we must therefore turn to genuinely historical concepts. It is probably now clear that the concept of 'conjunctive knowledge', in contrast to generalizing, universally valid knowledge, alluded to historical thought and that we will now accordingly attempt to grasp the distinctive nature of historical concepts.

If we want to find concepts that, although not general, are nevertheless not altogether concrete and individualizing, which are, in short, only applicable to a particular experiential space and in this sense perspectivistic, we must look for them in the field of interpretative history. All concepts which cannot be translated, which name something in a particular, historically conditioned experiential space and cannot be replaced by analogous concepts from our own experiential space without a distortion of their meaning, are what we mean when we speak about such conditional, stereotyping abstract concepts, which cannot be termed general concepts, despite their comparative generality, since they also possess an inclination towards individualization.[39,40]

The word *polis* and the untranslatable expressions 'cant' and 'flirt' fix objects that are attached to a particular experiential space. Within the space proper to them, the phenomena in question may well recur countless times, and the concepts are therefore general in relation to the many separate recurrences, each tied to a separate moment, which may transpire there. But they are at the same time completely individual, to the extent that they cannot be trans-

201

ferred to experiential spaces other than those in which they originated. To go so far as to subsume *polis* under the concept of 'state'
in general involves a special kind of dismissal of particular perspectivity and disregard of specific material contents. This can, of
course, be done in a generalizing consideration, which is a possibility and has its justifications, but from the viewpoint of genuinely
historical acquisition of knowledge such a procedure is a falsification rather than a designation of the subject matter in view. Similarly, the phenomenon intended by the English word 'cant' is not
simply replaceable by the concept of *Heuchelei,* the German term
for hypocrisy. Both words are attached to the particular experiential spaces within which the phenomena corresponding to them developed, and in which they have gained their names. From an
historical view, one grasps them altogether inadequately when one
catches them up in a conceptual net spread out over all time. They
are grasped with historical adequacy only through interpretation,
which consists in working out the existential relationships intended
by these concepts. And we can manage to bring these relationships
to life only if we also take into consideration the other correlatively
posited meanings belonging to the same experiential space, and
thus 'work our way into' the affected experiential space of the historical community to be investigated.

While a concept within the unhistorically generalizing type of
concept formation is comprehended only when one determines its
genus proximum and *differentia specifica,* the comprehension of a
conjunctive concept attached to a particular experiential space is
achieved only when one has managed to penetrate into that space.
The totality of that world must be mastered, and not the totality of
an abstract conceptual plane, if one is to understand a conjunctively determined concept in an historically interpretative way.
This is due to the fact that it is not only the concepts that are different in different experiential spaces, but also the phenomena
intended by them. This can be demonstrated in the phenomenon of
'flirting' mentioned earlier. This expression, and the phenomenon
to which it refers as well, derive from the Anglo-Saxon cultural
milieu, but have to all appearances spread throughout the entire
'cultivated world'. But it is altogether inappropriate, despite this
diffusion of the word, to designate all erotic playfulness between
young people as 'flirting'. The dependence of the usage upon the
racially conditioned capacity, probably shaped by Northern tem-
perament as well, which allows one to be erotically stimulated
'without danger', brings it about that a transfer of the usage to
peoples of the South will involve a change in the formation, to
bring it close to sexual brutality. 'Flirting' requires a certain

restraint, which is determined not only by race but also by cultural traditions and class customs, and these together give the phenomenon a special form and meaning. But if, for these reasons, the phenomenon is not transferable, then its name, which arises in the same lifespace, is also not to be transferred into foreign experiential spaces.

5 The power of conjunctive knowledge to form community

Historical concepts, then, permit the clearest demonstration that there exists a kind of stereotyping abstraction in the formation of concepts which moves in a direction altogether different from the generalizing that aims at definitions. The abstraction and relative generalization integral to conjunctive naming maintains perspectivity and the relatedness of the contents to a particular experiential space and a particular complex of practical knowledge.

Trans-conjunctive generalization, in contrast, aims to de-anthropomorphize concepts or at least to remove their meaning from a particular community and relocate them on to the level of universal validity. Von Weizsäcker[41] is therefore right to remark that while generalizing concept formation leads to universal validity, the inclusion of subjects into an experiential community, no matter how extensive, only leads to community-wide acceptation for these concepts. Here there is in fact a qualitative leap which is grounded in the material difference between the two types of concept. A general concept is potentially valid for everyone, even if in actuality only one person thinks it; a community-wide, conjunctive (historical) concept counts only for those who participate in an experiential space, even if in actuality everyone participates in it. The knowledge stored up in an historical, conjunctive concept is and remains perspectivistic; the general concept, in contrast, attempts to eliminate anything reminiscent of such perspectives. The conjunctive concept requires existential resonance and sympathy with a particular 'world', a community; the general concept arises on a level where the linkage with a particular community has been eradicated. It thus follows logically that we emphasize the community-forming power of conjunctive concepts but deny this power and capacity to general concepts.[42] The distinction between the two types of concept corresponds completely to Tönnies's parallel sociological distinction between community (*Gemeinschaft*) and society (*Gesellschaft*).[43] The first type of concept corresponds to community-consciousness, the second to societal consciousness.

The distinction also corresponds to another, stemming from the same root, that of 'culture' and 'civilization'. The general concepts of the natural sciences are civilizational concepts, those of conjunctive knowledge are the expression of a consciousness attached to a particular culture. I have tried to show elsewhere that historiography, philosophy and the art of interpretation in all its guises are relative to diverse cultural spheres, and I indicated there that all civilizational entities, in contrast, make up a single, unified system. It is for this reason that it is possible to transfer knowledge and to accumulate it progressively in the latter case, while all concepts attached to culture (concepts of philosophy, for example, but also genuinely historical concepts) radiate from particular systematizing and ultimately existential centres and can be understood only by reference to them.[44]

This presupposes that an experiential community, which was, to begin with, limited to two individuals in our example, can potentially expand into a 'sect', a cultural community or to the other types of community. The cultural community, however, is the most inclusive broadening of concrete conjunctive experiential community that we know up to now. We shall not deal here with whether humanity as a whole can now or ever develop into a conjunctive experiential community. That conjunctive naming concepts are indispensable to the construction and survival of concrete experiential community needs no proof. The perspectivistic pattern of experience is stored up in these concepts; new life is created through them; new lives are brought into being in their name; new arrivals, new generations are initiated into them; and understanding them means at the same time participating in the fabric of life of an experiential community. Not a word can be understood, unless the existential acts pertaining to it are also realized together with it; no course of life can be expressed and made understandable to others, unless it follows the route appropriate to such courses within that particular community.

6 The problem of conjunctive knowledge in historical application

In our analysis, which was a genealogy of meaning and, as such, altogether disregarded the problem of historical origins, we constructed an experiential community by first positing a single individual, whom we brought into existential relationship to a *vis-à-vis*, in order to depict his conjunction with this *vis-à-vis* (which at first was a thing) within a transitory segment of his existence. Then we posited a 'responding' object, which was at the same time also a subject, in place of the lifeless *vis-à-vis* and then had a conjunctive experiential space emerge from this constellation. This conjunctive experiential space was still filled with perspectivistic experiences, shaped by the moment and constantly changing in the flow of shared life. Then we considered the significance of concepts and language for conjunctive knowledge in order to characterize the phenomenon of experiential contextures being subjected to stereotyping. We described the distinctive character of this stereotyping in contrast to that which takes place in the general concept. Only when we reached this stage in our construction did we cause the number of participants in the experiential community to grow, in order to bring into being a group joined by shared experiential contextures and by the perspectivistic but already stereotyped concepts attached to them.

This is a construction of a phenomenon to be described, which clearly stands in open contradiction to the historical-sociological career of social consciousness – so far as we now have an idea of it. Since overcoming the errors of the social philosophy of the Enlightenment, which similarly proceeded in this regard from the isolated individual, in order to derive society from him, we now know that the group actually came before the individual, and that the individual was wholly absorbed within group consciousness long before he could stand there as an individual by himself. For it is at a later stage of development that the individual becomes aware of himself in his singularity and particularity. And it is at a still later stage of his self-reflection that he has progressed so far in the process of individuation that he not only cultivates and especially values what is individual in himself but also considers what is momentary in his life and experience as interesting and valuable.

Impressionism in art, science, and philosophy corresponded to this stage, comprising the cultivation of the momentary, and, culminating in a whole development of individualization, it signified an atomization of man and his experiential space as well. But the Enlightenment itself had already transcended the individualist point of departure of its constructs (which, viewed sociologically, were a reflection in theory of the atomization of the communal society of the Middle Ages), for it treated this derivation, which was originally meant as history, as a construct and applied it further as such. And it is in this form that we find the construct in Kant. As a construct, this derivation has a dual justification: on the one hand a pedagogical one, in that the subject matter can best be built up in this sequence; second, a material one, because it takes the layers which are confounded together in actual fact and orders them in accordance with their material interconnections in relation to meaning. In this case the derivation does not refer to historical time but to the meaningful, staged sequence of interconnections stored up within the phenomenon to be described. This dissociates a unitary phenomenon in a manner analogous to a schematic presentation of the logical syllogism, where the premises are separated from the conclusion and the latter derived from the former, even though it is precisely the coexistence of the parts and their logical interdependence which constitutes the very meaning of a syllogism.

In recognizing our presentation as a genealogy of meaning, we avoid the danger of the misunderstanding that we meant as historical succession something that can only be understood as genealogy of meaning. If we turn our attention to the historical origin of conjunctive experiential space, there can be no doubt that not the isolated individual but the community with its conjunctive experiential space and its language arose first. It is also clear that in the primeval stages of thought there was not only no individualized and time-fragmented grasping of surroundings but rather the opposite, a wholly stereotyped experiential field. In this experiential field there are what may be called prescribed courses of obligatory experiences, in which all the important events of the community are 'ritualized' and 'magically' stereotyped, with the result that if something not previously experienced were to surface within the particular individual there would be the greatest inhibitions against grasping it as something new. But one thing is clear: all experiences have their perspectivity, even if it is a stereotyped one, and the meanings of words receive their specific character from the communally elaborated conjunctive experiential space. Rites, transactions, war and work, erotic relationships and childbearing gain a meaning that is fixed for the community. They are organized into rigorously ordered ritual enactments, participation in which takes place in the same way for every member and grants apprehension of only one side of the phenomenon. The world is covered by collective representations, as Durkheim calls them,[45] which exercise a compelling force over the members of the group. The world is not an experiential space penetrable in innumerable directions but a particular configuration existing only for the community, a world of its own, to which only those can gain entrance who take part in it. Rites, cults, and magical activities still have the same standing as language and concepts: the latter have no tendency toward classification or working out general definitions, but rather toward fixing significances for the common experiential space. But this, too, takes place not in the theoretical spirit of ascertaining and ordering but in the spirit of a co-operative expression of life-relationships. The many-sided functionality of the concept, its origin in the configuration of life and existence for it, are as yet obvious; and it is for this reason that the capacity for abstraction, even in the sense of conjunctive abstraction, is only indefinitively present. Collective representations in Durkheim's sense thus spread themselves over all the things, events and relationships of life, and the significance of something for the concrete life-space overspreads, hides, and draws itself into the determinations of pure existence. We do not possess things as they might be in themselves but only as they exist for the community. To anticipate: our present-day pre-scientific conception of reality stands in direct continuity with this kind of life-experience. Even if the conception of reality in contemporary everyday life is not wholly a continuation of the primitive experience of the world, it is nevertheless so closely related to it in structure that in our everyday spontaneous experience of the world – notwithstanding our superior theoretical knowledge derived from natural science – the sun is still seen by us as a disk and, notwithstanding our knowledge of causality, magical ideas still govern our horizon of expectations. And we too control our fears through secret charms. Things have faces, and a lingering animism still leads us to see the objects and growths of a place not as bare but as charged with a mood (sometimes malevolent – a raging stream; sometimes joyful – a spring landscape).

The 'world' is given in this way, and the mighty wave of the rising natural-scientific, abstract mode of thought could not denude things of religious-magical and other shape-giving significations. The world does not exist for us as a sum of things merely extended in space, and in so far as and to the degree that a thing is more than a simple *res extensa,* this surplus derives from the world of collective representations. Viewed historically, then, the experiential space of our everyday is keeper of the most deep and original possibilities of human experience, which persist in structure, although greatly altered in detail, in the conjunctively perspectivistic quality inhering in this space. The alternative experiential and intellectual project, that aims at the abstraction and de-anthropomorphizing within which civilization runs its course, raised itself out of this experiential space. But today conjunctive experiential space is the site not only of our everyday life but also of our cultural creation in its entirety. The artist paints things in their collective significance and perspectivity of meaning; the poet portrays feelings in our relationships to them. Historiography, too (even if it is becoming increasingly scientific, that is, exact, in its critical relation to sources) retains, even at its highest level, its primal form as 'narration'; that is, a presentation, having reference to a particular experiential space, of an interconnected set of matters.

7   Analysis of collective representations

As noted earlier, then, collective representations are the precipitate of conjunctive experiences which are perspectivistic but stereotyped, that is, having reference to a specific experiential space. They can be grasped by and in this sense have full force only for those who existentially partake of them. As such, therefore, collective representations are already something more than experiential contextures. In comparison to these, they are objectivities, because they establish the significance of objects of possible experiences in a way going beyond the individual and the psyche. They are not supra-individual for all possible subjects, but only in relation to the members of a group who are actually present in fact. The individual as he has been assimilated to a community, guides himself by these ideas, after all, and submits himself to them. They exercise a compelling force over him. Durkheim is already wrestling with this problem when he tries to clear up what a social fact could be. Since he sees that one cannot call these social facts 'experiences' (since they do not coincide with the experiences of the single individual but rather are always there for a specific group even if they are not being actualized at the moment) he decides to treat them as things.[46] But to this it must be objected that this designation is extremely liable to misunderstanding, since things are something quite different again from the phenomena which we, like Durkheim, are trying to characterize. A thing exists in space, and is tied in its existence to a specific period of time. It does not change in its being in-and-for-itself in the same way as do, for instance, the collective representations which refer to it. As mountain, the mountain remains a mountain; in conjunctive experience, by contrast, the mountain may be a 'magic garden' for several generations and then become a landscape, or signify something different for the experiential community. The mountain exists, the collective representation refers to it. The collective representation may transform itself in contents, but its mode of being will nevertheless remain one of referring itself to existing things. One would be in danger of being thrown back to the earlier assumption that 'collective representations' are 'psychic existence', if it could not be maintained against this that as long as the collective representation that a mountain is a magic garden continues to prevail, this 'representation', this 'bestowal of significance' rises above the psychological realm, since the psychic can exist as reality only within the soul of the individual. But in giving effect to collective representations by thinking and experiencing, the individual psyches merely actualize something that was somehow there before this actualization and will still be there for a long time after it. The question is however: how is it there?

We can also adduce other arguments to show that collective representations go beyond the psychological, which can only mean going beyond the actualizations in individual psyches at a given point in time:

(1) No single individual in a group (especially when the experiential space of a group is very rich in collective representations) commands everything knowable that may be already available to the group in question in the form of group pieces of practical knowledge. The totality of what is knowable is divided among various individuals, each of whom only takes part in a particular segment of the representations possible in a collective experiential space. Nevertheless, the totality of these segments forms an organic whole, which 'exists in nobody's head' as a whole but in a certain sense is suspended over the group.

(2) Further, there are collective representations which by their very nature cannot be realized by an individual. Every cult, every ceremony, every dialogue is a contexture of meaning, a totality in which the individual has his function and role but where the whole is something which is dependent for its actualizability on a plurality of individuals and which in this sense reaches beyond the individual psyche.[47] An individual can well imagine the whole ceremony, but as a collective representation it is not primarily something to be thought, but rather something to be given effect through the interplay of various individuals. At this point, the elevation of the contexture of meaning above the individual psyche (which alone has psychic reality) becomes visible from a different side again.

If one follows up Durkheim's reflections, one can scarcely overlook the fact that German idealism in its most recent phase and in the phenomenological school (both of which refer back to the analyses of Kant, Lotze, and Bolzano) has worked out the suprapsychic mode of being of the sphere of validity. Durkheim is in fact on to something, and he would also be able to distinguish it adequately if he were not restricted in his thinking to the positivist tradition but instead had at his disposal as well the conceptual and analytical apparatus of idealistic philosophy. This logical-ontological product of the idealist tradition becomes important here and we want to put it to use, although it must be noted right away that it is employable in our context only with modifications.

Proceeding from impressions similar to the ones which we have considered in connection with Durkheim, neo-idealist philosophy (in the form of the so-called philosophy of validity) arrived at the insight that when one canvasses the whole realm of possible 'objects' (in the broadest sense of this work)[48] some turn up that cannot be wholly accommodated within the usual classification of all objects which are in any way possible. While two essential groups of objects possible were earlier distinguished (things taking up space and time, on the one hand, and psychic proceedings occurring in time but not occupying space, on the other), this classification proved insufficient in the course of time. Awareness of the inadequacy of this 'object-theoretical' classification came at first and above all in considering the mode of being of theoretical formations, and especially those of mathematics. Schematically, the argumentation in these reflections goes something like this: If I call to mind, say, the Pythagorean theorem, and direct my attention to its propositional contents, the latter is an 'object' which cannot be considered a spatio-temporal thing nor designated adequately as psychic proceeding, and, in consequence cannot be accommodated within the alternatives of 'things in space' and 'psychic act'. There is thus a third kind of objectification. That the Pythagorean theorem as a theoretical contexture of meaning is not a spatial phenomenon is doubtless immediately evident. Although it can be applied to 'triangles' that exist in space, the subject matter of geometry is not this or that concrete triangular wooden figure of the triangle drawn on the blackboard but rather the 'triangle in itself', which is a construct. The drawing and the wooden figure are only symbolizations of the ideal triangle. But the Pythagorean theorem is not an experience, not a mere psychic act, but is distinguished in its contents from the experiences that actualize it. If there are twenty people gathered in a room and all, simultaneously, while listening to a lecture, think the Pythagorean theorem, there is still only one *theorem* even though there are twenty psychic *acts*, which are not the theorem itself but merely actualize it. The contents of the theorem are thus a new kind of object that can be fitted neither into the world of things nor into the sphere of mental proceedings. It is *there* in a different way than are bodies and psychic occurrences, and if one does not want to force it into the categories of 'thing in space' or 'psychic being', which are inapplicable to it, then one must constitute a special category of mode of being for such objects. The Pythagorean theorem is a contexture of meaning, a set of contents with theoretical validity. If the mode of being of bodies and of psychic proceedings is to be called 'being' (*Sein*), then we can call the mode of being that is an attribute of propositional contents 'being valid' (*Gelten*), since the propositional contents are 'valid' for all times and subjects.

But a troubling ambiguity is still unhappily confounded in 'being valid' as a way of naming this, and it must be resolved. 'Being valid' designates, first of all, quite simply a specific mode of being, and it is as such an ontological category. Second, however, the thought is also articulated in the expression 'being valid' that the contents in question are not simply *there* in a certain mode of being but that they also have in them an injunctive character, that they signify a norm – and a norm, indeed, that holds for all imaginable subjects. From this point of view, the proposition termed valid has timeless validity. This characterization does apply in the case of the Pythagorean theorem: the semantic contents articulated in it not only represent a particular mode of being but also have the character of a claim valid for all possible thinking subjects. We nevertheless want to distinguish the mode of being encompassed in the expression 'being valid' from the injunctive character which it also encompasses.

The specific mode of being we should like to designate by the expression 'existing in the mode of significancies', which is designed to indicate that the objects denominated in this way (which have the character of being contextures of meaning, significations, collective representations, etc.) have their being neither in the mode of spatial objects nor in that of psychic proceedings. By means of this expression we also want to avoid using the concept of being valid, which always carries with it an injunctive character – and one, moreover, that is as far as possible timeless and compelling for all possible subjects. That the ontological character was confounded with that of injunction-and-validity had undesirable consequences, since the injunctive component was also carried over to formations which have nothing to do with validity and especially not with timeless validity, even though they do quite properly belong ontologically within the sphere of significancies. The amalgamation of these two moments came about chiefly because the phenomenon of this mode of being, which had not been analysed before, was first discovered in the sphere of mathematics, and because the characterization drawn from there was then transferred to all other significancies. We know now why the analysis was bound to take this turn. If it had been initiated in another field it would have turned out differently. But here, in the field of mathematics, where universal validity does exist in fact, where the idea of an experiential knowledge having only conjunctive validity cannot even arise, where from the very outset everything is directed towards providing supra-conjunctive standing for all meanings, the claim to validity accompanies every significancy as a matter of course. But this cannot disguise the fact that in other

211

fields there are formations and symbols to which the characterization 'to exist in the mode of significancies' applies but which do not present themselves at the same time in the character of possessing validity beyond time and community. The 'collective representations' of the Durkheimian school are just such 'objects', which 'exist in the mode of significancies', but which somehow are 'valid' only for the community that orients itself by reference to them. Even as such they are 'objective' in a certain sense in relation to individual experience, since they maintain their being, after all, even when the community pertaining to them is asleep – to take an extreme example – or when, for whatever reason, no one actualizes them. But they are not objective in that other sense and not valid as if they were of eternal truth and in any sense obligatory for all times and all communities. Their obligatoriness and exemplariness are bound up with a concrete group existence and restricted to a certain period in historical time. Every kind of Platonism as a doctrine of the pre-existence of these ideal significancies, is to be avoided in this conception.

This idea of a logical pre-existence of truth still makes some sense with regard to such semantic formations as the Pythagorean theorem, which can be correct in only one way and all of whose actualizations strive to achieve this one correct form. But this structure of validity is not transferable to semantic formations (such as works of art) which are 'normative' in a completely different sense than mathematical propositions. It would be nonsense to say of a work of art that it strives to achieve the sole correctness, the only 'beauty' of art; for we know that in art unified ideals in artistic styles exist for the duration of historical periods at most, and that they retain their 'validity' only as long as a correlative artistic volition exists. Even in the area of art, then, where it is still possible to speak of conformity to norms (although the norms change in essential ways from period to period) the mathematical notion of validity cannot be applied.

While we do not accept as applicable to semantic formations in general the quality of validity, which neo-idealist philosophy, overly oriented to theory, would like to demonstrate with regard to all areas of culture, we do nevertheless accept this thesis in so far as it asserts a certain objectivity, a relative abstractability of significancies from the psychic acts which actualize them. But here too we must make several essential qualifications. There is an essential distinction, after all, between contents of a theoretical proposition and collective representations – despite the common characteristic of being abstractable from the experiential act that actualizes them. While the social and historical constellation out of which they have originated does not enter into the theoretical contents, a collective representation incorporates the situation out of which it has arisen, its functionality for a particular community, into the meaning it contains. Not everyone can read this functionality in it. But anyone who does get to understand it grasps it by conceiving of the originating situation of the collective representation together with the meaning it contains. For the same reasons, all conjunctively determined concepts and collective representations possess expressive character as well as documentary meaning[49] with respect to the individual or collective subjects that produce them, while theoretical insights of the type of mathematical truths have no expressive value.

But collective representations are not only an expression of the community in which they arise; they also refer to the things of the inner and outer world with which the community comes in touch. Conjunctive significance attaches to things; and the naive person, the individual who is uncritically absorbed in the collective representations of the community, does not notice that he sees the things of his experiential horizon only in so far as they fit into collective meanings. For him, there is not a 'bare' 'sobre' reality, materially determined in space and time alone (nature), with collective representations superimposed upon it, but rather the unbroken unity of both.

We too, as we naively go about our lives, read the moments of signification into things as determinants of being, without being able to extract such determinants from bare existence. It is like a backward projection of our current self-critical division between being and meaning when we speak of either the naive practical knowledge of the world or of such knowledge in past ages, as if this duality had also existed for them.

8 The communal subject within us

It is part of the distinctive character of the methodology and epistemology which took universally valid thinking as the point of departure for its reflections and analyses that, just as it made a one-sided concept of knowledge and of the concept in general the point of departure for its theory, it also came to a one-sided definition of the knowing subject.

One can only call it an inner systematic consistency of the methodology and epistemology here criticized when its one-sidedness is repeated in the same sense, flows from the same source, as it were, in all phases of its approach; and it will probably have to be interpreted as a sign of our own consistency that we reach precisely opposite results in all the essential phases of the problem of know-ledge, including that of presenting the knowing subject.

As we know, Kant and all of post-Kantian epistemology works with a so-called epistemological concept of the subject. We have already pointed out that Dilthey, in contrast, placed the 'whole person' in the foreground of epistemological analysis; and while we consider this concept as still requiring further precision, the pattern of contradiction between the two methodologies is sufficiently indi-cated even in this form. If the model of thought that takes as its starting point the prototype of natural-scientific knowledge arrives at an epistemological subject, and the methodology which is orien-ted primarily to historical knowledge arrives at a more concrete, abundant subject, one should not make the mistake of thinking that either of these methodologies arrives at the subjects it intro-duces through direct psychological analysis of psychic life. Instead, both subjects originate as reconstructions of cognitive results having different natures. The subject of the former methodology is the structural correlate of the universally valid cognitive results; the subject of the latter is the adequate correlate of a result of knowledge that is anthropomorphically bound in a more profound way.

Everyone must grant that the so-called epistemological subject is not to be taken as a concrete reality, which would have to be present in isolation somewhere in the world. The epistemological concept of the subject is nothing other than a constructive concept. It has meaning and value as such, and we mistake this constructive design when we try to take it as a metaphysical reality or to look for it in the positive empirical world.[50]

To make this more precise: the epistemological subject is nothing but a subject constructed to accord with a certain type of cognitive result, one that is subject to a validity beyond time, persons, or conjunctions – which is to say, the results of mathema-tics and theoretical physics. As such, it is nowhere to be found free-floating, by itself (that is, there is no person who is only an epistemological subject), it is not arrived at by distinguishing an integrated capacity of human psychic life. The key and the starting point for this construction are, rather, certain results of the sciences which reached such a level of abstraction in their theoretical struc-ture that all reference to individual or collective determinants was extinguished within their contents and which could just for this reason lay claim to validity beyond conjunctivity. Not only all refer-ence to a particular experiential configuration bound to an indi-vidual or group is extinguished in them, but also all reference to the totality of mental powers; and it is for this reason that the subject

214

that can be structurally co-ordinated with them can be poised as a supra-individual, supra-social, supra-temporal one.

Although we must here leave open the question of how far the supra-temporality and universal validity of cognitive results having this nature extend, there is no doubt that not all types of thought can be adequately comprehended on the basis of such a supra-temporal subject, and that the philosophy which constructs its subject to accord with supra-temporally valid thought structures will have the greatest difficulties if it tries belatedly to work cognitions that are in essence historical and conjunctive into its system. Here, the systematic presuppositions directed towards a specific kind of knowledge and now applied to a new, qualitatively different area must fail completely. This is why it is so important for conjunctive knowledge to dispense with the supra-temporal, supra-social subject in methodology and epistemology. We do not object at all to the fact that the usual epistemological subject is a constructive formation. We ourselves can arrive at an adequate subject – which is not a reality like the soul or the spirit but rather a logical reference point – only through construction. Nor do we charge against it that it is falsely constructed for knowledge of a universally valid character, but only that it was represented as characteristic of all forms of knowledge. Where it is a matter of historical or some other form of conjunctively bound knowledge, the adequate construction of the subject is not the ego beyond community, consciousness in general, but rather the collective communal subject within us. The collective subject in us extends precisely as far as there exist in our total consciousness knowledge-contents which are bound to community and gathered in conjunctive experiential space. To this extent we are determined by community. The range of *consciousness in general within us*, in contrast, extends as far as there are supra-communal, generally valid, abstract items of knowledge to be found in us. One can bring out the domain of purely personally-bound knowledge elements in us as a third sphere, and correspondingly speak of a personal subject. Let us emphasize here again that whether knowledge is imputable to consciousness in general, to the communal subject, or to the personal subject in us, has nothing to do with its accuracy or truth. The peculiar conflation of the problem of universal validity (for how many subjects something can be made wholly communicable and irresistibly evident) with the question of truth had the unfortunate consequence that kinds of knowledge bound to personality and community were dismissed as unscientific. To refute this, one must recall that there are even sciences which are dependent in essence on experiential communities of a conjunctive kind. Art history, for example, is a science that arose from a specific form of experiential community of 'connoisseurs' and will not be able to do without this foundation no matter how exact a level it attains. An art historian, no matter how much he refines his methods of communication and his philosophical apparatus (which is absolutely necessary) always presupposes the 'connoisseur' in himself and the 'community of connoisseurs' as his audience.

By 'connoisseur' we mean a person who can take his experiential knowledge, relating to qualitative features, specialized, and intensively concentrated upon a single field, and make it evident to a circle of individuals who are associated with him through a specific experiential community, directed towards the same subject-matter-field and bound by tradition. Making such knowledge evident may succeed through bare indications, unarticulated gestures, the merest hints, or it may proceed through extensive analysis, exact dissections, and proving step by step what has to be demonstrated; but the basis of both kinds of communication and demonstration remains a capacity for intuition, which has been specifically formed and cultivated and which is present in all members of the experiential community. One must really have learned to 'see' in a special sense, to be able to go along step by step with the evidentiary force of what is shown.

Yet the experiential knowledge of a connoisseur – even though, by definition, it can be rendered communicable only to a circle which is culturally close-knit – is nevertheless knowledge comprising genuine penetrations of the object. Are superficial observations about art to be considered truer because they can be communicated to more people precisely on account of their superficiality? And is this not exactly the case with every observation in intellectual history and, more broadly, in the humanistic sciences? In brief, when we distinguish among an 'I' sphere and a 'subject in general' sphere, a communally-founded subject sphere and a subject sphere attached to personality in us, and variously impute experiential knowledge to one or the other of these, we do not mean to establish any distinction of rank by this, in the sense of greater or lesser measures of truth in these types of knowledge.

We have spoken of various subject spheres in us, and shall now concentrate on the 'communal subject sphere within us'. We have already indicated that we do not in any way mean by this some sort of point within the ego which could be ontologically grasped, but that we are rather concerned to show that a certain sphere of experiential knowledge actualized in the course of our life does not correspond to our most intimate conjunctions with things and men – which is to say, that it does not refer to the most highly personal experiential space, which is ultimately determined by momentary factors; and, on the other hand, that this sphere also does not proceed upon the level of abstraction which is the basis for the knowledge within a conceptual system rising above community, but that certain experiential contents actualized within our consciousness gain their meaning from their reference to a certain experiential contexture of which the community is the bearer. We do not create this type of experiential knowledge out of ourselves; it enters us from the community in which we live.

What is decisive is not this genetic characteristic but rather the fact that the objective structure and the contents of these experiences are specific and connected to this experiential space. The experiential knowledge from such an experiential space is not directly transferable to another, and 'one and the same thing' means something fundamentally different for different experiential spaces, because the supposedly identical 'thing' appears worked into the fabric of different collective representations. In our sphere of communal consciousness we are always actualizing contents, and we do so in a specific mode of carrying the experience through, which has its place within a contexture of significancy that extends beyond the particular subject.

With the 'contexture of significancy' just mentioned, however, we have found a new 'object' for our investigation. We have come to the sum and system of all the collective representations and things knowable which can be realized by a given community in a given historical period. We have already tried to show that the separate collective representations have a supra-individual, more than psychological mode of existence (without having supra-temporal validity, by the same token). Now we can specify a further property of this mode of existence, which is that no collective representation is ever postulated in isolation but rather is intimately related to and structurally connected with the other collective representations postulated at the same time. Just as one concept presupposes another (for which reason the doctrine of validity hypostasized the idea of a unitary system of all timeless truths) so a specific collective representation presupposes the whole experiential space of the relevant community in a given age. Similarly, every collective representation is structurally connected with the remaining components of its experiential space. While the methodology that aims its constructions towards the timeless acknowledges only one such contexture, by reference to which every production is seen, measured, and judged (which has its reasons in the case of knowledge like that of mathematics), we find as many spheres of significancy as there are communally-attached experiential spaces to be

217

distinguished. Thus every particular item of conjunctive knowledge is attached to a specific contexture of significancies, which can be actualized only in a specific community of experience and practical knowledge. That something like a single principle asserts itself within the collective representations belonging to one and the same experiential space, whereby the components, the individual collective representations, are structurally interrelated, can already be shown by the fact, for example, that the collective representations of a magically oriented experiential community ground their experiential totality upon a certain underlying magical 'system'. Or, to cite a different domain of collective representations, 'styles' assert themselves in artistic production, and such styles must also be considered principles, even if in the special sense of principles pertaining to visual signification. We are alleging, in short, a distinctive kind of existence that rises above the individual psyche, a communally-determined totality of conjunctive experiential contextures, though it should be noted that it is an existence which has nothing to do with existence in the metaphysical sense. Although the sphere of significancies which can be set over against the individual subject and his existence coincides in its contents in many respects with what Hegel called 'spirit', we dismiss all personalizing characterizations that would have spirit approach to an independent divine existence. As far as we are concerned, there is no existing subject – or at least none that can be empirically grasped by us – present behind the sum of systems of significancies, even though these systems do flow historically into one another; and if we shall nevertheless speak of a collective subject of the experiential community, this is only a figure of speech for the sake of brevity and a constructive formation in the same sense as what we have called the 'communal subject within us'.

The contextures of significancies, the systems of coherent collective representations, exist in the mode in which significancies exist; but the subject constructed as pertaining to them (as member of a logical relation) does not exist. It is nothing but a construction.

For the sake of flexibility and brevity one can speak of the collective subject of an experiential community and its fate; but this is always meant only metaphorically. Things and the psyches of individuals exist, as do, in a special way, significancies and also contextures of significancies of the most varied kind. But subjects of knowledge – individual as well as collective subjects – are only constructions, expressions of one of the two members of the logical relation of subject and object.

218

9   Dynamic aspects of the community's life-space

Let us return to the contrast between the logical-methodological construction oriented to exact natural science and that methodology which, through analysis of historical knowledge, tries to work out an altogether different type of thought. At this point, the difference is expressed in that the natural-scientific mode of thinking knows only static thought, while the historical mode of thinking must sooner or later begin to break through to a dynamic conception of knowledge. The difference between the two conceptions asserts itself most manifestly in the ways in which they conceive of the construction of the epistemological ego. While the natural-scientific mode of thought hypostasizes a static ego, that is, a knowing ego that remains identical for all times and all epistemological communities of knowledge, the alternate theory must invoke a dynamic subject, at least for the historical type of knowledge; i.e., it must first establish the changeable character of the cognitive basis of all conjunctive knowledge and then posit, by reconstruction, the communal subject corresponding to this basis as also changing. Although both theories paid attention to development and change, they did so in different ways, with different methods of incorporating change into the total system of the theory. And it had to be integrated differently, for different fundamental conditions prevailed in the two cases. If one focuses on the structure of the historical course of mathematics and of the exact sciences, one must reach the conclusion that the progress in the process of knowledge which is to be found there has a different structure than progress in history. In mathematics it is a question of the genesis of a single contexture of validity, which does not itself actually have a history. Here, only the human struggle to elaborate this sphere of knowledge has a history. The true system, the valid contexture can only be one, and a later insight corrects and refutes earlier ones as errors, if they were erroneous. In the exact disciplines the change characteristic of the historical plays no role other than that of searching, the gradual elaboration of a portrayal of truth which is once and for all.

But this is not history in the most genuine and profound sense of the word. The contexture of truth being sought itself has no history, only its conquest has a distinctive life-story.

But the structure of conjunctive knowledge and that of communal experiential space, with all the collective representations that make it up, are of a completely different nature. In connection with our semantic construction of conjunctive experience[51] we have pointed out that in existentially attached thinking of the most simple kind, where only two subjects take part in a life community, the collective basis of knowledge is already a dynamic one, one that changes. This mobility, this dynamic moment is verifiable and demonstrable in collective knowledge of wider distribution, in the conjunctive knowledge of a sect or a cultural community, where the shift in what is known collectively and in the total system becomes most readily graspable in the shift in the meaning of concepts. This change of meaning is a phenomenon that can occur only in the sphere attached to culture, in the sphere of the conjunctively bound experiential community, and the presence of the phenomenon of change in meaning can be used as an indirect criterion in judging how far the experiential community extends and where supra-conjunctive knowledge begins. Where concepts possess an unchanging meaning, where they can be defined once and for all, we are at the level of supra-conjunctive knowledge. Where they are essentially subject to a shift in meaning, they belong to the conjunctive level. The numerical system is a uniform conceptual system, identical for all time and derivable from nothing more than the principle of its formation. The conceptual system of exact physics similarly exists unconditioned by its cultural background; and in so far as changes in it do appear historically, they must be understood as corrections internal to a single systematic approach. With concepts which are bound to a culture, to a specific experiential space, it is not at all adequate to substitute for an earlier concept one which arose later in some line of continuity. It is meaningless, for example, to say that the Greek word *polis* really means state, since the object intended by the word *polis* – the collective representation in its institutional and other forms of existence – is something completely different from what we mean today by the word 'state', which derives from the Renaissance period. There is even a profound change in significance between the Renaissance concept 'status' and our present-day 'state', corresponding to the difference between a Renaissance state and a contemporary state, although they both stand in historical continuity with what preceded them. Here, then, the change in the meaning of the concepts is anchored in the change in the collective phenomena to which they refer, and the acoustical similarity of 'status' (*Status*) and 'state' (*Staat*) conceals a change in meaning that has come about in the concepts as well as in the historical phenomena corresponding to them.[52]

We have already pointed out that in a conjunctively integrated experiential and life-community, care is taken, by means of institutions and language, to inhibit through stereotyping this constant potential for change. Particularly effective in this regard is 'magical stereotyping' (Max Weber), which works to ensure that institutions, cults, rites, and all life-relationships are wherever possible performed in the same way and are perceived by the communal subject from a stereotyped perspective.

If the constant flow of collective representations is restrained through these stereotypings, there are, correspondingly, various levels of 'velocity' of changes. Thus it is correct to speak of static and dynamic cultures, although it must be borne in mind that this distinction is only one of degree, because even the most static culture undergoes change over the course of time. Accordingly one can make a distinction between magical and religious stereotypings, arrange the various types of stereotypings hierarchically, and then ask how the various social structures (clan, status group, or class society, for example) relate to these stereotypings and what tempo of change is connected with each specific social structure. But since this problem would direct us towards a different set of questions, we will not pursue it further here.

The communally determined life-space is constantly involved in a process of becoming, then, in its entire existential basis, together with the conjunctively determined conceptual apparatus appropriate to it, including collective representations; and any stereotyping amounts to nothing more than effective retardation of this process. In the preceding analysis, as well as in our example of the *polis*, it must have become evident that until now we have indiscriminately arranged conjunctively determined concepts which serve to name objects of a certain experiential space alongside the formations to which they refer. We have been able to do this up to this point because it did not lead to error, since it was simply a matter of establishing that both have their origin in a certain life-space and secure their specific significance from it. From now on, however, it will be necessary to distinguish between these two types of object – the collective formations on the one hand and the concepts which refer to them on the other – in order to be able to discuss them separately.

We must accordingly distinguish between such an object as a *polis* and the concept of this *polis* originating in the same experiential community. Both are phenomena that originate in conjunctive experiential community. They are also similar in that they change with the totality of the community and that, although most closely tied to the state of things within the community, they possess a measure of objectivity in relation to the individual experiential actualizations of separate individuals. Despite this similarity, however, the two are not identical. The *polis* is a formation that, during a given period of its historical career, has its existence in a certain form; and that form is as such independent of the form of existence which has substance in the reflections of the individuals who participate in and live in it. We shall put this in another way. In every period of its existence, the *polis* exists twice and in both respects as objective formation.

First, it exists as a distinctive 'framework-form'[53] of coexistence within the Greek life-community. As such it consists of the entirety of relationships and collective actions regulated primarily by cult. But the *polis* is not only the entirety, the sum of the relationships; it is at the same time their contexture, their system, their totality. In relation to this articulated, meaningfully contextural totality, any particular actions, entries into relationships, are only partial actualizations of a contexture that extends beyond them. These actualizations are indispensably necessary for the existence of the framework-form itself, since its history and fate depend on change in the individual performances and actualizations, but the framework-form is nevertheless not identical with either the individual performances or the sum of all of them, for neither the single individual nor the coexisting individuals are in a position to grasp the systematic totality of the reality of the *polis*, but can only take part in its realization. The ontological reality of the *polis* as such always escapes from the subjective consciousness of the individuals who are realizing it, just as every event is normally something more rich and universal than the 'cross-section' by means of which those who take part in it conceive of the event as a whole.

A second type of objectification (and both involved independence, elevation above any particular realization within any discrete individual) pertains to the *concept* of *polis*, which arises within the same life-community in the reflections of individuals concerning this formation. This concept fixes for the community the perspectivistically determined conceptions of the formation itself, while they are held by individuals. The being of the *polis* during a period of its existence is something different from the concept which the experiential community forms of it. (Similarly, for example, the being of a specific economic form is also something different from the concept of the economy that arises in the simultaneous contemporaneous reflections of the same community.)

Both – the *polis* as a formation having being, which individuals actualize in their coexistence, and the historical 'concept' of the *polis* that has its origin in the same life-community – are of the 'spiritual mode of existence', although in different ways. While the concept of the *polis* arises in reflection on the *polis* as it somehow has its being, one exists *in* the *polis*-in-being not by forming a concept of it but by having a place *in* the spiritual relationships that comprise the existence of the *polis*. (This is not to say that the concept which a specific community constructs of its framework-form coincides with being of that form even in contents.) The 'existence-in-a-non-reflective-way' within the *polis*, which is associated with the first of our two types of objectification, is itself a spiritual phenomenon; but it is not at the level of reflection. The community thus creates spiritual contextures and forms of living together that do not have their being at the reflective level characteristic of the concept.

The following example is best calculated to make it clear that the *polis* and the prevailing economic system are not formations of nature, relationships between things and persons, which are simply *there*. It would be easy to say that what we designate as a *polis* in being is nothing but the ensemble of relations resulting from the particular relations among the individuals in a group, and that these relations are no more 'spiritual' than a planetary constellation, which expresses the concourse of the stars at a given moment; and that the form of the state at any time is similarly nothing but the contexture of individual relations, each one of which might well be 'spiritual' in itself, but the sum of which is nothing but a contexture of individual functioning relationships.

It must be said against this, however, that there can be no doubt that the framework-form which the participation of everyone makes actual has a spiritual structure possessing a supra-individual objectivity. This is the case despite the fact that no single individual designs a plan like that of some legislator for the particular framework-form (as, for example, the *polis*) and despite the fact that for the most part the individual is spiritually oriented only toward his own circle of activity and functioning and has little or no awareness of the overall plan. Just because of the objective spiritual structure, which is nevertheless in being, the framework-form must not be regarded as merely a 'constellation' or 'configuration' of the relations, but only as meaningful contexture, as meaningful formation.

Men's spiritual nature is already operative (unconsciously and involuntarily) in the structure of their coexistence, and it is for this reason that Max Adler's[54] interpretation of Marx is completely correct and fully adequate when he regards the economic sphere as a spiritual sphere and not as a material and natural one. Here too, the spirituality manifests itself (unconsciously), which is the same as that spirituality which at the reflexive level can comprehend and deliberately change itself. Even in our social and economic exist-

223

ence, then, we are not living in mere constellations and natural relations any more, but rather adjusting, accommodating the purely
natural givens of our existence to spiritual contextures of the most
various kinds.

Once it is granted that these framework-forms of communal
existence are spiritual contextures, it is nevertheless important to
present them clearly in their own objectivity, that is, in their
independence of the subjective representations which are entertained about them. Max Weber's exaggerated theoretical nominalism[55] led him to construe these formations so that they coin-
cided with the intended 'meanings' of individual experiencing
subjects.

Nominalism proceeds from the unjustifiable assumption that
only the individual subject exists and that meaningful contextures
and formations have being only to the extent that individual subjects think them or are somehow oriented toward them in a conscious manner. But this is just as much a prejudice determined by
philosophical-systematic factors as is the opposite assertion that
significancies are to be thought of as ontological realities, which is
to say, that they are to be hypostasized in the manner of the doctrine of conceptual realism. Here we are called on to have recourse
to an exact analysis of the phenomena and to modify prejudices in
accordance with the true phenomena rather than to falsify the
phenomena for the sake of the prejudices. If one proceeds from the
prejudice that there can only be individuals and that significancies,
formations and contextures of meaning exist only to the extent one
thinks of them, one must go on interpreting such phenomena as, for
example, the *polis* in being or the 'ceremony' until they have been
interpreted as a mutual orientation toward one another on the part
of single individuals, and as the probability of such orientation. It is
not to be doubted – and this we emphasize in contrast to an exaggerated conceptual realism – that *polis*, ceremony, and all other
more than subjective formations only exist in the form and to the
degree that they are actualized by individuals. Nevertheless – and
this opposes nominalism – the contexture of meaning (dynamic as
such) is something which ranges above the individual consciousnesses taking part in it and which holds them together. Therefore,
when the historian and the sociologist asks (with Ranke) 'how it
actually occurred', he is concerned with these supra-individual contextures and not with conceptions about them. What is of interest
when one is trying to comprehend the historical being of cere-
monies in an age is not what X and Y imagined about a ceremony in
the course of it, not what the contemporary theory asserted about
'ceremony', and equally not the 'idea' and the 'ideal' of a ceremony

in general, or the ceremonial ideal of a given epoch. What is of interest is the spiritual-systematic contexture ranging beyond the conceptions of the separate individuals, which resulted from the meaningful interplay of individual acts of consciousness at the time at which the ceremony took place.

When the argument presented earlier fails, nominalists try to remedy things by subjecting this totality, since somehow or other it simply is *there*, to further reinterpretation, now as a methodological construction of the observing subject (the historian or sociologist). According to this theory, we, who are directing our attention to the composition of the past course of things, originate this unity of contextures and then project it back on to historical reality, while this reality has being only by virtue of the fact and to the extent that the individuals think it. In the knowledge of nature, this would correspond to a theory that would assert that in and of itself there is nothing but things, and that relations are constructed by the observing subject. With reference to natural-scientific knowledge one could properly object that one must either take one's stand on the theoretical ground that the knowing subject himself originates all categories (and thus the categories of substance as well as those of relation), in which case it is meaningless to cite this moment of autonomous positing of categories on the part of the knowing subject exclusively in connection with relations; or one must rest on a foundation of empiricism, according to which concepts govern themselves by reality, in which case concepts of relation are just as much 'copies' of reality as are concepts of substance. The same holds in the humanistic sciences. Here as well one would have to say that the concept of contextures of meaning that connect people corresponds to reality just as much as does the concept of these people as individual beings. The concept of inter-human contextures of meaning is directed towards reality in the same way as is the concept of substance which refers to individual people.

Once the spiritual reality of such formations as ceremony and *polis* has been established in this manner, we must on the other hand prevent them from being confused with those other meanings which circulate under the names of 'the idea of the *polis*', 'the essence of the *polis*', 'the idea of the *polis* at a particular point in time', etc., and which clearly refer to something other than this formation-in-being. This is the place to distinguish the distinctive objectivity of the *polis* itself – as a supra-individual contexture of existence, as a meaningful formation, as historical reality – from the objectivity attaching to the meanings which arose by virtue of the fact that the members of some experiential community in which

225

the *polis* arose sought to gain reflective clarity about this reality within their experiential space. This concept will of necessity have only perspectivistic and conjunctive validity, but as such it will possess a distinctive objectivity ranging above the individual psyche and graspable by the other members of the community. Here too one can observe what we demonstrated in the example of the Pythagorean theorem: that when twenty individuals actualize in themselves the same perspectivistically and conjunctively determined concept of the *polis* that is meant by the theory of the state of a certain period, the meaning of this concept exists only once, while the mental process that actualizes it exists twenty times. The meaning itself thus has an objectivity that distinguishes itself from the individual's stream of consciousness. And if several theories arise in the same period, each of these *polis*-concepts will possess a distinguishable identity and objectivity in relation to the majority of individuals who share this understanding. But this objectivity must be understood in a sense different from that which is present in the Pythagorean theorem, and also in a sense different from the objectivity which characterizes existing formations.

Whereas the Pythagorean theorem is valid for all possible subjects and in its contents displays no perspectivity bound to a specific experiential community, the concept of the *polis* as it appears in the Greeks' political theory can only be adequately understood when one can penetrate into the experiential community from whose point of view the *polis* is intended to be reflectively comprehended by men who exist in it, in its character as a spiritual reality. In their concept of the *polis* its significance for them is reflected and preserved. Although it is they who identify the *polis* itself, they comprehend it only in the perspective of the significancy in being for them. This significancy is of the greatest importance for us. Since the unconscious creation of spiritual formations springs from the same communal forces as their historical concept, it is quite certain that the connection between concept and object in existence gives concepts of this kind a quite special significance. Nevertheless, there are two objectifications before us, both of a spiritual kind: the *polis* is a spiritual reality created by the unconscious spiritual forces of community life. The concept of the *polis*, in contrast, is a perspectivistically and conjunctively determined reflective item of knowledge about the spiritual reality created by that same community.

It should be noted that there are extremely interesting existential relationships between the spiritual realities of an age and the reflective, conjunctive knowledge concerning them. Both take shape in and radiate from the same experiential and life-space; but while first effectuation and constantly repeated actualization of the spiritual realities takes place, as it were, behind the reflective consciousness of the particular individual, the individual himself is consciously aiming at knowledge of these formations-in-being: he thinks them and recognizes them. Yet in this knowledge he does not draw on himself or on a pool of timeless, supra-conjunctive concepts and knowledge, but rather on the conjunctively determined accumulation of experiential knowledge of the community in question, to which he belongs. The extent to which and the direction in which the objective formation, the spiritual reality of the *polis* can be known at all, is determined by the conceptual apparatus and the points of view within which knowledge of this sort has hitherto proceeded. The spirit of the community creates and forms its spiritual realities at a completely different level, so to speak, than that on which they can enter into its own reflections. While the spiritual reality is something global, and, like every reality, contains an unending plenitude within itself, knowledge of it is always only cross-sectional, perspectivistic, bound to a point of view and angle of vision. One must, therefore, look at the spiritual reality as one would look at a body in space, from various sides and standpoints. With regard to spiritual phenomena (where it is after all not a question of spatial multi-dimensionality encirclement of reality), this emergence of new standpoints takes place within the historical process itself. The new angles of vision, the new standpoints, with their resulting perspectives, come into being inasmuch as the basis of life shifts. A particular period in the history of Greek life or of its *polis* became visible to the Greeks in the course of their history in ever new aspects. It gained ever new significance in every present, as something past. These new significancies, however, did not grow out of an immanent theoretical interest but rather out of the existential needs of the community as it continued its life. (This implies that all historical knowledge is tied to the historical and social process out of which it arises – something which is even more true of sociological knowledge.)

All conjunctive knowledge of a historical space is not only tied in its origins to the social experiential space and to the spiritual realities which fill it, but it is also taken back into further life and changes the actualization and thereby the spiritual state of these realities. The notion of the *polis* or of 'ceremony' entertained by citizens concerning these formations does not constitute the *polis* or the ceremony as a spiritual reality, since the one does not, after all, coincide with the other, but the actualization of these spiritual realities does nevertheless proceed differently when the conceptions referring to them have changed. Although neither the *polis* nor the

227

ceremony change to fit the conceptions individuals have of them, both are nevertheless altered by the change in those conceptions. As a result, there arises a connection resembling interaction between reflection and new creation, between the further development of the spiritual realities and thinking them over. The prospects for reflective penetration of the experiential space filled by spiritual realities and the perspectives possible at a given level of reflection both depend on the state of previously accomplished reflections on this matter; but this in turn is dependent on the state of the overall spiritual reality – and every new illumination growing out of this reality again changes the spiritual realities.

We are thus dealing with the closely interconnected dynamics of spiritual realities and the dynamics of the conceptual level as the cognitive basis of the conjunctive comprehensibility of these realities – in short, with knowledge of a dynamic object achieved upon a dynamic basis of knowledge, where the movement of the one factor is connected with the movement of the other and both together constitute the total spiritual movement. This, by the way, is the justification of two of Hegel's theses concerning the identity of subject and object, knowledge and the dynamic conception of knowing. It follows, however, that in the nature of the case, no single concept can be adequate to a spiritual reality (as, for example, the *polis*), since every spiritual reality, in the course of history, changes its spiritual being. It would have to be covered by a different single correct concept for each age, but such a correct absolute concept for one of its morphological states could not be comprehended absolutely either, could itself only be seen and formulated perspectivistically.

We must now consider the distinctive dynamic of the spiritual realities apart from the movement of the conjunctive knowledge referring to them and then determine their connection.

10   The dynamics of spiritual realities

The reader will have noticed that in our presentation we have continually refined our most important concepts and that we have attempted further to differentiate and illustrate them through new examples. If we spoke at first of a unitary complex of collective representations conditioned by community, we later divided them into two different groups: that of the 'spiritual realities' themselves and that of conjunctively valid concept their arising in the same experiential community. If we now turn our attention to the first group alone and try to characterize it still more precisely, this graded refinement and illustration deliberately proceeds by gradual progression, because it is our view that the communicability of these things is itself dynamic, although in a sense different from the motility we have been discussing. This is not a case where the clarity and unambiguousness of the concepts employed can be fixed by a work of definition guaranteed from the beginning by a static system, but rather one where we have to do with a graduated penetration into an object whose concrete fullness is to unfold progressively and about which observations are to be made which are to acquire increasing depth. A similar process runs through the course of intellectual history. The process of imparting knowledge is more organic when one does not begin right at the end and premise the definitions, which can be end results at best. Communication is itself a dynamism, but one whose nature we cannot pursue further here.

Before we can attempt a more precise characterization of spiritual realities and their dynamic, we must first take a closer look at the scope and breadth to which they fill out the experiential space, and we may have to distinguish various types of spiritual reality. Our illustration of spiritual realities has proceeded from things that are inter-personally determined. Cult, *polis*, etc. are all collective representations, for which Durkheim in *The Rules of Sociological Method* has already coined the concept *institutions*. One might assume in consequence that the sphere of spiritual realities consists of nothing but these collective activities, borne by a plurality of persons and regulated by prescriptions of operation. We began with them because their objectivity, ranging above the individual consciousness, could be demonstrated through their mode of existence, which is dependent on a plurality of persons. But formations and representations which do not have their being in the reflective mode of concepts belong to the same kind of reality, even if they are not based upon a multiplicity of persons. Let us first consider a spiritual reality which is rooted in only two persons, which simultaneously represents an existential and a spiritual relationship, but which does not coincide as such with the concepts formed of it: an erotic relationship between two individuals belonging to the same group. However much the sexual relationship of two individuals may be a natural datum and as such not a contexture of meaning in itself, and however much it may remain the same in its purely physical aspect (*Naturhaftigkeit*) at all levels of cultural existence, the meaning ascribed to this physical relationship in different communities of the historical universe is always a different one. In what follows, then, we have in mind the spiritual but not theoretical ascriptions of meaning in terms of which the lovers live: not the poetic conceptions of love – which are already reflective impressions of the spontaneous ascriptions of meaning in terms of which two individuals live in so far as they love one another – but the unreflective form of loving one another or erotic relatedness which is spiritual and meaningful, notwithstanding the absence of adequate conceptual formulation.

The spiritual reality of the love relationship, with which we are here concerned and which we want to delineate, must be marked off in two directions. It must be distinguished from the purely physically determined sexual relationship, which is, in the last analysis, more or less the same in all human communities, and from the reflective theoretical formulations arrived at by a 'theory of love' or by the participants in love when they reflect on it. Clearly there is a third alternative between these two poles, one which is not equivalent to the merely physical relatedness of the subjects and which also does not secure its primary form from a reflective act of concept formation, but which is rather to be sought in the spontaneous spiritualization of the physical relationship, which is actualized in existential acts (in feelings, transactions, and intentions). This third alternative is different in every cultural community and historically changing in each one. We know that 'love' means different things in different societies, that 'romantic love', for instance, is only one of the possible erotic relationships, and that this relationship, like all other spiritual love relationships, contains a measure of stereotyping for certain cultural circles, which are socially and historically determined. In their most spontaneous turns toward the other, the lovers unconsciously and involuntarily actualize one of the types of meaning that is possible in a particular life-space, and even the wholly personal expression of the relationship having the most individual coloration still gains its distinctiveness in relation to this basis, and is thus determined by it in this event as well. When we undertake to address 'love' as a spiritual reality like *polis* and 'ceremony', we have in view this pretheoretical, pre-reflective ascription of meaning, which always incorporates and works in the ever identical physical relationship, but always gives it meaningful form in a different way. Like the institutions, love may be said to transform itself behind the backs of individuals, who merely actualize it.

If one attends to the fundamental theme brought out in this example, it becomes evident that a spiritual community in time takes all the facts of nature (trees, springs, mountains, rivers) as well as the phenomena of psychic life (feelings, love, longing, fear, etc.) and physical relationships and states (birth, death, sexual relationship, search for sustenance, etc.) and overlays them with specifically spiritual and cultural meanings (which are present prior

230

to theoretical reflection), and that the theoretical reflection of every experiential community, when it attempts to grasp the nature of things in concepts, comes upon a nature which is already cloaked in meaning and shaped by spirit, and not upon pristine nature. The conjunctive community, its spirit, is to be found within these objectifications in its full development, and it spreads itself over all things, living not only in the souls of subjects but also in the space environing them. And when this spirit tries to grasp the spirit of its environment and inner world, what it finds is always itself.

We have already distinguished two types of such spiritual realities: first, those which with Durkheim we called 'institutions'; second, those ascriptions of meaning which reworked the natural environment and inner world into meaningful formations. Now we want to note a third kind of pre-theoretical collective meaning formation, which we shall simply call 'works' (*Werke*). It is clearly not the case that experiential space is wholly occupied by inner and outer nature become meaningful, alongside of social relationships and framework-forms regulated by prescription. There are also other spiritual realities which are formations of meaning in a distinctive way, although, like the meaning contents already cited, they help to build up the experiential and life-space of society. Probably no extensive analysis is needed to show what we mean by 'works' in this context: all the artifacts that the single individual creates, to all appearances simply out of himself, in isolation, which he introduces as new things into the world of nature in that he originates a meaning consciously, though that consciousness need not be theoretical. The significancies previously discussed were only superimposed upon 'inner' and 'outer' nature. They did not transform the natural thing that underlay them, but merely took it up into their meaning-contents. Sacred images, idols, utensils, clothing, dwellings, buildings, and so on are all characterized by the fact that the natural is used as means, as medium for realizing a contexture of meaning envisioned beforehand. While the 'inner' and 'outer' world becomes meaningful, is pre-given to the single individual because he grows into it and usually apprehends significancy as determination, attribute of nature itself (for it came into being 'behind his back'), the significancy 'work' comes into being before his eyes and at his hands; and the one who has not made or created it but merely views it, also associates with it the idea of its having been formed, the idea of its having the quality of a work. (This does not apply equally at all levels of culture. For a primitive, a work, a sacred image, has ontological character despite its character as work: it is the divinity itself.) Although this work has an individual creator, it is not the work and expression of

231

him alone; in all that concerns technique, stylistic intention, etc., the collective ego of the community is at work. Everything stored up in earlier works asserts itself in any new creations and moves the execution of the individual work in the direction of the collective process.

Spiritual realities (nature interwoven with meanings, institutions, works) are distinguished from one another only by incremental steps and degrees, and our presentation would not be complete if we neglected to interpolate between the works of individuals and the category of institutions those institutions without prescription, those collective works created by a plurality of persons, which are not correctly characterized as either works or institutions. We have in mind such formations as language, custom and other unregulated but self-regulating social relations, which are all totalities of meaning, all in a state of becoming, which arise spontaneously but can nevertheless not be identified with 'works' nor equated to a nature with significancies superimposed on it.

We cannot conduct in this place a thorough analysis of all the distinctions among the types of spiritual reality which have been noted. But we had to give some account of them in order to point out with some breadth how sociological space is completely occupied by the collective creations of life-community. There is no corner in which the spirit of the conjunctive life-community is not embodied. All of these things taken together comprise the world of meaning and of significancies. From this one can see that we are using the concept of a meaning in a very broad sense, very different from the theoretical concept (which refers, e.g., to the Pythagorean theorem). Neither artistic creations nor religious formations are theoretical formations of meaning. Nor are the meaningful relationships of feeling, such as the various forms of love, asceticism, or commitment, theoretical contextures of meaning (even though they may to some extent employ conceptual expression). They are nevertheless meanings, first because they possess that certain ontological abstractability from any individual subjective-psychic occurrence (even though they have their origins in such occurrences and must always be actualized by them, and are therefore most intimately bound up with them), and second, because they can therefore be attended to as realities in their own right. But they are not nature. They sometimes refer to natural things and incorporate things determined by nature into the stock of spiritual things. That these meanings are nevertheless not identical with the determinations of nature is proved by the circumstance that mankind, while always surrounded by the same three-dimensional reality governed by natural laws, and determined by the same naturally-determined psychological processes, has always created within the contexture of its life a different outer and inner world for itself out of these natural givens, and has thus always constructed an ever-different life-space for itself inside of the space determined by nature.

The argument that this spiritual reality, in any of the four types cited earlier, has a mode of being different from thing-like being as well as from the psychological course of things in individuals can be further strengthened by calling attention to a characteristic peculiar to this mode of being: its distinctive structure. We had already pointed out that the spiritual formations in being for a community in any period of time are not present piecemeal and independent of one another, but only as parts of a spiritual totality that is dynamic as a whole. All the spiritual entities, elements, occurring in the life-space of a given epoch undergo change in time, but each one in conjunction with the remaining elements of that life-space, not by itself. Change in one field is co-determined by change in the others. A common spirit, a common tendency, is at work in the direction taken by change at any particular time. Sensitive and precise historical analyses in art history, but also in linguistic, literary, religious, economic and social history have shown us that the general process of development within the individual fields within a common life- and culture-space, though actualized by different individuals, moves in a common direction. In art history Riegl coined the useful term 'artistic volition' (*Kunstwollen*). Artistic volition refers to the tendency operating unconsciously in the creative artist which impels him to move in the direction of the dominant style even in his most spontaneous expressions and productions.[56] Such a communally-conditioned will resides in each field of culture and determines its attributions of meaning, its productions, and its language. For this reason one could also speak of an 'economic volition', a 'social volition', and ultimately introduce the concept of a 'will to a world'. By this term we would understand not only the direction of the specific spirituality manifesting itself in works but also the deepest unity of style belonging to the consciousness of the community in all of its objectifications, conscious or unconscious.

That every individual production within a spiritual totality moves in a direction prescribed by its age, however individualistic the age may be, results not only from the fact that a similar kind of world volition has entered into every individual consciousness in a community, but also from the objective structure of the formations. In every style, in every artistic creative form there clearly lies (aside from the aspect of the creative design relating to the creator as subject) a principle (but not a theoretical one) that can be creati-

233

vely carried through to its conclusion (as an idea is thought through to its conclusion). The fact that the Baroque developed out of the Renaissance is due partly to the fact that baroque tendencies were already embedded in the artistic forms of the Renaissance, tendencies which had merely to be isolated and pursued further. An early baroque painting or building already contains the tendencies whose logical conclusion can well be considered to constitute late baroque. These objective tendencies embedded in individual formations also demonstrate that the latter have a distinctive existence of their own, even if it is not wholly independent of the existence of the community that stands behind them. Several different objective tendencies reside, in potential, within every formation, and each of them could in principle be carried to its logical conclusion if its distinctive direction were pursued. Which of these tendencies is taken up by the overall volition (*Gesamtwollen*) can only be explained by reference to the existence of the living community and not by reference to the structure of the formations alone. Nothing can better demonstrate that it is a matter of volition which of these tendencies residing within a formation is taken up and brought to fruition than the fact that the repertory of forms which originated in antiquity and blended itself with the artistic forms and volitions of the Christianized peoples of the great migration could still belatedly unfold, as classical element, several of its potential directions. On the basis of these classical elements contained in our repertory of forms, we have managed repeatedly to gain a new understanding of antiquity, and to take out and carry to creative conclusions distinct tendencies from among its objective possibilities, in the art of the Renaissance, as in classicism. Individual formations as well as the complex of such formations comprehensible as stylistic unity have an objective structure, which frees them, to some extent, from dependence on life, in its fluctuations.

Each individual carries on his life, of course, brings about some change in the general process, if only through the temporary creation of a new word, and thereby furthers the dynamics of the whole; but this ongoing existence does not take place in a vacuum devoid of tradition, but rather rests upon the given state of the life-community, which manifests itself in tendencies of will and structures of objects. Upbringing, teaching and daily life draws the individual into this life-space pervaded by volitional tendencies and stylistic orientations. Although the creative genius may soar up to a sphere above society, this sphere is supra-social only in a relative sense, for it arises out of the accumulation of accomplishments established by tradition. The genius merely advances the growth of

seeds already embedded in the spiritual subsoil, and every innovation, however creative, is always drawn back into the general
process.

When we now say that every life-community has a different
world, we mean that the totality of spiritual realities of all four
types is different in different communal life-spaces. The community is thus not only (as may have appeared in the first stage of
our presentation) a totality bound together by common life-
actions; it is also bound together by those spiritual formations that
arise in it and contain the precipitate of its collective life. At the
same time, however, this precipitate is something objective that
can be considered in itself, something which, like an object, can be
distinguished from its substratum, something which contains within
itself in the form of tendencies and directions the independent
germs of its potential for further development.

But every society survives by taking up new generations, in their
designs; and the new generations become the bearers of what is fact
and the shapers of what is to come, by virtue of their incorporation
of new designs into the life-space of the community. This means
that there is a steady, continuous process of revolutionizing the
whole spiritual structure, so that two experiential spaces widely
removed from one another in time already represent two different
worlds throughout. And yet two depictions of the world emanating
from the same community will be in very close contact with one
another, provided that they have arisen within the same tradition
(i.e., when there is also an existential continuity of generations
behind them). The significance of this for interpretative understanding we shall be able to appreciate only later. The world-views
are closely bound to one another, not only because this bond is
guaranteed by the continuity of the existential designs of the community and its merely gradual transformation but also because
what is later is connected with what is earlier by the objective side
of the matter: that the later versions of spiritual formations have
come out of seeds and tendencies present at the beginning. For this
reason it is possible for cultural communities to encompass a wider
range than life-communities. A life-community extends only as far
as there is immediate existential contact. A cultural community
also joins into a whole those individuals and groups who are only
united in the designs and tendencies of objectifications. Wherever
there is cultural community, there must also have been, some time
and somewhere, immediate existential contact. It is accordingly
not necessary that those who are members of one cultural community must also live simultaneously in existential community
together, but there must have been mutual existential contact at

235

some time. Where a unity can be uncovered in the later cultural heritage of scattered communities, there must have been an existential fusion in history. It may be that the dispersed members of the community, having once more gone their separate ways after such existential contact, are variously living to a conclusion a different tendency among the possibilities and seeds they have taken up. They take these tendencies, individually, to distinctive conclusions, along the lines of their particular designs upon the world, but still continue to form a whole at this stage, because it is the same seeds that they have developed, if also differently. This circumstance implies a connection for a long time to come, even if partial or total isolation should ensue. The European-American cultural community is such a cultural community, but only to the extent that it is living off common objective and subjective (intentional) traditions. Within this entity, it constitutes nations, landscapes and spiritual dialects which are nothing but further developments of common seminal possibilities caught up in different specific existential life-communities.

It follows that we have several kinds of community, with cultural community as the most encompassing, and with family and friendship as the narrowest. The narrower communities subsist within the wider ones, and they are characterized by the fact that their distinctive 'wills' and 'objectifications' are sustained by those of the wider community, and, even in so far as they are different, refer themselves to this common store. They render themselves distinct from the common basis by contrast with it.

Reviewing the ways in which the presence of these diverse spheres is reflected in a cross-section of contents of an individual's consciousness and in his designs, it becomes clear that he belongs to different communities with regard to different contents and subdivisions.[57] In his total existence, then, the individual participates in various levels and spheres of communities; and only historical analysis, which must also be sociologically discriminating, can tell us where to refer an individual with regard to any given matter. In his consciousness the individual also accommodates contents belonging to some historically earlier system, as well as contents and existential orientations which may be present nowhere else, having originated in him as innovations, and which must be ascribed to one personality alone, being subject to socialization only later. Through self-exploration the individual may indeed discover 'experience' areas of psychic space never as yet experienced by others, but the direction (and even the opportunity for taking this new direction) is provided by the general state of consciousness, the general structure, the stage of the world in general which he shares with the other members of his community. His contributions to forward movement and continuing achievement arise out of the movement of the whole and return to it. While the ongoing creation is achievable only within the different individual consciousnesses and becomes dynamic only in these individual existences, these are in their turn altogether bound to the whole of the life and designs of the community, which ranges far above them.

11   The dynamics of conjunctive knowledge

If we are to understand conjunctive knowledge aright, we must also firmly connect it to these general dynamics of communally-attached spiritual processes, where no part moves independent of the others and where a whole world changes with the fate of the community to which it belongs; we must situate it within this totality of life and experiential space determined by community.

When conjunctive knowledge pursues knowledge of the world, it always grasps these spiritual realities: not somehow the world 'in itself', as it might be, but rather the world as it actually is at some specific stage in the destiny and developmental process of the community. Conjunctive knowledge thus everywhere comes upon nothing but spiritual realities. It takes in institutions, works, and collective creations – in short, nothing but formations of meaning, although of the most varied kinds. It always takes in things spiritual filled with the same spirit. It takes in the meaning-filled experiential and life-space from a specific perspective, and every cognitive penetration into social events succeeds only in so far as allowed by the general state of the social process, and only to the extent to which it appears necessary as a 'next step' in the continued existence of society. For the knowledge and self-knowledge of the social community is also a part of the general dynamic, and society must know its formations to a certain specific degree, so that its self-development will take effect in the direction of the next step.

The questions, points of view, and conceptual apparatus with which one deals with the totality of the collective experiential space depend completely on the state of development and direction in which earlier approaches and concepts have moved. The next step, however revolutionary it may be, is possible only from the platform of what is already known.

Thus if one wants to understand the emergence of a theoretical line of inquiry or a new point of view in the social sciences or in historical study, one must keep two things in mind: first, the stage that reflective knowledge has reached in the historical community in question prior to the emergence of this line of inquiry, and second,

237

the overall state of the historical-social process for which the new knowledge is to be existential, that is, for which it is destined to be a factor in the making of history. For historical space is not like a landscape, where one can walk around and describe things one after another, just as they happen to be put next to each other: here is a mountain, there is a river, it is green here, it is gray there. What there is about the social and cultural process of the present and the past that becomes visible at all, and the sequence and perspectives in which it is to be seen, depend on the extent to which this knowledge is necessary to the continued existence and work achievement of the knowing community, the extent to which it has an integral function in the process as a whole and gains meaning for the process on this basis.

In exact natural-scientific knowledge, once it has made its appearance, one can notice that lines of inquiry are largely immanent, because one problem generates the other out of itself with theoretical necessity. But in the social sciences and the humanities there are only short stretches of immanent theoretical necessity, and the framework, the general state of the problem can be shown to grow out of the social process, most often out of social conflict.

From this there arises a powerful set of tasks and an important problem area for the sociology of cognition and of social cognition in particular, because this discipline is concerned to reconnect all knowledge of society and of cultural history with its anchoring point in the social process in which it originated; to understand the particular perspective of a line of inquiry by reference to the general process for whose sake this thinking has proceeded, and to establish the relationship between the partial movement directly served by a certain idea and the general movement. Only by beginning with this complex of questions is it possible to explain why sociology arose as late as it did (not until the eighteenth century, in fact) and why this line of inquiry, having begun so late, underwent a transformation whose points of view and conceptual apparatus can only be understood on the basis of the totality of the general movement.

Not only the origins of sociology, however, but also the particular perspectivity inherent in every historical and sociological line of inquiry can be understood in its particularity only by reference to the direction and meaning of the general movement. We have already seen that perspectivity is an essential feature of all conjunctive knowledge in general, but the reason why one perspective is appropriate to one experiential space and a different one to another (whereby the distinctiveness of the perspectives finds expression in the axioms of concept-formation in each case) can only be explained by reference to the determination of the function of those cognitions for the general movement.

And here we must bring up an unusual and important circumstance that we have already encountered in the course of our study. Every spiritual reality, despite the fact that it has arisen in and for a specific historical space for the sake of a historical life-community, is something global and total compared to the particular perspectivity, the particular reflective cognition – even when the latter comes into being in the same life-space, in the same community, and at the same time as the formations to be known. That is to say, that the spiritual reality of the *polis* in a certain period, for example, was not necessarily understood best and most adequately by the theory of its time. It is quite possible that a subsequent state of theory, with its distinctive line of inquiry, sides, and aspects, could have a more profound understanding of the *polis* of that epoch than the theory which originated at the same time as the *polis*. This circumstance, this discrepancy between formations and their being understood can also be explained by considering that reflective theoretical cognition occurs, in the individual too, at a completely different level of consciousness than naive-spiritual attunement to meaning-contents. To live in the *polis*, to act spiritually within it, and in this sense to actualize it, is also a spiritual mode of conduct (and thus no mere vegetative life), but this spiritual existence in the *polis* has nothing to do with reflective knowledge of it. Grounding one's life upon the spirit of the *polis* is different from gaining cognition of this spirit. One of the most important questions in the sociology of thought concerns the stage of spiritual existence of a spiritual formation at which reflection upon it becomes necessary out of its very spirit, whether this signals the dissolution (as Hegel thought) or the perfection of its spiritual development.

That non-theoretical spiritual creation aims at spiritual matters, and that the spiritual formations, if they are to be known, represent a cognitive goal that extends beyond that particular historical space and remains for all ages, a goal having an objectivity beyond time, can already be observed in the spiritual conduct and reflective activity of the single individual. An artistic creation or a philosophical system has a distinctive objectivity that confronts even the creative subject who created it as an independent autonomous entity. One would think that the creative subject would be the one most likely to understand his work, and yet once the work has been created it represents an interpretative task even for its creator. He, of course, knows best what he intended in his work (it is in this sense that we want to define the intended meaning of a spiritual formation), but

239

he is not necessarily the one most competent to judge when it comes to the interpretation of his work as an objective formation existing in itself. He can make it his own task to understand the work, once set forth, by reference to the tendencies that lie deepest within it. In the course of his life he may leave the work behind him or he may understand it ever more deeply and only later grasp – as if marvelling at his own greatness – the meaning of what he has himself created. Only in this connection do such phrases as 'understanding Kant better than he understood himself' or 'to understand Kant means to go beyond him' have a meaning.

The seemingly incredible fact that someone can create something that not even he can wholly understand can be explained in light of our recent reflections by recalling that a work always takes up out of the historical community and retains numerous moments, motifs and elements, as well as, most importantly, deep inclinations towards purposes deemed proper to works. These motifs adhere to the community's collective project, and they are absorbed by the creative subject at the level of that pre-reflective spiritual perspectivity of which we have been speaking, and then utilized by him as material for his work. In this state of things it can easily happen that the creator, while taking up some motif of the community in his work, has grasped it only one-sidedly, and that this motif comes to full effect in the plenitude of its inherent possibilities only in the course of intellectual history, according to the capacity of later tendencies and surroundings to capture a different side of it. One can adduce as an example here the Hegelian element in Marx. Whether Marx was aware of the full scope of Hegel's dialectical idea when he incorporated it into his system, or whether it was only coquetry and frivolity that led him to adorn his text with Hegelian phrases, is a secondary question when it comes to understanding the objective meaning of the Marxian system. Although it can be an important and pertinent task to establish Marx's 'intended meaning', this is not something to be given primary consideration in our line of inquiry. What interests us about this is that the dialectical moment, which entered into Marx's work from a particular current of the spirit of his age (*Zeitgeist*), could become important once more for a later age, because this later age, on the basis of its new constellations of ideas and problems, is in a position to discover in the dialectic an important methodological form of cognition, something which may not have been even visible in this way at an earlier time.

Many fruitful objective germs for further development lie similarly buried in works and spiritual formations of the most varied kinds, and only a theory that grasps and establishes the process of appropriating and understanding spiritual formations which proceeds at two levels of consciousness, as well as the independent objectivity of these formations in relation to any conceivable interpretation, can do justice to these distinctive findings.

Every formation, then, possesses an intended and an objective meaning, whose comprehension can equally become the objective for an interpretation. But this objectivity of meaningful formations has nothing to do with timelessness. What the *polis* actually is at a given moment in time has nothing to do with the idea of what a *polis* as such having timeless validity (comparable to the example of finding how the timeless Pythagorean theorem must go) could be. This line of inquiry is a meaningless importation from the theoretical sphere, which is completely different from this conjunctive sphere in which the only spiritual realities are those attached to specific experiential spaces.

To return to our central point and to summarize what has been said: spiritual formations of the most varied kinds fill the experiential space of the community and are objectivities in relation to subjects, who can take these formations in two ways on two different levels: first, in pre-reflexive spiritual intentionality by actualizing them (one also calls this 'living in the formations'); second, by being attuned to them in theory and reflection. One can be attuned to spiritual formations only perspectivistically. If it is attempted to see them schematically, objectively, they disappear as spiritual formations from the eye of the beholder, just as a landscape disappears if it is attempted to view it as on a map, construed without perspective. For this reason all substantive, qualitative cognition of meaning always moves essentially within a conjunctively determined, collective experiential context. If it decides to rise above the conjunctive and to elevate itself to the level of abstraction where one works with pre-defined, systematically timeless concepts, it can still reveal a good deal about social life in general, but it renounces the comprehension of the concrete richness of spiritual contents, the view of historical life 'from the inside', and thus the truly interpretative aspect of historical-social knowledge.

Every conjunctive cognition is the carrier of some tendency towards a certain project in thinking and knowing, whose objective precipitate is to be found in the conceptual level it employs. Any given epoch in the life of a cultural community is shot through with several competing 'cosmic projects', each of which has some intellectual project corresponding to it. In certain ages, the capacity for expansion of such projects is so great and so significant that, as we have seen, they subordinate all conceivable objects to themselves and at least make the effort to transform and penetrate the entire

241

life-space in their own spirit. Such an intellectual project relates anything new to this life-space and comprehends it on this basis. Just as an African native incorporates the objects of civilization into his own experiential space and endeavours somehow to give them magical meaning, so do we, upon seeing and touching new things, annex them to our life-space and read spiritual features into every individual form.

One of the most important inclusions of heterogeneous data into one's own life- and learning-space is the reception of historical memorials into our experiential space. In so far as historical knowledge is interpretation, it is the orderly incorporation of spiritual realities of heterogeneous origin into our historical life- and learning-space. To understand the true scope of this assertion, we must reiterate what we previously said in passing about interpretation and now make this problem of interpretation the focus of our inquiry.

12 The problem of interpretation

We discussed the particular mode of being of spiritual formations in some detail since this is of fundamental significance for a theory of interpretation.

Interpretative understanding has two meanings. The first is a *contagion-like relation* to an alien *psyche* (as in the ideal-typical case of someone entering a room and our 'getting' him, through instinctive psychic contagion, without his having spoken a single word).[58] The second is a penetration *into a life contexture* by virtue of the fact that we gradually work up to an empathic involvement (*Teilnahme*) within a conjunctive experiential space, with its specific collective representations. Whereas the first form of interpretative understanding is made possible only by our capacity for entering into *psychic* contagion, the second is made possible by our spiritual capacity for comprehending meaningful formations of the most diverse kinds. Even when we presuppose an experiential community to which we existentially belong and in whose experiential contextures we take part for sizeable stretches, it still requires a special capacity to be able to grasp in their significance the formations issued forth from the experiential contexture and, conversely, to find a way into the pertinent experiential contexture with the formation as starting point. This is precisely why we had to distinguish carefully between the two types of formation and to show that significancies are not congruent with experiential configurations. While the former arise from the latter and return to them, they nevertheless have their own special contents and their own special mode of existence. They are not merely symbols of something else, but contents which have attained independent standing. That is why the capacity to respond experientially and psychically and to make contact does not suffice for understanding. Although the capacity for grasping spiritual realities belonging to an experiential space or subject is built upon the capacity for direct contagion, it is, in relation to that one, a different, new capacity within us. Accordingly, we distinguish the *understanding of existence* (existential, psychic contagion) from the *understanding of significancies* (semantic comprehension, spiritual understanding). In real life, the one blends into the other. At one moment we rely on instinctive, existential contagion to enter into the Other, and at the next, we proceed by way of his spiritual objectifications (cf. Spranger). On the other hand, in understanding the spiritual realities belonging to a particular experiential space (*Erfahrungsraum*) we can grasp the particular, existentially bound, perspectivistic meanings only if we somehow can make our own the space and contexture (*Erlebnisraum und-zusammenhang*) underlying them.[59]

Although it is possible to call the grasping of a trans-conjunctive, general propositional contexture (such as the Pythagorean theorem) 'understanding', we deliberately and emphatically prefer to segregate this type of semantic comprehension from the two forms of understanding just described and to call it 'apprehension' (*Ergreifen*). In accordance with our distinction between conjunctive and universally valid semantic formations, we should like to reserve 'understanding' for penetrating into a conjunctive experiential space. The differentiation between universally valid exact natural science and history also corresponds to this difference. The specific 'art' of the historian – interpretation – is applicable only to formations bound to a conjunctive existential space and is altogether different from analysing and explicating an unambiguous, objective set of propositions, such as a mathematical proof.

In sum, then, interpretative understanding means penetration into an experiential space, bound to a community, into its formations of meaning and their existential bases.

We should like to distinguish further between both understanding and interpretation in a stricter sense. Following our distinction between the pre-reflective grasp of phenomena and their theoretically reflective, conceptual comprehension, we shall take mere understanding to mean either the existential, contagion-like grasping of the externally existent or the spiritual, pre-reflective grasping of formations, and we shall take interpretation to mean the theoretically reflective explication of what is understood, always resting on

243

what it has formed, the existential bases of an experiential space as well as its spiritual realities; but we have already indicated how certain it is that this reflective comprehension, conditioned as it is by the state of 'theory' at the time and by the state of the historical-social organisms in general, will always turn out to be essentially perspectivistic and never wholly adequate.

Limiting ourselves to the simple understanding and interpretation of spiritual formations, the perspectivism just noted holds not only for reflective comprehension in interpretation but also for the existential relatedness of the subject to formations belonging to foreign subjects and worlds which may stand in a relation of predecessor (*Vorwelt*) to him within a historical tradition. The subject only apprehends as much in foreign formations and in foreign existences as is encompassed within the tendency of his own line of sight. Here, too, we can clearly see the completely dynamic quality of all cultural, spiritual-psychic understanding, as well as the primacy of the non-contemplative, active aspect within understanding. The individual or the community should never be conceived as though surrounded by a fixed and finished rigid world of spiritual realities to which they attune themselves contemplatively. It is rather the case that grasping anything as 'factual' is carried out within the tensions of a will to the world. Once it has incorporated or generated a volitional direction and expectancy, the entire community attempts to perfect and to realize this will in every spiritual act. An artistic volition is intent upon permeating the whole of an individual reality. A style does not only realize its intentions in works, pictures and statues, but also enters into the formation of the most trivial objects, into the design of clothing and furniture, and in the rhythm of life expresses itself in gestures. A religion seeks to put into effect a system penetrating the world, from the reformation of the soul to the shaping of institutions. And cultures are bound to be slowed down in their dynamics, and do indeed slow themselves down; explicating themselves and permeating the world and experiential space is an existential necessity for them because a will to the world (*Weltwollen*) becomes conscious of itself only in the course of its explication. It is only in this way that a dynamic destiny takes shape. A new will, then, grows imperceptibly out of the expansive capacity of every will to the world, in direct continuity with it, and this alone can accommodate the earlier stream of development, but only in order to lead all this forward in the direction of its own new dynamism. This is where the Hegelian concept of 'overturning' (*Umschlagen*) applies.

It becomes evident from the phenomena just described that every member of a cultural sphere and every subject within it constantly exists in a state of spiritual tension, and that this is no less the case for static cultures. Every spiritual formation is apprehended, not in static contemplation but from within a certain tensioning. This tension takes the form of a hovering, anticipatory vision of a world that is sought, and it takes its departure from a world vision in a state which either has already been or is about to be left behind. In so far as it persists in formations, memorials, etc., the past is apprehended in the experiential space being newly fashioned from within this tension; and the past is considered part of one's own experiential space, and one sets the past in motion, in that one projects into it the direction of movement in which one lives. In this way, the past ceases to be something different from us, a sequence of experiential spaces cellularly shut off from one another; it turns into a becoming that leads on right to our own becoming, our own will to the world. If we did not have movement, dynamism, tension in us, we would not grasp the world of history as something which is becoming; and the more intense the tempo of dynamism is in us, the more active and not static do we perceive the past in its complexity. This may let us explain how it is that India, for example, has no genuine conception of history and no historical sense of time: as long as one's own experiential space is so thoroughly stereotyped that the dynamism is slowed to such an extent that the shifts are not discernible within a single generation, the apprehension of the past of one's own experiential space is a static one; that is, one deals with past spiritual realities as though they belonged to one's own experiential space. In addition, all cultural phenomena are, of course, spontaneously reinterpreted, but this dynamic change is too gradual to enter into reflective consciousness. The data of the past are not ordered in succession, as in a developmental sequence, but side by side, as if in space. Events and formations are interchangeable, as if everything could have happened at any time: no thing exists for reflection except an eternal now.

Past spiritual realities are ordered according to the model of development only when one does not merely live poised in a certain tension, but when this stress also becomes graspable by reflection. By becoming visible, it becomes the methodological form of object-construction when history is being constructed. It is well known that while seeing things in developmental terms is of very recent origin, seeing things historically in the sense of a tensing from a world having being towards a world which ought to have being is well established in the Western tradition. This can be traced back to the Prophets, with whom the feeling of being tensed for (*Spannungsgefühl*) the messianic kingdom originates. This conception entered into Christianity. In Augustine, for example, there is a tension of this world towards the City of God, but no concrete ordering of historical events comes about by virtue of this, even though a philosophy of history is already implicit in it (cf. Troeltsch). The Middle Ages were relatively stable, because here there was a fusion of these Graeco-Judaeo-Christian elements with the will to the world of primitive, strongly stereotyping peoples. That this world did not remain static, as did the oriental cultures which were similar in these respects, is doubtless because this experience of stress was taken up within it and broke through in the Renaissance, which is, in fact, a resumption of elements from classical antiquity (humanism), on the one hand, and prophetic-Judaic elements (Reformation) on the other.

This stress expresses itself in the field of reflective thinking in that conjunctive knowledge, as soon as it becomes dynamic, becomes acquainted with a certain type of concept, the ideal, and, with regard to the vision of the world as a whole, the utopia. Utopia is nothing but the theoretical anticipation of the will to the world upon which stress is concentrated, and every cognitive penetration of social and cultural experiential space characteristically occurs within this tension, this expectant straining towards an ideal, a utopia. Utopia contains the direction, the point of view, the perspective, and the set of questions from which the present and the past first become comprehensible at all. Investigating the structure of utopia is therefore one of the most essential tasks of the sociology of thought.

Upon typological consideration, we can distinguish two sorts of utopia at the very outset: the idea (*Idee*) and the ideal *(Ideal)*. What is distinctive of the idea is that it is the experience of expectancy, of tension, without a conception of development focused upon history: the desired world towards which aspiration strives is hypostatized into a world above. The ideas, the perfect formations, pre-existently have their being, all at once, in a spiritual supramundane space. Our world with its formations participates in it (Platonic participation) but it does not move toward it in a systematic, serial process of approximation. In the ideal (Kant's 'idea'), the idea has become a dynamic goal and the whole will to the world moves toward it in a progression of linked terms.

Pure utopianism is a pre-scientific form of historical-sociological cognition, but even excluding enthusiasm for utopia (which must by all means be done) cannot change the fact that the concepts which originated in this tension between existence and imperative retain the perspectivity which entered into them by virtue of this origin. Historical-sociological cognition is perspectivistic in this sense as well, and every concept within a reflection which has become dynamic in the way discussed earlier contains a dynamic perspectivity: the general stress lives on within it. Words like 'capitalism', 'proletariat' and 'culture' do not contain or denote a mere summation, but rather a direction of movement as seen from a particular location within the historical stream. Needless to say, these concepts are directional not in abstract distillation but only in their concrete substantiality. When a socialist utters the word 'capitalism' the thought of a self-transformation of this system is included in his determination of the concept. The contents of the concept are determined by the stress controlling the socialist vision of the world. That is what we mean by the unavoidable perspectivity of historical-sociological concept-formation. What concept of sociology was not complicated and constituted out of some political stress? Value-freedom is possible in sociology and social knowledge in the sense that one ought not to praise or blame phenomena to be described, or, in other words, that one ought to refrain from any valuation. But at a much deeper level, valuation cannot be excluded; namely, at the level of the perspectivity that has entered into the formation of concepts. We believe that questions for the discussion concerning value-freedom must be reformulated along these lines, and that the last word on this is far from having been spoken (cf. Max Weber).

Understanding and interpreting the spiritual realities of past epochs means setting these realities into our own experiential space. But, as is apparent from discussion earlier in this chapter, this can happen in two ways:

(1) It can be done naively, by treating these realities as contemporary, as though the interpreter's experiential space had simply expanded in time. This happens in periods when its own stress has not yet become visible for the period, and its dynamics have not yet been discovered as an ordering principle. An example of this would be when, unconcerned about the anachronism involved, a Baroque completion is imposed upon a Gothic cathedral or statues from antiquity are placed in a Romanesque church and drawn into experience as formations belonging to one's own experiential and creative space.

(2) Or it can be done dynamically, when the tension is alive, when the world is comprehended as becoming, and seen as developing in relation to our own tension. The construe of the world as in a state of becoming, which construes the world in relation to ourselves, as did Hegel, or, like Marx, in relation to one of our utopias, is already dynamic. But its grasp of the world remains perspectivistically adapted to our own experiential space and it grasps

247

only as much of past formations as fits into this retrospective pro-
longation of our tension. Fundamentally, then, it remains a way of
comprehending foreign worlds by taking them up within our own
experiential space. This essential element of every philosophy of
history is also present in every way of considering history, for there
is no consideration of history which does not ultimately rest on a
philosophy of history.[60]

In addition to these two types of comprehending and experiencing the past there is a third: understanding the formations of an
experiential space from its own perspective. This we shall call
immanent understanding and interpretation (cf. Troeltsch). This
sort of understanding can arise only in ages that have become very
sensitive historically, and consists in trying to penetrate into the
existential background of an experiential space by way of its formations. But this attempt can succeed only with regard to experiential
spaces with which we stand in historical continuity. Furthermore, it
is possible only in an epoch that is differentiated enough to contain
within its experiential space several more particularized experiential spaces, whereby the interpreting individual acquires existentially the inner state of mind which alone makes it possible to
penetrate a variety of identical spaces.

We must not forget that in a particular period several experiential spaces can exist within the same space. An urban dweller who
happens into a rural milieu or a peasant who becomes a worker
migrates from one experiential space into another; and even in the
movement from childhood to age, one traverses several experiential spaces existentially. We do not penetrate such new spaces
through their spiritual formations alone, but also through being
existentially accepted in several communities of life and lore. In
this living process we learn to understand formations, to see them
differently than we did before, and we become acquainted with the
way in which particular modes of consideration are anchored in
particular cultural spaces. The result is that we first become critical
of the exclusiveness and inevitability of the mode of consideration
which happens to have been taught us. This loosening of the exclus-
ivity of our own world-view can only take place, however, when
existential rootedness has already become looser in our experiential space through some historical or individual course of events. If
this does not happen, we shut ourselves off from reception within a
new experiential community. The peasant girl in the city continues
to see the formations of a new world in terms of the experiential
intentions of the old one. Only where the exclusiveness of inherited
modes of conduct has somehow become subject to question is
'empathy' possible.

Here, in the multi-layered experiential community of the present, there takes place the earliest schooling for turning oneself about, for opening oneself to receiving 'from the inside' the contents of other experiential spaces: in a word, for immanent understanding, immanent interpretation. But in life this shifting of one's own position can occur organically. It proceeds organically from existential reception to the understanding of spiritual formations, and it follows the same course as that taken by the child in its development, being received existentially to understanding formations.

The way of immanent understanding of foreign historical spaces, in contrast, follows the opposite course, starting out from memorials and formations, and proceeding gradually and step by step to the conquest of foreign experiential space itself. This requires a systematic retraction of all linguistic meanings that are current today. Even if a present word were historically continuous with a word from the past and were acoustically identical with it, understanding the past word would still require historical reconstruction. Here, too, leverage points of some existential sort are necessary. Immanent interpretation is not limited to cultural spaces out of which our world originated; we have access to all spaces in which seminal particles of our epoch have returned to life. Interpretation succeeds only when our own cultural process, in one of its tides of movement, raises to the surface an element from the past, and the interpreter is touched by both the tide and the element. Through these existential points of contact, which make up the Archimedean point for world reconstruction, it may be possible for the interpreter, by means of critical work, to sweep away all of the interpretations which epochs blind to history have laid over phenomena. Such points may also be available wherever, in contemporary experiential communities to which one has existential access (e.g., peasant communities), one finds preserved formations and cognitive perspectives which resemble those of the past and which have persisted only within a certain form of community (thus the meaning and forms of ancient paganism are preserved in peasant religiosity).

It is clear, then, that immanent interpretation is also most intimately linked with the general stress of contemporary will, even though it takes a direction different from other sorts of interpretation. And it should be emphasized once more that formations comprehended in immanent interpretation cannot by any means lay claim to being beyond perspectivity, since, as we saw, not even contemporaries are in a position fully to comprehend their own formations (nor can individual creators do so with their own work). As we saw, the *polis* is not only what it appeared to its contemporaries to be. Now we can add to this that only the intended meaning can be comprehended by immanent interpretation and that this does not coincide with objective meaning but must be recognized as one possible perspective with regard to the objective contents.

13   The problem of reliability in conjunctive knowledge

From the very outset, we obstruct our own way to the proper comprehension of spiritual realities, formations of meaning, by interposing a prejudice which consists in dealing with them without necessarily meaning to do so, on the tacit analogy of material realities. A stone or some other object in space has something about it that human knowledge cannot penetrate, while all formations of meaning present us with something we can penetrate. As we are taking in a formation of meaning, subjecting it to interpretative understanding, we have the feeling of grasping it from the inside – a matter already noted earlier from another angle. Contrasting the kind of comprehension that proceeds by means of sharply defined universal concepts (*Begreifen*) with interpretative understanding, we would consider it to be an incomplete penetration of its subject matter. When we comprehend a logical pattern, such as a mathematical proof, it already happens that this, compared to the comprehension of a material configuration of external causality in physical nature, provides a feeling of greater closeness and certainty, an impression of being at the heart of the matter, of having possessed ourselves of the principle of construction governing the proof. But even this penetration to the core of a train of thought is still remote from the inner certainty of evidentness which accompanies a correct grasp of spiritual realities in interpretative understanding. Spiritual realities are creations of our spirit; and this manifests itself above all in the fact that understanding always gives us the feeling of having made our way to the creative centre of the formation in question. In such interpretative understanding one is aware of it when one is still moving on the periphery of understanding a formation or feels it when one is approaching its centre. One also knows (or at least can know) when one has fully penetrated to the centre, from which point, though it is not possible to show the logical necessity of the formation, one can freshly gain access to all parts of it.

Anyone who has ever really understood a piece of music, a painting, or a conjunctive contexture of experience of a theoretical and reflective kind knows that it is not adequately taken in when one simply takes cognizance of its contents but only when one also spiritually recreates it while taking it in. People of a receptive nature are easily able to advance thought or artistic creation along the lines of a particular style, because in the course of understanding they also grasp the formative principle, the creative core. This grasp of a formative principle of spirit and soul resembles, but is far from identical with, that inner structure of necessity pertaining to the grasp of mathematical trains of thought together with their purely theoretical principles, which enable one to advance thinking on the same problems, and to carry further the universally valid conditions and connections of the system-model, and to represent them in a way that commands the assent of all thinking beings. When one grasps the compositional principle as the key to the inner necessity underlying the organization of the representational material in a painting which is properly interpreted, these connections have a necessity quite different from but also more deeply compelling than the connections of theory. And it does not amount to any disparagement of the characteristic of necessity if it is also known at the same time that this evidentness can only be conveyed to a restricted, experiential community. This distinctive feature, that one cannot avoid letting the ultimate support of evidentness rest on elements in the experienced object which are qualitative in content, attaches to every kind of qualitative knowing, and accordingly applies to conjunctive knowledge of formations and configurations of meaning, as well as to every sort of cultural reality.

It would be altogether wrong, then, to conclude from the essential perspectivity of spiritual knowledge, from the dependence on historical standpoint, and from the conjunctive conditionality of any proof of correctness of this sort that, first, everything runs into diffuse unverifiability in this domain, or, second, that there are no items of knowledge accumulated here, no objects grasped, but simply a pursuit of illusions.

The position that this sort of cognition has no objective reference will only be maintained by those who model the criteria of truth and scientific status upon universally valid mathematical knowledge. As far as disciplines built upon necessities which cannot be rationally contested are concerned, we may leave aside the question whether particular truths can be derived immanently from the validity of logical principles. Yet even in these 'exact disciplines' there is a dilemma. Mathematical knowledge is either based on intuition, so that here, too, knowledge would be dependent on intuitions; or, as is increasingly assumed today, all individual assertions flow from a few axioms – which raises the question whether the givenness of these axioms has a source. If the latter assumption is correct, the ultimate criteria for concrete statements are rooted

251

in contents and not in pure logical forms here too, except that the self-evidence of the truth of these contents is inherently associated with our general human nature and not with our historically conditioned culture.

Nothing is proved against the scientific character of this kind of knowledge by the ultimate recourse to the qualitative which is inevitable in all conjunctive knowledge. In these fields of study, which aim for qualitative knowledge, it is in any case not so much a question of demonstration or proof (*Beweis*) as it is of exhibition or showing (*Aufweis*). Experiment is replaced by display, although only the conjunctive learning community can gain access to what is displayed. Formal methods of describing what is being shown can become ever more precise; and in this regard there is in fact coming to be something like a generally applicable technique, which is developing progressively. Among these methods, capable of general employment, are those of pictorial description and the study of historical sources. But even historical interpretation has formal criteria and methods which can be made independent of the conjunctive foundation, such as the formal criterion of the internal consistency of any interpretation of a formation. But we must not make the mistake of supposing that evidentness is guaranteed by these formal methods, but must rather recognize that it ultimately derives from a grasp of the qualitative, and that the graspability of the qualitative is not the *result* of applying these methods but the precondition of their being applicable at all.

If all this had to be said to answer charges against conjunctive knowledge, it is now possible to note that there are also elements in this knowledge which assure deeper penetration into its object than is ever possible in the exact sciences. There is a moment within qualitative knowledge by virtue of which it is unquestionably superior to natural-scientific knowledge. This moment manifests itself as the phenomenon of genuineness. Genuineness is a phenomenon which can occur as a determinative quality only in the case of qualitative knowledge and represents a surplus over and above the mere correctness of a cognition. Something which has being can be genuine, and a cognition founded in being can be genuine. It signifies the integrity of an existence and the integrity of an inclination to knowledge. If the essential perspectivity of all conjunctive knowledge is taken as given, there are genuine and ungenuine existences within this perspectivity, as well as genuine and ungenuine reports of what has been learned. An existence is genuine if it founds its existence upon the principle of its being; a cognition is genuine if its perspectivity is determined by nothing but the perspectivity of its location and not by heterogeneous concerns, which always lead to falsification. A party politician may see things in a certain perspective from where he stands, and we are able to say, when we see those same things and also comprehend where he is looking from, that it seems reasonable and highly logical to us that he sees things in such and such a way; but we can also say with a high degree of certainty that at this point falsifications set in which cannot be put to the account of the place from which he is looking, but have their origin in dubious ambitions. The case is the same here as in the representation of a landscape: there is no landscape without perspective; but it is in principle possible for us to test all landscapes from our point of view and to determine that the one feature is consistent with the point of view portrayed, but the other misrepresented. Genuineness is also subject to testing, if also only in the way that the qualitative can be tested.

The brand of philosophy that wants to build truth solely upon a conceptual level valid for all time knows nothing but the criterion of 'truth in general' and would prefer nothing better than to bring this into being out of itself alone, without reference to existence. It is internally consistent only when it ultimately strives for the elimination of ontological premises and attempts to derive the world in the last analysis from a formally rational consciousness. Corresponding to its points of departure is a concept of truth that is immanent and formal and that finds its highest ideal in logical deduction. But it is no less consistent for a philosophy which grounds itself in existence (ontology) to stop seeking the criterion of truth in a doctrine of validity suspended above existing things, and to locate truth, though by circuitous paths, in a certain way of orienting oneself to the object. Genuineness is simply the expression of the search for such an ontological criterion of truth.

If we consider the historical fate of qualitative conclusions from experience, we notice something else. While what is true and correct establishes itself in an immanent way, with the unequivocal insistence of the rational necessity inherent in it, observation reveals that, in their own way, genuine and significant conjunctive cognitions, as well as spiritual formations of a non-theoretical sort, are bound to outlive – given enough time – the problems of their own time. It can indeed be said that important achievements in the humanistic sciences as well as important works of art, poetry and philosophy are not denied eventual recognition in this domain, seemingly so lacking in uniform standards. Those who anticipated a subsequent direction and were denied recognition in their time may well have been discovered only belatedly, but a complete obliteration of really important achievements has hardly been possible (or only to a very slight extent), so that the saying that time will tell concerning the true worth of works has its truth. But how is this possible? Can it really be the case that the judgment of the masses, the democratic principle, proves to be correct even in the securing of spiritual and conjunctive knowledge? Sociological objections to the tribunal of the masses are well known. They include Simmel's subtle analysis in his *Soziologie*, in which he tries to show that of necessity only that spiritual level can prevail in a mass which corresponds to the spiritual minimum of the individuals involved, since the mass can be socially constituted in spirit only in the measure permitted by this lowest common denominator. But in this regard it should be noted that we are not dealing in our case with popular jury of individuals assembled at a particular time, but rather with a conjunctive experiential community dispersed over time, united by cultural continuity, sharing cultural direction – which is to say that we are dealing with the sociological type we have called 'connoisseurs'. Judgments concerning the value of works only flow into general consciousness from the critical assessment of connoisseurs, who gradually discover what is significant. It must be admitted that a conjunctive experiential community of connoisseurs tends to be conservative, bound by stringent tradition, and easily inclined to rate highly values which go along with what has already been adjudged excellent. This takes us very close to the failure by contemporaries to give recognition to works which have already grasped the 'next step'. And the chances of finding acceptance are correspondingly greater for those works which, in their creations, undertake to fit wholly within the horizon of expectations of the past. If one lives thoroughly in the present and observes it carefully, one realizes that directions of development are not a simple matter. Several possibilities for the future are simultaneously present at any given time, and it is a question of destiny which of them comes to prevail. Accordingly, works and forms containing genuine things may be brought under because they pursued what is next possible in a direction which will not prevail tomorrow, but the day after, or later still. But since the germs remain within the cultural space as possibilities and since, as one can assume, everything that is somehow present as a possibility will ultimately come to fruition within the cultural realm, even if only at a later stage, it may be said to be certain that these buried impulses will prove of value to a subsequent will to the world and that the works will be rediscovered.

The possibility of being denied recognition is naturally greater in communities whose qualitative assurance has become insecure (which depends on the degree of integration of the experiential community); and this enables us to understand why the denial of recognition of achievements by contemporaries is a modern rather than an ancient phenomenon, if for no other reason than that the conjunctively integrated community of connoisseurs has detached itself as a separate office from the mass, from the underlying community. Connoisseurship today means *avant-garde*, while in the more closely integrated medieval times the entire community was a qualitatively oriented connoisseurship, particularly with regard to religion and art, which were at the centre of cultural life, although the community was of course internally differentiated.

In any case, this self-assertion of the genuine and true over time is a phenomenon peculiar to conjunctively conditioned spiritual entities. In the creative process (such as in language and art) the individual is always less important than the collectivity, and he is correspondingly less certain in his judgment. The part assigned to external fate as criterion of conjunctive knowledge is also connected with the pragmatic character of this whole sphere of thinking.

But the suggestions in this chapter cannot pretend to dispose of this most difficult problem of the conjunctive sphere of thought, as the epistemological analysis of this problem does not belong to the topic of this essay. We are satisfied to present the most conspicuous phenomena – as raw material, so to speak – for an epistemological treatment of the problem of truth as it arises in this connection.

14 The splitting of the community and of consciousness

It is probably only at the primitive level of communal association, in the clan, that we find complete unity in the direction towards which the community is tensioned, and, as consequence of this unity, a will to the world and formation of the world which are uniform in contents. The clan can be thought of as a conjunctive life- and learning-community in which each member commands what is knowable about this world with equal right, in principle, and in the same way, a community in which each member feels himself supported by the creative as well as receptive tendencies of the others, running parallel and mutually reinforcing, and, finally, a community in which there are at most the differences which depend on the natural determinants of disposition and talent in individuals. There are also, however, organically determined distinctions among age cohorts and kinship units;[61] and age distinctions in fact present us with the most primitive original classification of the group. (Classification by kinship, *gentes*, does not come into consideration here, because the group originally stems from such a natural unit, and conjunctive life-community is initially

255

founded upon consanguinity.)

As long as communal meals continue, there is as yet no splitting of the contents of consciousness either in the sense of one framework-community containing two narrower ones, each possessing its own world, or in the sense of there being only one world of knowables, but having some of its contents taken out and denied to the public as a mystery. Where and in so far as this patriarchial form is preserved even in class society, there is difference in power among table-companions, but not in conceptions. They form a community of conjunctive experience in every sense of the word.

A splitting of this unitary world occurs only when oppressed and overlords come into being by virtue of conquest (cf. Oppenheimer). Under these conditions, a split takes place for two reasons. To begin with, because the defeated group was itself originally a distinct conjunctive experiential community and brought with it distinctive ideas and traditions, a distinctive will to the world, and a tensioning in a different direction. This alone, however, would not account for the continuing difference, since a unified conjunctive experiential community would come about from the subsequent coexistence of the two groups, in the course of which the two wills to the world could, so to speak, unite. That this happens only in part is because matters are arranged by institution so as to bring about a relative separation of the two life communities, such that the existential and ideational space of the rulers and the existential and world space of the conquered constitute spiritual 'states within the state'. While a common association arises with regard to the realities where the two experiential communities touch, an impenetrable space encompasses each side, in spiritual matters too, and each of these remains a mystery to the members of the other group. And, in general, the rulers consciously treat their mysteries as mysteries. Acceptance into the cultural community takes on symbolic importance in this case. And even where a state religion prevails it is important to know whether the religion does not mean something quite different to the dominant strata than it does to the subordinate. It remains a question for an immanent approach whether the same spiritual realities are not seen and experienced in a different perspective from the ruler's standpoint than from that of the ruled. It is well known, for example, that the Roman Catholic church, which in this regard brings about the maximum amount of unity, provided peasants with the perspective of peasant religiosity (predominance of superstition, favouring of sacrifice over prayer, transfer of originally orgiastic elements into religious contents, etc.). Here we find that type of understanding in operation which we described as the absolutely naive acceptance into one's own

world of spiritual realities from other worlds, whereby one proceeds altogether 'unhistorically', under cover of the fiction that one
is dealing with realities belonging to one's own world. The same
spiritual realities which are held 'in common', chiefly institutions,
are thus seen from two sides, from above and from below. Their
immanent experience is different from above and from below, and,
once advanced from this experience to reflective awareness in
theory, is also differently interpreted. (This double vision is important if we call to mind that there is always a sociology 'from
above' and another 'from below'. The rulers just see the social
structure differently from the ruled.) The institutional formations
which bind the community, despite its split, into the higher unity of
the whole group, form the medium in which the component groups
meet one another externally while in fact seeing quite differently.
Through this common possession of formations upon a quasi-
supra-conjunctive level, a certain kind of capacity for abstraction
enters into operation, a capacity which enables us to see the very
things that appear different from the inside in a different way,
which can be considered relatively unperspectivistic, compared to
conjunctive scrutiny, which is always perspectivistic. This
expresses itself in language first of all, which originally comprises in
its words nothing but conjunctively determined ideas, and which
originally intends, proceeding within a specific perspectivity, spiritual realities which are always concretely linked to a specific, historical experiential space, but which gradually turns ever more into
a language of commerce between the social strata, into a means for
abstract agreement. The same acoustical sound complexes may
then at one time signify something conjunctively determined, and
at another something removed, by the greatest possible abstraction
from conjunction, from particular things of meaning.

To clarify the conditions obtaining here by means of a simple
example, we must digress briefly. The worlds of the child and adult
also differ in their experiential perspective. Although the two sides
always mean and learn something different using the same words,
some sort of communication (which we deliberately do not want to
call understanding) does come to pass, at a shared level which positions itself like an intermediate realm between the worlds of the
child and the adult. Let us assume that a child is playing with a
puppet. No matter how much we try, we shall probably never be
able to understand in full concreteness the specific conceptions of
this thing possessed by the child; but enough is already accessible
for us to know that, fully absorbed in play, it deals with the thing as
with a living being, that it is existentially bound up with it in a way
we could never achieve. The child experiences adventures and

psychic contagions with it that we could never analogously enter into with a puppet. When the child utters the word 'plaything' or 'puppet', there are for the child associated with the word the conceptions that originated in the child's particular conjunction with the thing, conceptions which may also become adequately transmissible in a possible extended conjunctive community with other children. We have our own conjunctively determined ideas about puppets and playthings in as much as, in our everyday life experience with other adults, we do conduct ourselves in some stereotyped way towards these things. For us the child and the world of childhood signify a spiritual reality of a particular coloration, and one that has not been the same in all societies. History reveals the most varied ways of experiencing the world of childhood and the child from the standpoint of the adult world. Children have been seen by society as sacred, as small adults, as grotesque, as darling and sentimental. Society saw the child with various ascriptions of meaning of which the child knows nothing. It may be that the plaything is something grotesque and comical for us (an experience which finds complete expression as work in puppet shows for adults); again, the child knows nothing of this. We simply do have our own conjunctively determined knowledge concerning this spiritual reality, concerning the accumulation of meanings by virtue of which the puppet is more than wood and rags; but we nevertheless simply say to the child, for example, 'Give me that plaything'. In saying so, we enter into a communicative relation with the child. We mean to signify only the determinations which are sufficient to secure compliance with the demand for surrender of the physical object. In the abstractness it assumes in communication, the word 'plaything' retains only very restricted features in its make-up. It merely designates the object as something with which one can play, thus distinguishing only a general function that can be transferred from a particular experiential community to other experiential spaces. 'Thing' (*Zeug*) is a colourless word and designates the category of artifacts in general. 'Play', although more concrete, leaves open what concrete playful relationships are meant to be included in the word's definition. We encounter the child by and large upon this abstract level of communicative conceptual definition and the illusion is created that we have thoroughly understood one another. In yielding to our demand, the child has already taken the first step towards emerging from its conjunctively determined experiential space, and we ourselves have completely gone over to the communicative level at least for the duration of our statement. What is remarkable is that once communicative abstraction has come into being, human beings can live in its space for stretches of time, and there is a tendency, even though it is not constant to experience even spiritual realities only in so far as they come into consideration for a communicative significancy. This brings about the remarkable phenomenon that one is gradually altogether absorbed in communicative abstractness and that one virtually experiences nothing of the plaything other than its being a mere function: just a 'thing' with which one can 'play'. This initially communicative level itself then becomes the object of experience, so that things can only be experienced in so far as they are subsumed under these conceptual meanings, and conceptual meaning in this sense is drawn back into life. To the extent that this happens, the world itself emerges upon a level of concrete absence of spirit, relatively independent from concrete experiential space. It becomes transmissible through communication, and the accumulated experiences, detached from the community, can be furthered within alien communities. This is the origin of the sphere of civilization.[62]

The basis of knowledge undergoes a stabilization, which has an analogue (which is not fully adequate) in the fixing of the literary language in relation to the dialects. This thinking is static, relatively supra-conjunctive, and impersonal. This knowledge divests itself of its genetic bondedness to a particular experiential space, but only in so far as it continues at this level of concepts as they are laid down within a system. Methodologists of the natural sciences have oriented themselves exclusively to such experiencing and thinking. Although such an abstract, supra-conjunctive level of concepts and a line of knowledge attuned to purely functional relationships emerges in every stratified community, this level attains to world-forming predominance only at a time when the conjunctive experiential community is rendered less closely knit, when an economy based on barter and local transactions gives way to a commercial economy and finally to a capitalism based on calculation. With regard to spirit and soul, the symbol of this dissolution is the disintegration of the religious world-view, from whose exclusive dominion the individual spheres of culture gradually emerge and become autonomous. Although the individual social strata already exist apart under the sway of dynamics which are bound by religion and are restrained – each having its own peculiar world and culture within the framework of the culture as whole – the world is not perceived as truly split until the dynamism, which had always been present but inhibited, somehow becomes apparent to the community. It is striking and remarkable that at the very time that the movement for autonomy comes to the fore among the individual spheres which had formerly been bound and amalgamated in religious consciousness, the community which had been integrated by estates or something of the sort turns into a class society, with each of the classes sooner or later assuming a dynamism of its own, of which it becomes conscious. It is also interesting to observe how the various classes, in their upward striving and in the course of their subsequent careers, relate to these now autonomous currents. In general they take up a direction which was only an inner current in the integrated state of the community. They affix it to their shields, so to speak, establish something like a community of interest with it, and, by rendering the undercurrent independent, carry the conduct and objective system appropriate to it to completion. We can observe this autonomization and systematic elaboration not only in art, where the emergence of 'bourgeois art', for example, is a recognized phenomenon, but also in the history of thought. We saw in the first part of this study that the rising bourgeoisie allied itself in all areas with the rationalism of supra-conjunctive abstraction, a rationalism which had already attained a high stage of development in antiquity but which had been reintegrated into conjunctive knowledge of the world in the Middle Ages. This is to say that in the Middle Ages purely abstract communicative thinking, in so far as it was already developed, was worked back into theology, thereby becoming a component part of a conjunctive world picture once more. A theological world picture, accordingly, includes stretches of abstract, supra-conjunctive thinking, but these always flow back once more into the conjunctively determined world picture and into irrational realities which can be knowingly handled only within a particular community (cf. Max Weber and Georg Lukács).

Such thinking, beyond conjunction and freed from theology, achieves autonomous power when the will to the world of the rising bourgeoisie takes it up. First within the religious realm and then in connection with a struggle against religion, it removes all 'significancies' from things, since these are always conjunctively determined. In consequence, it ends up in the physical world with mere spatial objects and their relations. And even these are comprehended only in so far as they are a 'something' which can be referred in all their determinations to a numerical system, and in so far as they are wholly commensurable to it and calculable in terms of its relations, since a numerical system is, after all, the most extreme case of a supra-conjunctive system of relations.

The eradication of ascribed meanings in the external, spatial world has its counterpart in the eradication of meaning contents in 'inner experience'. By stripping away all the particular relations of significance by virtue of which psychic life had been a field fitted into the concrete religious world picture, one arrived at the pure intentional act and at the psychological processes and functions devoid of meaning that are studied by physical psychology only in so far as they can be related to measurable external things and events.

In the world of the social, as well, proceeding in this way leads to a generalizing sociology and thereby to discovery of the social as such. In this intellectual undertaking all institutions with concrete, historical contents, as well as all other spiritual contents, are seen only in abstraction and studied only in their functionality for any cohabitation in general. (Underlying this is the same process that we observed in the case of the formation of the abstract concept 'plaything', where we tried to show how in such concepts the concrete richness of the conjunctive knowledge of an object is replaced by a purely functional relation.)

For a generalizing sociology, in other words, all concrete phenomena come into consideration only to the extent that they can be comprehended as parts of a purposive connection. This mode of conceptualization has been developed with the greatest logical rigour by Max Weber in *Economy and Society*, where he himself admits that the purposive reinterpretation of non-rational social formations is, as it were, a fiction of sociology. This is putting very sharply the fact that purposive-rational calculability in the social field most nearly approximates to mathematization in the physical sciences. While it even approaches actual quantification on occasions, the dissolution of every spiritual reality into a functional connection (where the notion of the maximum result with the most economical means is the ideal of construction) is in any case well qualified to constitute a supra-conjunctive principle of demonstration, which stands in far-reaching affinity with quantification and causal inquiry in the physical sciences. This affinity consists first of all in the fact that this type of rationalization makes it possible to eradicate everything that is conjunctively determined, qualitative, and, accordingly, not to represent the existence of 'institutions' and spiritual realities 'seen from the inside', as they are present to the particular community. An additional affinity to physical science is that this rationalization contains within itself the possibility for trans-conjunctive generalization, since all human transactions can be viewed as in a means-end relationship, and, just as the consideration of external connections can always be fitted to the schema of causality, so every 'transaction' can be examined schematically for its purposive-rationality. From this point of view it is understandable that Max Weber finds it necessary to reinterpret all social 'formations' into 'transactions'.

We do not need to pursue in this place the question whether this procedure actually does achieve supra-conjunctivity. But it is beyond any doubt that the tendency to see everything as in a means-end relationship can only develop in an era in which our way of considering life, and, indeed, life itself, has become predominantly purposive-rational. Perhaps this projection of purposive-rationality into all past conditions and the explanation of the spiritual by reference to the economic and social is itself a perspective on things that is most closely connected with where we stand today. But whether it is perspectivistic or supra-conjunctive is not our problem here.

In our present context it is only important to show that sociology as a generalizing scheme – as a science of the social process in general, as a structural science of society – is a counterpart to the rational, supra-conjunctive physical sciences; and it was this intellectual design which sociology consciously set itself as programme at its first appearance (Comte).

History is the only scientific discipline that sets itself the task of grasping concrete formations in their uniqueness and richness and in their historicity, which is to say, without abstracting from their contents and concreteness. Only history has remained in continuity with conjunctive, perspectivistic thinking. And it could not have been otherwise, for what is contentful and concrete about spiritual formations disappears if one tries to grasp them non-perspectivistically. Scientific consciousness continues to proceed in this matter except for its critical method in chronology and the investigation of sources, just as one now grasps reality nowhere except in that everyday life which remains bound up with community. The kind of 'religious consciousness' that grasped the qualitative in its concreteness was also alive in both history and everyday life.

Here we must insert a reflection that takes as problem precisely this phenomenon of everyday pre-scientific thought. We spoke earlier of a splitting of consciousness connected with the social splitting of the group. Our comments were concerned with a splitting by means of which several experiential spaces emerged within the same framework group and in consequence of which one group in the overall community associated itself with one such space and another group with a different one. An example from our own life is the still persisting difference in world-view between peasantry and feudal aristocracy.

But we also spoke of a supra-conjunctive layer of communicative conceptual meanings detaching itself. Until now, however, we have simply been tracing how the sphere of rationalization arose out of the necessity of communication and developed itself in the course of time into an autonomous current which, as 'civilized thinking', became the source of the generalizing sciences (including the exact physical sciences, experimental psychology, and general sociology). But we must now return to that stage of the communicative sphere in which it had not separated itself so completely and profoundly from the spiritual totality of what experience teaches as it has today, but rather only had the function of providing a connection among the various conjunctively integrated groups belonging to the same framework. In this capacity, the communicative sphere had to enter into and to be understood by every single consciousness in the larger group, or it could not have fulfilled this communicative function. By acceptance of such a 'conceptual level', however, a doubling of ideas and concepts concerning the same realities arises in the consciousness of individuals: first, the ideas and concepts which are completely conjunctively rooted, and then, superimposed upon them, meanings that belong to the communicative level. An earlier, conjunctive way of thinking and communicative thought penetrate one another, and each seeks to absorb the other. We can observe that while we encounter the world in unsophisticated experience, we push our exact knowledge about things aside or at least apply it only in rudimentary fashion. In everyday knowledge of other men and in assessment of situations (all of which do after all signify a kind of knowing) we usually forget what we know and understand from natural-scientific psychology and generalizing sociology. We act according to methods quite different from those which these sciences could provide. These sciences, moreover, can only determine general relationships and regularities; but the capacity for judgment, for recognizing what is at issue in just *one* of the cases possible, for 'grasping a situation', is an intellectual activity that differs completely from what is called scientific activity. In such cases we are attending to wholly concrete spiritual realities, full of contents, and we are doing this in just the way in which our counterpart is attending to them. Just in this way, we react more adequately than if we sought to comprehend objectifications by reference to a supra-conjunctive contexture.

And when we are considering history, we do not alter anything in this preservation of the conjunctive attitude: we simply render it more consistent, more precise, more critical, but it remains an extension of the mode of knowledge and bearing which marks our experience of everyday. Nothing demonstrates more effectively how far everyday life experience is independent of scientific knowledge and how much it thinks in collective representations which are hardly susceptible to rational and reflective analysis than that we care so little, in our natural experience and penetration of our life-space, that we know from other sources that the sun is a fixed star and that day and night are not substances but phenomena of the rotation of of the earth. Every time that we experience them phenomenologically as elements in the world around us and enter into an experiential relationship to them, our scientific knowledge about them sinks out of sight: they are sun and day and night for us, parts of a myth. Although the encroaching civilizational way of knowing increasingly drives these mythical elements out of every-day practical knowledge, mythical and magical components do nevertheless survive in our everyday knowledge of life even today. Even where the contents of myth have completely faded away, mythic structure persists in everyday thinking to the extent that all these things are construed and known with reference to ourselves just as in myth: things are not objects in any sort of absolute space, but things and events in a life-space. This comprises their specific perspectivity, and it is on the strength of this sign that we venture to assert that the structure of everyday knowledge is a continuation and legacy of conjunctively bound knowledge, after it has gone through the stages of magical and mythical thought. While these modes of thinking were once in sole command, fashioning a unified world picture, they now form part of an under-current of our thinking and experience of the world: the thinking of everyday.

The consciousness of the individual, then, may be likened to a petrification of past ages in the history of consciousness, and just as geology can reconstruct the history of the earth from the successively layered strata of the earth's crust, so the career of consciousness is preserved in stratified layers in the make-up of the individual consciousness of the present. Needless to say, consciousness is not a petrification in the sense of there being clearly separated remnants and strata of past modes of experiencing the world, lying on top of one another. In consciousness everything interpenetrates, and only a circumstantial analysis can separate the fused elements so as to reveal historical origins. It is not really geology which has a comparable task, but philology, for which every contemporary linguistic form, every word, may be considered as a particular product of a general development, and for which the historical reconstruction of the total process requires recourse to the historically established linguistic forms as well as to geographically locatable languages, as derivatives of the same linguistic family, and to variations in the form of dialects. It remains to be seen whether, in view of the ways in which the contents constantly flow into one another, it will ever be possible to subject the development of consciousness to as exact a reconstruction as the history of language. Here we wanted only to show that scientific history and everyday practical knowledge both follow the same conjunctive, perspectivistic, and qualitative methods of acquiring knowledge.

If a layer of conjunctive knowing which is relatively unspoiled, even if flecked with scientific insights, remains present in us, and if a communicative layer is added to this quite soon, what results in practice is a duality in the ways in which individuals bear themselves, in relation to concepts as well as realities. Let us amplify this by an example. When bearing himself in an immanently religious manner, the individual believer stands in the same relationship to God, worship, and religion as do the other members of the same cultural community: he possesses these contents in the way of the existential community, a way which is wholly concrete and perspectivistic and which can only be shared conjunctively. But he is also capable of attaining to a completely abstract relationship to these realities, as when, for example, he wants to take a stand in a political struggle for his religion and comprehends all of these realities not as they are seen from 'inside' but as they appear to the others, as just another religion. When he speaks of religion in this sense, his consciousness shifts up into a supra-conjunctive attitude, to comprehension of the phenomenon of religion as it also exists for 'those without'. But it is not religion alone, but all spiritual realities which have become subject to being taken in this two-fold way; and from this follows an amalgamation of two ways of bearing oneself towards things and taking them in, present in every individual consciousness. In this, individual consciousness reflects a splitting which may well have its origin in the objective splitting of community.

The phenomenon we call 'cultivated culture' (*Bildungskultur*) does not quite measure up to this degree of detachement, which already points to the civilizational layer of communicative definitions, but it nevertheless has its place at a considerable distance from the original existential rootedness of cultural creation.

While the spiritual realities of community-culture (*Gemeinschaftskultur*) rest upon an immediate existential association among individuals (taking the word 'immediate' in its literal sense, as 'unmediated') and its objectifications express without mediation the existential course of the community (its transformation) and while this community-culture only stretches as far as the geographical boundaries of the space occupied by its bearers, the phenomenon we are calling 'cultivated culture' arises partly out of the widening of the community, but also from a mixing of social

265

spheres. The place of formation of cultivated culture is the city, as is well known, where strata from cultural spaces which are widely divergent, while continuing to belong to the same framework-form, intermingle and come in touch with one another. Cultivated culture is a culture that has been rendered relatively independent from the particular, narrowly bounded life community and its existential connectedness. It is just as conjunctively determined as the original culture, although not as strictly tied to existence. The discoveries to be made there are just as perspectivistic as those to be sought in the 'original experiential community', but there is nevertheless a relative loosening of ties to the concrete basis of the particular community.

In cultivated culture, the various group communities belonging to one framework-community can meet one another, although they are usually led, directed and sustained by one of them, because the further development of the cultural process does not proceed here immediately on the basis of the life-community; but it is rather that the 'tendencies', 'germs' (*Keime*) and global projects that flow from these various communities are independently worked out. At the level of cultivated culture one survives on the germs and volitions that flow from communal life and not directly on the strength of the particular community itself. This implies an enormous acceleration of the cultural process. While the slightest material change in cultural objectifications within a primary cultural community presupposes a corresponding, infinitely slow alteration of existence, the 'germs' and 'tendencies' detached from life are able to be grasped and to develop, to unfold more or less freely.

While the style of a folksong changes only with infinite slowness, because every anonymous poet and modifier of the song only revises it imperceptibly in the direction of the new stylistic and global volition, the artistic poet (*Kunstdichter*) is already focused (if not reflectively, conceptually) upon the stylistic tendency of the song and immanently, on this basis alone (without awaiting any accompanying alteration of the basis in life), forces the development in the direction of carrying the style to its culmination. Correspondingly, creative personalities in a primary culture are quite properly anonymous, since it is actually society that creates itself in and through them. In cultivated culture, on the other hand, an inner differentiation of the group has already taken place, and the creator of works, precisely because he does not need to wait for life to issue the form of artistic creation next possible, does not to this extent merely live out the life of the group, but grasps the tendency set free in the formations (which is itself already an individual creative achievement) and carries it forward in the direction of the next step.

This leads to a certain laxness in cultivated culture, in comparison with primary culture, in which every step in the creation of world and work was bought at the cost of life, and there prevailed a greater genuineness, depth, and simplicity and in which the congruence with existence provided for a more gradual development, a full unfolding and differentiation of all possibilities. If one lives ever more off the possibilities themselves, in contrast, this is bound to mean considerable frivolity and can lead to a more rapid consumption of substance. The positive aspect of cultivated culture is precisely the 'cultivation' that it brings about which implies adaptability, a widening of spiritual horizons, and a heightened sensibility.

But not even cultivated culture is free-floating (*freischwebend*). This is mostly because it can only arise out of the combination of cultural communities which live in the same historical continuum; which is to say that they are successors to a once-unified existential community (hence the inner affinity of the 'germs' and 'tendencies' stored up in cultivated culture); or, where there are cultural injections (i.e. foreign elements), these have been incorporated into its own cultural space by existential contagion at an earlier stage. Cultivated culture is not free-floating, furthermore, because the 'cultivated' who work away at it always come from the various existential communities and introduce the tendencies which originate in those communities into the common stream of cultivation, which is why that stream is not uniform but polyphonic and dialectical in constitution. Within that stream, tendencies which differ from one another and even struggle among themselves parallel and cross one another; and all of them flow out of narrower, more primary communities, and, despite their internal struggles, all are parts of one general communal process. Cultivated culture cannot in fact generate new germs, a new stress, on its own; and that is why the absorption of new motifs flooding in from existential backgrounds is constantly taking place. For this reason cultivated culture, while related to communicative thinking in removing itself from a particular community, differs from it in preserving its perspectivity and qualitative directedness. This is true even when it becomes the spiritual representative of an extensive cultural community. While it transcends community in one sense, cultivated culture remains conjunctive nevertheless.

There is also a thinking and reflective knowing which proceeds along the lines of the cultivated culture and remains conjunctive, even though it is elevated into the cultivated stratum. While communicative thinking, together with the entire sphere of civilization,

267

is in principle transferable to all communities (if they have attained the maturity necessary to take it in), conjunctive thinking, even at the more elevated 'cultivated' level, cannot be transferred in its totality. This explains the fact that, while the exact sciences can be taken up and advanced by all nations, we encounter inhibitions determined by cultural boundaries in the humanistic sciences, especially in history and above all with regard to the interpretative dimension; and the advancement of these sciences in any of the directions they have taken is restricted to a specific cultural territory.

Earlier we observed the two levels of individual consciousness corresponding to the two-fold nature of conjunctive and communicative thinking. Such two-dimensionality also holds for cultivated culture. The individual at first grows into the perspectives of a particular community, and only penetrates into the strata of cultivated culture from this starting point. Just as one begins in language by learning a dialect and has the literary language imparted only later, and just as living language continues to take shape in the dialects, despite the presence of a literary language, and the literary language must constantly be revised accordingly, so does a person (not excluding the cultivated) live in a duality of experiential knowledge concerning cultural formations. Here, too, something that has come into being in the course of history is mirrored in the individual consciousness. To mention a further analogy: just as literary language was the stabilization of a dialect, so does the cultivated level originate in the emancipation and hypostatization of the culture of a particular stratum, that of the social stratum that first came to rule (viz., aristocratic culture). Only later do the other strata gradually grow into this culture, whereby it is not only possible but actually the case that through a shift in the social structure the next stratum is able to assume the leadership and co-ordination of this level of culture. Every new stratum to penetrate this level naturally brings new stresses and volitions into the total dynamic of this level (which do carry the tendencies of the existential background to their final conclusion, if also in a form detached from their basis). And those enter immediately into conflict with the other volitions and tendencies. Although it is most natural and common that each individual who makes his way into the ranks of the cultivated should continue to work and create in the direction of the global volitions which have entered into him from his community of origin in the course of his life, there remains a certain freedom of choice concerning the global volition to which one attaches oneself. Biography and convictions can bring it about that experiences at the cultivated level modify the original stress and global volition, so that the individual puts himself at the service of a group volition different from that of his origins. And because emphasis and direction have become somewhat free-floating at this level, it is possible to take sides with a different emphasis, either out of conviction or interest, especially for socially free-floating existences, such as impoverished gentry or Jews. It is only because cultural creation itself now takes place at the level of cultivated culture, that it is no argument against the sociological determination of thinking to point out that the theory and philosophy of the proletariat was partly created and propagated by elements of the bourgeoisie. The stress, the global volition of the proletariat, derives from the direction of its social movement, as it is in being, and it is just because this volition has become free-floating, and because cultivated culture lives on germinal elements and not directly on the basis of existence, that it is possible for individuals from other strata to make it their own.

We have now pursued conjunctive thinking to its highest stage, since what holds for cultivated culture in general holds as well for one of its parts, reflective comprehension of its contents, conjunctive thinking at the level of cultivation. It is only at this stage that conjunctive thinking about culture itself really becomes a science. In primitive cultures reflection about their own culture and surroundings is still myth and fable. The tendencies present in a narrative, mythological grasp of how the environing world has come to be, are later perpetuated in the philosophy of history and historiography, and we have already indicated that the latter, even as science, clings to the basic form of representing and taking in the world, the narrative form, in which alien historical entities are incorporated into one's own experiential space. We have frequently stressed that historical narration, however positivistic it may be, is bound to retain the pattern of construing events by reference to oneself, which is to incorporate all the features through which the perspectivity of conjunctive experience manifests itself. But while there was only one direction towards which a primary cultural community was tensed, and while every such community worked out the details of only one such dynamically shifting standpoint in the course of considering and assessing historical things, there are in cultivated cultures, as the previous discussion makes clear, a plurality of directions of stress, a number of global volitions, corresponding to the social strata underlying them, and that there are consequently present at any one time a number of standpoints for reflective knowledge of the cultural space. The unified standpoint of primary culture was already to be grasped as a dynamic one, and each of these multiple standpoints within one cultural community is

269

also to be regarded as dynamic. The working out and development of these standpoints proves to be the most essential task of every sociology of culture and thinking.

No matter how much these standpoints may differ in original stress and global volition and how much they may seem to work against one another, they nevertheless always form a unity, when viewed from a higher viewpoint. They are after all differentiations within a single general movement, and can be overviewed in their function from the perspective of that movement, when one of its phases comes to an end. The standpoints are nothing but functions of this general movement. For a sociology of thought that proceeds in a historical manner, the understanding and grouping of these standpoints is a problem in so far as it has to present them not as a confusion of tendencies but rather must try to group them around a common fundamental movement of the cultural process. To accomplish this, it is necessary to assume a fundamental movement of the cultural process and grasp one of its currents as leading and directing it. But the direction of this predominant movement itself can only ever be grasped perspectivistically. If we are nowadays inclined to refer the predominant dynamism to the development of economic-social forms, to define the standpoints according to the extent to which the groups on which they rest have an interest in the development of the present dominant economic and social form of capitalism, and if we are inclined to distinguish reactionary, conservative, and progressive strata accordingly, it may well be that this identification of the predominant dynamism, as well as the assignment of the leading role to the class that brought about this economic form, is a one-sided view, to be understood existentially and sociologically as arising from the fact that for capitalism (in other words for our era) the centre really has shifted to the social-economic. It is clear that if we were to orient the general dynamics towards the movement of another form, such as religion, and to define the stratum bearing the cultural development on the basis of such a view, the perspectival picture would have quite a different character. There can be no doubt that we are talking about a time-bound moment in our construction of history, and that to this extent it yields a perspectivistic picture of history. But it has a double mark of genuineness and correctness: first, that the social and economic has in fact become existentially the centre of reality for us, and this ensures the genuineness of history seen from this standpoint, and, second, that we do succeed in understanding all cultural material, the totality of spiritual realities, by reference to this line of development. Since we master the total process in this way, if only from a one-sided perspective, a subsequent perspective, organized by reference to a different centre, will equally have to comprehend the same happenings, after appropriate reinterpretations, just as a different aspect of a given object must be understandable from an accurate picture with spatial perspective.

Once one recognizes that every social tendency adopts a different spiritual tendency and that this goes so far that a certain volition to think in a certain way is tied to each particular volition to have the world a certain way, and that this world volition becomes a system to such an extent that it even reproduces itself at the level of double reflexivity – which is to say that even methodology is filled with this volition (as we tried to show in the course of the historical analysis of the first chapter) – then it becomes clear that the historical analysis provided in the first part serves to confirm the results gained by the systematic reflections of the second.

This closes the first circle of our investigations. In the first part we tried to show through historical and sociological analysis how that methodological theory originated in conjunction with a certain thought- and world-volition and how it was related to the totality of the general movement; and in the second we sought to build up this theory from its starting point to its logical systematic conclusions, and thereby to provide the foundations of a theory which was already presupposed by the historical analysis. Thus the final goal of all thinking that maintains that thinking is nothing but one of the organs through which that which has come into being, the spirit, becomes conscious of itself is to recognize its place: the systematic *place* of the historical-philosophical sociological theory in the second part, just as, at the conclusion of the first part, the historical-philosophical *place* of the theory which has just now been expounded. It is not that we believe with Hegel that this brings us to the end of history, but simply that knowledge of the place from which we think must shed a special light on the nature of the ideas presented.

271

Appendix
The sociological genesis of cultural sociology

1 The task of a cultural sociology

While we investigated, in the first of the preceding studies, the coming into being of the constitutive problems of methodology, in its conjunction with the social process as a whole, in an attempt to provide a contribution concerning the sociological connectedness of the theory of method, the second study served to work out a systematic basis for the sociology of thinking which had already been employed in the first study and which will also be employed in the studies to follow. This overlap between the two undertakings is to be explained by the fact that they mutually presuppose one another: if one studies the thinking of an epoch from a sociological standpoint, one must utilize one of the historically developed methods of thinking we considered in our first study. But if one employs such a method, it is necessary to recognize its rootedness in the total process, like a sociologist, and to take that rootedness into account. It is not necessary for us to deal in this place with the philosophical consequences of such reciprocal presupposition between two ways of considering things; we have addressed ourselves in another context to the problem of a philosophy – and indeed of any theory – that takes its own basis in historical presuppositions into account.[63] Here we were interested to take certain systematic problems normally relegated to a single specialized discipline and to view them in an historical-sociological way as well; and, above all, it was our primary aim in the first study to comprehend so far-reaching and abstract a discipline as methodology (it is, after all, second-order reflection) in its conjunction with the sociologically-determined general process.

Studies of ideology are normally only carried up to the furthest point where manifest class interests obtrude into theory and the formation of ideas. But the ultimate goal of the study of ideology must be to grasp the 'total ideological superstructure' in its sociological determination. We do not believe that this can succeed down to the last detail, since personal elements also determine ideas and since the specialized contents also determine the forms of knowledge. But we do believe that the connection with social factors can be pursued up to the ultimate points of departure for abstract theory. It must be possible to show, for example, that a particular type of methodology is, in its systematic point of departure, the expression of a particular thought-volition (*Denkwollen*), and that the latter is part of a particular global volition, which in turn, by virtue of its distinctive stress, can be shown to coincide immediately with a particular social stratum in a particular constellation of the social process. If cultural sociology and the study of ideology are to be more than a collection of occasional observations of thoughts that are determined by interests, then they must use this refined method.

As part of this method we must introduce the concepts of 'immediate interest' (*unmittelbare Interessiertheit*) and 'mediated involvement' (*mittelbares Engagiertsein*). It would be a vulgarization even of the economic interpretation of history to view the entire superstructure in all of its parts as immediately connected with interests deriving from the social base. There are elements of political ideology, economic theory and historical representation that can be shown to be completely determined by interest, which constitutes their ideological character even to the point of conscious falsification. These instances of determination by interest must of course be uncovered and analysed. But the real problem only begins when one goes beyond these points of departure and attempts to show that every political volition is anchored in a global volition and either arises from it (as in the case of conservative ideologies) or itself broadens out from a political and social volition into a global volition (as in the case of rising social strata). In other words, the more we are convinced of a deep *structural* connection between social and cultural process, that is, the more we study the way in which not only individual ideas are sociologically determined but the fundamental construction of world-views is determined by the social process, the less we will emphasize particulars that are determined by interests. Instead we will seek the truth of theories of cultural sociology in the variety of socially determined structural relations.

This requires a theory such as ours, which stresses the complete sociological determination of all thought, including our own, to locate ourselves upon a standpoint according to which all sociological studies can be initiated and carried out *sine ira et studio* so far as possible. Accordingly it must analyse both conservative and pro-

273

gressive thought so searchingly that their functions for the total process can be grasped.

Precisely when the essential perspectivity of all interpretative knowledge is emphasized, it cannot be construed in a superficial manner, as an expression of falsifications or positions in a struggle. The notion of *essential perspectivity* must not serve as the good conscience of a deliberately propagandistic science. It is not a sanction for regarding our knowledge as more genuine, the more we structure our world-view and the course of history in accordance with our own wishes and interests – that is, the more we engage in conscious falsification. These falsifications are not hard to unmask, and this falls within the range of the problem of the authenticity or inauthenticity of a particular perspective. In contrast to this false and superficial view, the theory of perspectivity asserts that even when we take the greatest trouble to eradicate all conscious and unconscious falsifications from our construction of history, it still contains an inevitable residue that expresses the standpoint from which we are regarding history. The sort of rootedness in a standpoint that we find in any falsification undertaken for the sake of propaganda can always be unmasked and avoided. Essential perspectivity, in contrast, is the foundation of order for a historical world-view. This inevitable perspectivity thus resides in the fact that particular historical contents can only become visible, in particular aspects, from particular life centres that occur within this history itself. Only the historical process itself can perhaps bring to the fore all of the possible standpoints from which history can be grasped; and even if we could unite all previous perspectives in a comprehensive construction without once more becoming perspectivistic, we could still possess such a construction only as a relative totality.

In so saying, we are also conceding that at particular moments the historical process allows a synthesis of past intellectual methods and world-views. To see the totality of the historical process, one must recognize the contribution of divergent points of view: progressive thinkers must recognize the role of conservative thought, and vice versa. But even in such syntheses one's own standpoint will eventually manifest itself, primarily in establishing the significance and role of individual strata in the entire historical process and in defining the direction of this process. This is part of the ineradicable rootedness of every mode of thought and of every synthesis that can be made on the basis of and within history. As long as we do not believe in some kind of supra-historical standpoint that suddenly descends upon us, and instead keep firmly in mind that we are trying to understand the historical from a standpoint which is itself historical, we shall not only be incapable of overcoming our point of departure: we shall not want to overcome it. We are only too deeply familiar with the experience that every attempt to jump free of history can succeed only by hypostatizing a partial standpoint. We are much more likely to escape from the dangers of hypostatizing the finite by drawing into consideration the entire available range of things in time than by laying claim to an 'absolute standpoint'.

Accordingly, a sociological theory of culture and of thought is concerned with the study not of the immediate interest of certain strata in particular ideational contents but of their mediated involvement with the entire world-view that pertains to these contents. With regard to their sociological implications, the results of such study will be less striking but more significant. For it will appear that not only do group interests struggle with other group interests in the world, but worlds fight against worlds, and the total cultural process is the result of such existentially rooted conflict. Anyone who has thought through to the end the living implications of a theory, or participated in a social struggle, or even been subject to the pressure of different social strata, will have come to the conclusion that social conflict also has its precipitate in ethical conceptions, modes of thought, fashions, etc. and that these are interconnected. He knows that styles of life and styles of thought are outposts of a struggle that carries on the immediately visible frictions of the economic and political spheres. Every thinker and every existing person feels that certain thoughts imply a commitment to particular volitions in and toward the world. Hence, if the task of cultural sociology and the study of ideology are to be the investigation not only of areas where immediate interest is at work but also of the mediated involvement of social groups, then research methods must unquestionably be refined.

This refinement consists primarily in not limiting the framework of inquiry to the category of means-end relations, of which the concept of 'interest' is one instance. Interest means that a person interested in an ideology sees certain ideas as the best means to an immediate end. But the total sphere of culture cannot be derived from this energizing principle, and can be comprehended by reference to it only in so far as culture is itself a process of nature. If human history were nothing but a struggle for existence, an organic process, conflicting social strata would not need to fight one another with world-views. Under such circumstances, given the presence of spirit to any degree, political ideologies would suffice as supplements to the tools of brutal combat. But it is due to the human sphere beyond physical nature that man also has world-

275

views, in which these ideologies are incorporated, and that the ideologies are effective only because of this deep anchoring. On the other hand, this cultural sphere of world-views is not so free-floating that its starting points are not connected with concrete existence and with the natural and social side of societal life – not in the sense of being immediately determined by it, but rather in the sense of being mediately anchored in it.

This implies, however, that taken as a whole the sociology of culture or study of ideology represents a combination and connection of natural-scientific and social-scientific methods. It joins a natural-scientific theory of the social process with a particularly oriented interpretation of the entire cultural superstructure. While generalizing sociology can grasp the social process with its means, it can at best deal with those ideational contents that are to be seen as immediately determined by this process (i.e., that are definable in accordance with means-end relations). If it wants to get any farther and locate the mediations that anchor these contents in the totality of a world-view, it must have recourse to *Verstehen*, to interpretation. It must use a completely different method, which is related to historical interpretation but not identical with it, to investigate the internal connections of world-view elements.

If we take a closer look, we shall notice that even the first step of interpretation in terms of interest occurs within the framework of interpretative understanding. In this sense Max Weber was right to speak of a *verstehende* sociology. But this purposive-rational interpretation to which sociology is supposed to limit itself occurs within the dimension of grasping other minds and their contents which we have called 'apprehension' and intentionally distinguished from existential, interpretative understanding. True, the grasping of means-end relations is the grasping of meaning, which makes it correct to call it interpretation in the widest sense of that term. Yet it does not occur in the dimension of genuine interpretative understanding, since this understanding projects the subject into a supra-conjunctive relationship by its own intellectual operations, and grasps a general connection on the basis of its own rational presuppositions as does natural-scientific thought in general. The means-end relation is the psychological extrapolation of natural-scientific causality and can be successfully applied only to the extent that the latter operates in reality. It does, in fact, apply to psychic life in the area of immediate interest. As such, this method of explanation is a link between being and spirit, and qualifies for building a bridge, across which being nature can be carried to spirit.

In this way cultural sociology is the boundary-creation of the present, uniting natural-scientific and interpretative, historical inquiry, which previously followed separate paths. That is why this discipline, both in its historical origins and its methodological problems, is one of the most valuable subjects of inquiry. It is thus also understandable that for cultural sociology at this stage the whole problem of conjunctive knowledge and of interpretative understanding, which previously appeared within the conservative tradition alone, is relevant to this union.

2 The emergence of the problem of culture

If we want to give separate consideration, as we have done so far, to the sociologically conditioned emergence and development of the problems that concern us, and then to their systematic meaning and methodological problems, we must first at least roughly sketch the development of cultural sociology. From the foregoing it is clear that the development of those sciences that study the historical process must be a special problem. While the development of the natural sciences is propelled by an immanent logic of things, so that only the way in which they become possible is a sociological problem, each phase of the social sciences is connected in both content and method with the total process.

Quite aside from our own interest in these things, it must appear astonishing in itself that these sciences constituted themselves at such a late date. We can speak of sociology proper as existing only since Saint-Simon and Comte, that is, since the first half of the nineteenth century; and cultural sociology is a completely recent development. How is it that the knowledge of nature progressed quite early to increasingly more complicated questions, whereas the intellectual elucidation of the social process and of cultural evolution occurred only quite late? If anything shows that knowledge is not pure contemplation and the solving of puzzles but rather originates in action and in connection with action, it is this. The social process only becomes recognizable when people try to affect it and confront it with their interests. The contemplative desk-work of theory can only take the results gained in struggle and systematize them, order them according to various points of view, and think things out from such points of departure. It cannot, out of its own activity, deduce one problem from another. And even this desk-work becomes productive only when it lives, at least in a mediated fashion, within one of the stresses that animates its historical surroundings. A particular manner of life is required for knowledge; and it is not the willing subject itself that knows, but rather collective volitions that know in and through the knowing

277

subject. Hence if one wants to understand the emergence of cultural sociology out of the total process, one must investigate it in several directions, according to the complexity of its intellectual structure. Clearly, the possibility of a cultural sociology is connected (1) with the fact of culture itself becoming problematic, (2) with the emergence of a science that makes the social process as such the object of investigation, and (3) with the genesis of a specific method and new orientation to cultural formations, which found its scientific expression in the study of ideology. None of the three originates within science; instead they codify something produced by life itself. It is appropriate to our dynamic conception to endeavour to locate the origins and development of these factors in the total process.

The problem of culture did not arise because of someone's ratiocination, but because culture itself became problematic. Culture cannot become problematic as such as long as it remains a culture of a primary sort. Only in the stage of cultivated culture does the possibility of its becoming problematic appear. In the first stage all meanings are grasped as substantial realities. They are part of the immutable realm of nature and of the facts of fate that cannot be changed. People relate to them as unproblematical, adapting to them as one adapts to death and the passage of time. As witnessed by technical thinking, it is at most possible to attend to the existing and immutable laws of nature and attempt to exploit them in one's own interest. This is why one of the most established methods of conservative thought is to consider the social and cultural poverty of the oppressed as belonging to the order of the universe and as part of the nature of things. The critique and problematization of culture is possible only at the stage where human beings become conscious that culture is to be ascribed not so much to nature as to the sphere of works; that is, a sphere that people do not simply inhabit and adapt to but form themselves. It is interesting that the passive reception of culture as Being ultimately turned into its opposite, so that culture was seen essentially as a 'work', as an 'individual creation'. This was the case in the first period of the Enlightenment, dominated by the theory of the wise and clever legislator, where institutions and all other factors that we now regard as collective creations were treated as works. This period lacked a phenomenology that could adequately distinguish among being, forms, and the third group of phenomena that lies between them and whose attribute is collective growth. When confronted by false or too narrow alternatives, people always proceed from the failure of one extreme to the choice of the other. That is why here the static, ontological view of spiritual realities was followed by a view of spirit as works. This extreme individualization corresponds to the spiritual attitude of the beginnings of the modern period and of capitalism, and is an orientation that impeded the discovery of the actual characteristics of the social sphere, since it interpreted society as the sum of all individuals. Atomistic thinking, the tendency to reduce everything to individuals, and the 'work conception' belong together, for they are aspects of the same global volition and express the striving for individual freedom.*

---

* *Editors' note:* Here the manuscript ends abruptly. The last, incomplete sentence is: 'This emancipation – the goal of those first entrepreneurial spirits who wanted to burst asunder the organic formations of the Middle Ages – did not lead, as we know, to the actual atomization of society, since capitalism itself created a new "order", but it . . .' Mannheim adds: 'Here follows the analysis of Rousseau's critique of culture, etc.'

Notes

1 A valuable account of the development of these sciences and their appropriate methodology can be found in Ernst Cassirer, 'Die Entstehung der exakten Wissenschaft' (The Emergence of Exact Science), in his *Das Erkenntnisproblem in der Philosophie und Wissenschaft der neueren Zeit* (The Problem of Knowledge in the Philosophy and Science of the Early Modern Age), vol. 1, Berlin: Bruno Cassirer, 1911, pp. 314ff.

2 *Ibid.*, p. 317.

3 On this cf. Erich Frank, *Plato und die sogenannten Pythagoräer* (Plato and the So-called Pythagoreans), Halle a.d.S.: M. Niemeyer, 1923, p. 143.

4 *Ibid.*, p. 147.

5 A fine characterization of the Aristotelian view of the world is contained in Werner Jaeger, *Aristoteles: Grundlegung einer Geschichte seiner Entwicklung*, Berlin: Weidmannsche Buchhandlung, 1923. [*Aristotle: Fundamentals of the History of His Development*, trans. Richard Robinson, Oxford: Clarendon Press, 1934.]

6 On anthropomorphism in the philosophy of nature see Karl Joël, *Der Ursprung der Naturphilosophie aus dem Geiste der Mystik* (The Birth of the Philosophy of Nature out of the Spirit of Mysticism), Jena: Diederichs, 1906.

7 Cf. Ernst Cassirer, *op. cit.*, pp. 345 and 353ff.

8 All such investigations doubtless go back to Marx's *Capital*, and especially to the chapter in volume I entitled 'The Fetishism of Commodities'. Simmel, for instance, has richly characterized the change in the manner of experiencing the objects of the world which comes into the world with the money-form (*Philosophy of Money*). But in doing so he took the capitalist money-form quite unhistorically out of its capitalist context and imputed the characteristic structural change to 'money as such'. Sombart and Max Weber, among others, have also spoken of a progressive process of rationalization which reaches its cul-

mination in the modern age, but they have still not brought into view what is most essential, that there have been rationalisms in earlier times and also monetary calculation, but that the category of commodity became the universal category forming a whole presentation of the world peculiarly in modern capitalism and only there. This had already been seen by Marx and has been elaborated by Lukács in his essay, 'Reification and the Consciousness of the Proletariat' (1923) in *History and Class Consciousness*, London: Merlin, 1971.

9 'No matter, then, what we may think of the parts played by the different classes of people themselves in this society (in the Middle Ages – K.M.), the social relations between individuals in the performance of their labour appear at all events as their own mutual personal relations, and are not disguised under the shape of social relations between the products of labour' (Marx, *Kapital*, vol. 1, 7th edn, Hamburg: Otto Meissner, 1906, p. 44). [Here quoted from *Capital*, vol. 1, New York: International Publishers, 1967, p. 77.]

10 This is only to claim that there is present a sociological attribution-relationship between the modern striving for universally valid truths and the democratic principle, but not that the thought of universal validity could not occur historically in other social settings as well.

11 In the next chapter we shall have the opportunity, primarily in the introductory parts of each section, to pursue in detail the differences of principle between the two methodologies.

12 Cf. Werner Sombart, *Der moderne Kapitalismus* (Modern Capitalism), 2nd edn, Leipzig: Duncker & Humblot, 1916.

13 The advantage of looking at knowledge from the point of view of existence is active in Kierkegaard and in the representatives of the phenomenological school. Our essay in the sociological theory of thinking emerges from this tendency, taken to its logical conclusion in that one proceeds from a social existence which is dynamically changing and not from the existence of the individual.

14 On this see Rudolf Unger, *Hamann und die Aufklärung: Studien zur Vorgeschichte des romantischen Geistes im 18. Jahrhundert* (Hamann and the Enlightenment: Studies on the Prehistory of the Romantic Spirit in the 18th Century), Jena: Diederichs, 1911. See also Josef Nadler, *Die Berliner Romantik, 1800–1814* (Berlin Romanticism), Berlin: E. Reiss, 1921. On the strata supporting the Romantic movement see Gottfried Salomon, *Das Mittelalter als Ideal in der Romantik* (The Middle Ages as Ideal in Romanticism), Munich: Drei Masken Verlag, 1922; and also Franz Oppenheimer, *System der Soziologie* (System of Sociology), vol. 1, Jena: Fischer, 1922, pp. 3ff.

15 Oppenheimer recommends the expression 'spiritual counter-revolution' instead of 'Romanticism' and wants to refer its origins, from the standpoint of semantic genealogy, to Tarde's principle of 'imitation par opposition'. There would be nothing objectionable in this if it were not that Romanticism contains, in addition to mere negation, something positive distinctly its own; namely, the accumulated positive matter of sunken epochs (as Oppenheimer recognizes, by the way).

We must therefore distinguish two factors in Romanticism: one factor by virtue of which it appears as a spiritual counter-movement against the Enlightenment (on all these points it is conditioned by the opponent against which it struggles), and, second, its function as heir to a style of thinking and living repressed by capitalism.

16 Gottfried Salomon (*op. cit.*, p. 15) has pregnantly epitomized the lifeline of Romanticism as follows: 'Romanticism is a movement that parallels the Reformation and Renaissance. It grows in religious soil, i.e. Pietism and Mysticism, becomes aesthetic and political rationalism and terminates in Catholicism, which like Classicism is an international phenomenon. Belief in the mission of the German spirit led to drawing on the Middle Ages as an apology for the past. Here, too, the idea of a rebirth, a "renaissance", is linked with Restoration and reaction.'

17 Modern phenomenology amalgamates two layers: a rationalistic systematics, which asserts itself in the ontology, and an irrationalist, fundamental attitude, which comes into effect in the distinctively phenomenological portions.

18 Where the sociological sources for this methodologism may be located cannot be readily established beyond doubt. One can make a beginning by recourse to contributing factors and thus derive the methodological attitude from the predominance of the technical spirit, whose basic formula is 'how is it made'. On the other hand, this methodologism also doubtless flows from the spirit of positivism, whose primary characteristic is the decomposing of comprehensive science into distinct disciplines, and which cannot allow philosophy to count as more than a science of method. It is doubtless superfluous to emphasize that the same spirit rules Kantianism in this respect as does Positivism, inasmuch as it is also familiar with the dualism between particular disciplines, on the one hand, and logic (in the form of theory of knowledge and methodology) on the other. We have come far enough to be able to discern the contours of this positivist-methodological spirit, but not so far as to be able to transcend this stage without further ado, at a single 'leap'.

19 Cf. Troeltsch, *Der Historismus und seine Probleme* (Historicism and its Problems), Tübingen: J. C. B. Mohr (Paul Siebeck), 1922, pp. 743ff.

20 Cf. Gottfried Salomon, *op. cit.*, p. 111.

21 In so far as there is still calculation present, it is not exploration of general regularities but seizing hold of a line of destiny.

22 Max Weber, Alfred Weber, Max Scheler *et al.* all merely modify this basic scheme and are dependent on it, even if they do proclaim the occasional or absolute priority of the ideal over the substructural.

23 In contrast to a product of knowledge tied to a community.

24 Let us adduce as an example that the empiricism of the English bourgeois world grew out of the nominalism of Franciscan philosophy. It thus adopted a mode of thought that had already come into existence in the Middle Ages, and developed it in the direction of the new bourgeois will to the world. On this example, cf. Paul Honigsheim, 'Zur

Soziologie der mittelalterlichen Scholastik: Die soziologische Bedeu-
tung der nominalistischen Philosophie' (On the Sociology of Medieval
Scholasticism: The Sociological Significance of Nominalist Philosophy), in *Hauptprobleme der Soziologie: Erinnerungsgabe für Max
Weber*, ed. Melchior Palyi, Munich and Leipzig: Duncker & Humblot,
1923. Further, Otto Bauer, 'Das Weltbild des Kapitalismus' (Capitalism's Image of the World), in *Der lebendige Marxismus*, Festschrift for
Karl Kautsky on the occasion of his 70th birthday, section IV, p. 417,
Jena: Thüringer Verlagsanstalt, 1924.

25 This was probably first consciously pursued by Max Weber, who
already spoke of a *verstehende* sociology. Cf. 'Über einige Kategorien
der verstehenden Soziologie' (On Some Categories of Interpretative
Sociology), in *Gesammelte Aufsätze zur Wissenschaftslehre*, Tübing-
en: J. C. B. Mohr, 1922.

26 For the Kantian epistemology the route to proceeding from the existential subject-object relationship is blocked because it wants to build
up epistemology apart from ontology (metaphysics). For it the
subject–object relation as an existent relation between existing subjects and things is not at all given as a point of departure, and it would
call such a standpoint 'dogmatism'. To this we must reply that the
attempt to construct an epistemology without ontological presuppositions must today be regarded as having already failed. Epistemology
itself presupposes correlations (the concept of knowledge of something, the subject–object relation, the opposition of immanence and
transcendence) which, no matter how much one sublimates them, are
of ontological origin. In its very name, the philosophy of immanence
presupposes an ontological distinction between consciousness and
non-consciousness, even if it stands in an agnostic relation to the latter.
Only when the route that has been blocked by these prejudices is
opened does one gain the courage to start out from the epistemic relation as an existential one. And only then is it revealed that Kantianism's immanent concept of knowledge was nothing other than a
hypostatization of a specific ontological knowing-relationship. On the
primacy of ontology cf. my 'Strukturanalyse der Erkenntnistheorie',
supplement to *Kant-Studien*, no. 57, Berlin, 1922. ['Structural Analysis
of Epistemology', in Paul Kecskemeti, ed., *Essays on Sociology and
Social Psychology*, London: Routledge & Kegan Paul, 1953.]

27 The idea that the experience of another self can be explicated only
through the indirect paths of a theory of empathy and analogical
inference derives from the false assumption, explicable by the history
of thought, that one must always proceed from a monadically closed,
'windowless' individual consciousness, and that a connection, an immediate contagion between 'outer' and 'inner' worlds could be conceived only as proceeding through the organs of sense. This
assumption corresponds to an experience of the world in which man
and the world are completely alienated from the subject and it is believed that these can only be 'thought'. Addressing the question of the
possibility of understanding the other while starting from this point, it

was necessary to take the most convoluted detours in order to deny the most self-evident fact: namely, the fact of psychic contagion; and then to replace it by a theory of empathy and of reasoning by analogy.

Against this, the following must be objected: although it is also possible to 'think' the other person and his characteristics, this thinking is always only a partial aspect of *having* the *vis-à-vis*. This psychic having of the alien soul is structured similarly to the sensory having of the bodily attributes of the *vis-à-vis*. It has all the characteristics of unmediated contagion, since the soul of the *vis-à-vis*, in its qualitative richness, is most suddenly present, incomparable and unique. That the theory of empathy and analogical inferences from our own soul cannot possibly be correct is shown by the circumstance that what could emerge as a finding along this route could provide us with anything at all except the alien soul as something incomparable and unique, in its otherness, as it is wholly different from us. This fact of the qualitative distinctness of the other self not being gained by empathy or reached by analogy from our own inner world can be most strikingly shown where it is a question of being affected erotically. Surely no one would wish to assert that when a man experiences the specific 'fascination' of a woman, he is experiencing this 'ontic aspect' of her by means of empathy based on his own qualities or by analogy to the contents of his own psyche. It cannot be doubted that here the psychic-erotic quality of the other affects us in just as immediate a way as do the sense impressions in which it is admittedly embedded.

In these matters, we are in agreement with Scheler's theory, without sharing his contention that there exist what may be likened to superpersonal psychic contents. We see in the latter assertion of Scheler an unverifiable metaphysical assumption, which, even as a hypothesis, would needlessly complicate the explanation of our understanding of the other. On this, cf. Max Scheler, 'Über den Grund zur Annahme des fremden Ich', published as an appendix to *Zur Phänomenologie und Theorie der Sympathiegefühle und von Liebe und Haß*, Halle, a.d.S.: M. Niemeyer, 1913. ['Other Minds', part three of *The Nature of Sympathy*, trans. Peter Heath, London: Routledge & Kegan Paul, 1954.]

28 On similar problems, cf. Gerda Walther: 'Zur Ontologie der sozialen Gemeinschaften' (On the Ontology of Social Collectivities) in *Jahrbuch für Philosophie und phänomenologische Forschung*, vol. 6, 1923, pp. 1–158.

29 'The connection of the thing (or person) with me I therefore call "conjunction", and the validity of this knowing "conjunctive". As we now see, it is historical, personal, and living. What distinguishes this knowledge, however, is not objectivity but conjunctivity' (Victor Freiherr von Weizsäcker, 'Das Antilogische', in *Psychologische Forschung*, III (1923), p. 302).

30 We often have a much less unitary image of ourselves than we do of our fellow men, and this not only because we know our own characteristics better than those of others (so that unification of the image is already in

and of itself more complicated) but also because here the perspectivity (which is the only thing that allows us to draw sharp and unambiguous contours) is constantly being dialectically superseded. We let ourselves be influenced by the various images that our fellow men have of us, suspend the validity of the one and then again of the other image, waver as to the principles in accordance with which we ought to measure ourselves, and do not have – as language spontaneously expresses it – the 'necessary distance'. If it nevertheless happens that an image does emerge, it is because, despite all difficulties, we effect a relationship to ourselves in the second person (and one does, after all, address oneself in the second person when engaged in self-reflection), and 'settling accounts with oneself' is nothing but securing the most fruitful distance from our own life.

31 Weizsäcker, 'Das Antilogische', *loc. cit*

32 A term used by Weizsäcker.

33 An expression of Adolf Reinach in 'Die apriorischen Grundlagen des bürgerlichen Rechtes', in *Jahrbuch für Philosophie und phänomenologische Forschung*, vol. 1, part I, 1913, pp. 685–847.

34 The frequently re-emerging idea of a 'universal mathematics' in Descartes, Malebranche and Leibniz points in the direction of this endeavour. Its history can be read in Cassirer, *Das Erkenntnisproblem in der Philosophie und Wissenschaft der neueren Zeit*, vol. 1, Berlin: Bruno Cassirer, 1911, pp. 446ff., 563ff.; vol. II, pp. 138ff. We should like to give here a citation from Malebranche also cited by Cassirer:

> 'Of these three sorts of truth (between ideas, between things and their ideas, and between things alone) those that exist between ideas are eternal and immutable and, because of their immutability, they are also the rules and measures of all others. For every rule or measure must be invariable' (Cassirer, 1, pp. 564).

35 A meaning that is individual in two respects: in that it dialectically suspends and preserves the general abstract meaning, and in that it designates things according to the way and in the particulars in which they exist for the specific community.

36 See Lucien Lévy-Bruhl, *Das Denken der Naturvölker*, translated from the French [*Les fonctions mentales dans les sociétés inférieures*, Paris: F. Alcan 1910] by Paul Friedländer; edited and introduced by Wilhelm Jerusalem, Braumüller: Vienna-Leipzig, 1921, pp. 148 ff. [*How Natives Think*, trans. Lilian A. Clare, New York: Alfred A. Knopf, 1925.] See also Ernst Cassirer, *Die Begriffsform im mythischen Denken* (The Form of the Concept in Mythical Thought), Leipzig-Berlin: B. G. Teubner, 1922, I, p. 20.

37 At the instance of this example it is demonstrable that concepts accordingly not only mean different things, as the existential basis from which they arise varies, but also that the direction which objectification enters upon may be diverse. (We have already referred to this fact, without being able to demonstrate it. See p. 152 of this manuscript.) If objectification takes the direction of fitting what is experienced into a

timeless system of concepts, then the formative principle of the concept-formation is moving in the direction of an ideal in whose utopian structure all perspectivity would be eliminated, as on a map. This way of removing what is learned from experience out of the stream of experience is completely different from the one we have just discussed. The latter would also, to be sure, overcome the transient and flowing within all experience, but it essays objectification in a direction in which relatedness to the unique experience and its communally rooted embeddedness is preserved. Let this be considered evidence for the assertion that concepts can differ for a variety of reasons.

38 Here experience is thus not only embedded in an existential relation, but the experience, the knowledge itself creates an existential change. Theory and praxis are thus – as is quite clear here – not so different in their contours as one tends to think.

39 On the rootedness of every institution and every concept in its own experiential space, and on the historian's task of grasping these formations in terms of the historical experiential space in which they arose, cf. the fine introduction by Fustel de Coulanges to his *La cité antique*, Paris: Hachette, 1919, 25th edn: 'We cannot fail to deceive ourselves about these ancient peoples when we look at them through the opinions and facts of our time.'

40 Max Weber has already attempted to articulate the distinctive nature of historical concept-formation in contrast to the general concept, by reference to the ideal type. See the second part of his essay, 'Die Objektivität sozialwissenschaftlicher und sozialpolitischer Erkenntnis', now reprinted in his *Gesammelte Aufsätze zur Wissenschaftslehre*, Tübingen: J. C. B. Mohr, 1922. [' "Objectivity" in Social Science', in E. A. Shils and H. A. Finch (eds), *Max Weber on the Methodology of the Social Sciences*, Chicago: The Free Press, 1949.] Alexander von Schelting, in his essay 'Die logische Theorie der historischen Kulturwissenschaft von Max Weber und im besonderen sein Begriff des Idealtypus', in *Archiv für Sozialwissenschaft und Sozialpolitik* 49, 3 (1922), has pointed out that the apparently unitary concept of the ideal type confounds two types of concept. 'Medieval city economy' and 'bureaucracy' are not ideal types in the same sense; and von Schelting would only admit the latter kind of concept as a genuine ideal type (pp. 74–50). All of these studies are already moving in the direction of working out the distinctive nature of historical concepts and striving to determine their difference from general concepts, but they are limited by the fact that they are not familiar with the sociological point of view in methodological analysis and are consequently bound to pass over the essential difference between historical and general concepts. Only the essential connectedness of every historical phenomenon (and thus the concepts that grasp them as well) with a specific historical conjunctive experiential space constitutes the essential characteristic of these concepts and lets us distinguish them from all trans-conjunctive generalizations.

41 'Das Antilogische', p. 303.

42 See Weizsäcker, *ibid*. It is to show the obverse of this state of affairs when Max Adler points out that man has the capacity to form society by virtue of 'consciousness as such' present in him, and his ability to create universally valid and communicable propositions. See his *Das Soziologische in Kants Erkenntniskritik* (The Sociological Element in Kant's Critique of Knowledge), Vienna: Verlag der Wiener Volksbuchhandlung, 1924. We shall not go into the question of whether Adler's sociological revision of Kantian doctrine is correct as interpretation. It is correct, in any case, to say that only the type of thinking that we have characterized as formed by construction and generalizing (and which we do not at all intend to demean but to complement with the other type of thinking pertaining to conjunctive experience, which has been barely noticed until now) makes possible that communication out of which humanity can arise as a society. But if 'universal validity' makes the formation of society possible, the formation of community arises only to the extent and degree that conjunctive attachment takes place. The farther the latter process progresses, with an increasing number of groups and peoples uniting in an historical experiential community, the closer humanity approaches the stage of a universal community which is more than a generalized society.

43 Ferdinand Tönnies, *Gemeinschaft und Gesellschaft: Grundbegriffe der reinen Soziologie*, 3rd rev. edn, Berlin: K. Curtius, 1920. [*Community and Society*, trans. and ed. Charles P. Loomis, New York: Harper & Row, 1957.]

44 Karl Mannheim, 'Historismus', in *Archiv für Sozialwissenschaft und Sozialpolitik*, 52, 1 (1924), in particular p. 39. See also Alfred Weber, 'Prinzipielles zur Kultursoziologie' (Fundamental Considerations on Cultural Sociology), in *Archiv für Sozialwissenschaft und Sozialpolitik*, 47, 1 (1920).

45 Emile Durkheim, *Die Methode der Soziologie*. [*Les règles de la méthode sociologique*, Paris: F. Alcan, 1895.] Philosophische-soziologische Bücherei, vol. 5, Leipzig: A. Kröner, 1908. [*The Rules of Sociological Method*, 8th edn, trans. Sarah A. Solovay and John H. Miller; ed. George E. G. Catlin, Chicago: University of Chicago Press, 1938.]

46 *Ibid*.

47 Stoltenberg calls knowledge of objects of this kind psychosociology. Cf. Hans Lorenz Stoltenberg, part 2 of his *Sozialpsychologie: 'Seelgrupplehre'*, Berlin: K. Curtius, 1922. See the preface.

48 In the terminology of object theory (as developed by Meinong and Husserl), 'object' (*Gegenstand*) does not mean a thing in space but anything about which one can make correct statements, which is to say anything that can become the subject of a proposition.

49 On the distinction between expressive and documentary meaning see the more detailed exposition in Karl Mannheim, 'Beiträge zur Theorie der Weltanschauungs-Interpretation', in *Jahrbuch für Kunstgeschichte*, I, (XV), 1921–2. ['On the Interpretation of *Weltanschauung*', in *Essays on the Sociology of Knowledge*, ed. Paul

Kecskemeti, London: Routledge & Kegan Paul, 1952.]

50 Post-Kantian German idealism has in view the first kind of misperception when it makes of consciousness as such a metaphysical entity; Max Adler's work is typical of the second kind of misinterpretation.

51 See p. 158 of this book.

52 This discussion of the concept of the state is based on a discussion in Professor Alfred Weber's seminar.

53 *Rahmengruppe* ('frame-work group') is an expression of Oppenheimer's which he derived from Simmel. Cf. Franz Oppenheimer, *System der Soziologie*, vol. 1, p. 465.

54 Max Adler, *Marxistische Probleme, Beiträge zur Theorie der materialistischen Geschichtsauffassung und Dialektik* (Marxist Problems, Contributions to a Theory of the Materialist View of History and Dialectics), Stuttgart: T. H. W. Dietz, 1913.

55 Max Weber, *Wirtschaft und Gesellschaft*, Tübingen: J. C. B. Mohr, 1922. [*Economy and Society: An Outline of Interpretive Sociology*, ed. Guenther Roth and Claus Wittich; trans. Ephraim Fischoff *et al.*, New York: Bedminster Press, 1968.]

56 Riegl also speaks of an individual's artistic volition, by which he means that unconsciously developing unity in the direction of which the constructions of a creative individual move. On this cf. Erwin Panofsky, 'Der Begriff des Kunstwollens' (The Concept of Artistic Volition), in *Zeitschrift für Ästhetik und allgemeine Kunstwissenschaft*, XIV, 4.

57 Georg Simmel, *Soziologie, Untersuchungen über die Formen der Vergesellschaftung* (Sociology, Studies of the Forms of Sociation), Leipzig: Duncker & Humblot, 1908.

58 The contagious character of this understanding is not affected by the fact that it may be illusory in a particular instance. To the contrary: illusion is a phenomenon in the realm of perception that corresponds to error in the realm of thought. See Sobeler, *Idole der Selbsterkenntnis* (Idols of Self-Knowledge). [Cannot be bibliographically located. The Editors.]

59 Edmund Husserl, *Logische Untersuchungen*, 2nd rev., Halle a.d.S.: M. Niemeyer, 1913, vol. 2, 1st Investigation. [*Logical Investigations*, trans. J. N. Findlay, vol. 2, London: Routledge & Kegan Paul, 1970.]

60 For a more detailed presentation see Karl Mannheim, 'Historismus'.

61 Heinrich Schurtz, *Altersklassen und Männerbünde. Eine Darstellung der Grundformen der Gesellschaft* (Age-groups and Men's Societies: An Exposition of the Primary Forms of Society), Berlin: G. Reimer, 1902.

62 See my essay 'Historismus' and Alfred Weber's essay 'Prinzipielles zur Kultursoziologie'.

63 'Historismus'.

Index

Note: Italicized page numbers indicate references contained in the note sections. References appearing throughout the text, e.g. interpretation, cultural sociology, types of sociology, have not been included in the index.

289

Routledge Social Science Series

Routledge & Kegan Paul
London and New York

Contents

*Authors wishing to submit manuscripts for any series
in this catalogue should send them to the Social Science Editor,
Routledge & Kegan Paul Ltd, 11 New Fetter Lane,
London, EC4P 4EE.*
● *Books so marked are available in paperback also.*
○ *Books so marked are available in paperback only.*
*All books are in metric Demy 8vo format (216 × 138mm approx.)
unless otherwise stated.*

International Library of Sociology
General Editor John Rex

GENERAL SOCIOLOGY

Alexander, J. Theoretical Logic in Sociology.
Volume 1: Positivism, Presuppositions and Current Controversies. *234 pp.*
Volume 2: The Antinomies of Classical Thought: *Marx and Durkheim.*
Volume 3: The Classical Attempt at Theoretical Synthesis: *Max Weber.*
Volume 4: The Modern Reconstruction of Classical Thought: *Talcott Parsons.*
Barnsley, J. H. The Social Reality of Ethics. *464 pp.*
Brown,. Robert. Explanation in Social Science. *208 pp.*
● Rules and Laws in Sociology. *192 pp.*
Bruford, W. H. Chekhov and His Russia. *A Sociological Study. 244 pp.*
Burton, F. and **Carlen, P.** Official Discourse. *On Discourse Analysis, Government Publications, Ideology. 160 pp.*
Cain, Maureen E. Society and the Policeman's Role. *326 pp.*
● **Fletcher, Colin.** Beneath the Surface. *An Account of Three Styles of Sociological Research. 221 pp.*
Gibson, Quentin. The Logic of Social Enquiry. *240 pp.*
Glassner, B. Essential Interactionism. *208 pp.*
Glucksmann, M. Structuralist Analysis in Contemporary Social Thought. *212 pp.*
Gurvitch, Georges. Sociology of Law. *Foreword by Roscoe Pound. 264 pp.*
Hinkle, R. Founding Theory of American Sociology 1881–1913. *376 pp.*
Homans, George C. Sentiments and Activities. *336 pp.*
Johnson, Harry M. Sociology: *A Systematic Introduction. Foreword by Robert K. Merton. 710 pp.*
● **Keat, Russell** and **Urry, John.** Social Theory as Science. *Second Edition. 278 pp.*
Mannheim, Karl. Essays on Sociology and Social Psychology. *Edited by Paul Keckskemeti. With Editorial Note by Adolph Lowe. 344 pp.*
Martindale, Don. The Nature and Types of Sociological Theory. *292 pp.*
● **Maus, Heinz.** A Short History of Sociology. *234 pp.*
Merquior, J. G. Rousseau and Weber. *A Study in the Theory of Legitimacy. 240 pp.*
Myrdal, Gunnar. Value in Social Theory: *A Collection of Essays on Methodology. Edited by Paul Streeten. 332 pp.*
Ogburn, William F. and **Nimkoff, Meyer F.** A Handbook of Sociology. *Preface by Karl Mannheim. 656 pp. 46 figures. 35 tables.*
Parsons, Talcott and **Smelser, Neil J.** Economy and Society: *A Study in the Integration of Economic and Social Theory. 362 pp.*
Payne, G., Dingwall, R., Payne, J. and **Carter, M.** Sociology and Social Research. *336 pp.*
Podgórecki, A. Practical Social Sciences. *144 pp.*
Podgórecki, A. and **Łos, M.** Multidimensional Sociology. *268 pp.*
Raffel, S. Matters of Fact. *A Sociological Inquiry. 152 pp.*
● **Rex, John.** Key Problems of Sociological Theory. *220 pp.*
Sociology and the Demystification of the Modern World. *282 pp.*
● **Rex, John.** (Ed.) Approaches to Sociology. *Contributions by Peter Abell, Frank Bechhofer, Basil Bernstein, Ronald Fletcher, David Frisby, Miriam Glucksmann, Peter Lassman, Herminio Martins, John Rex, Roland Robertson, John Westergaard and Jock Young. 302 pp.*
Rigby, A. Alternative Realities. *352 pp.*
Roche, M. Phenomenology, Language and the Social Sciences. *374 pp.*
Sahay, A. Sociological Analysis. *220 pp.*
Strasser, Hermann. The Normative Structure of Sociology. *Conservative and Emancipatory Themes in Social Thought. 286 pp.*

SOCIAL PSYCHOLOGY

Bagley, Christopher. The Social Psychology of the Epileptic Child. *320 pp.*

Brittan, Arthur. Meanings and Situations. *224 pp.*

Carroll, J. Break-Out from the Crystal Palace. *200 pp.*

● **Fleming, C. M.** Adolescence: Its Social Psychology. *With an Introduction to recent findings from the fields of Anthropology, Physiology, Medicine, Psychometrics and Sociometry. 288 pp.*

● The Social Psychology of Education: *An Introduction and Guide to Its Study. 136 pp.*

Linton, Ralph. The Cultural Background of Personality. *132 pp.*

● **Mayo, Elton.** The Social Problems of an Industrial Civilization. *With an Appendix on the Political Problem. 180 pp.*

Ottaway, A. K. C. Learning Through Group Experience. *176 pp.*

Plummer, Ken. Sexual Stigma. *An Interactionist Account. 254 pp.*

● **Rose, Arnold M.** (Ed.) Human Behaviour and Social Processes: *an Interactionist Approach. Contributions by Arnold M. Rose, Ralph H. Turner, Anselm Strauss, Everett C. Hughes, E. Franklin Frazier, Howard S. Becker et al. 696 pp.*

Smelser, Neil J. Theory of Collective Behaviour. *448 pp.*

Stephenson, Geoffrey M. The Development of Conscience. *128 pp.*

Young, Kimball. Handbook of Social Psychology. *658 pp. 16 figures. 10 tables.*

SOCIOLOGY OF THE FAMILY

Bell, Colin R. Middle Class Families: *Social and Geographical Mobility. 224 pp.*

Burton, Lindy. Vulnerable Children. *272 pp.*

Gavron, Hannah. The Captive Wife: *Conflicts of Household Mothers. 190 pp.*

George, Victor and **Wilding, Paul.** Motherless Families. *248 pp.*

Klein, Josephine. Samples from English Cultures.
   1. Three Preliminary Studies and Aspects of Adult Life in England. *447 pp.*
   2. Child-Rearing Practices and Index. *247 pp.*

Klein, Viola. The Feminine Character. *History of an Ideology. 244 pp.*

McWhinnie, Alexina M. Adopted Children. *How They Grow Up. 304 pp.*

● **Morgan, D. H. J.** Social Theory and the Family. *188 pp.*

● **Myrdal, Alva** and **Klein, Viola.** Women's Two Roles: *Home and Work. 238 pp. 27 tables.*

Parsons, Talcott and **Bales, Robert F.** Family: Socialization and Interaction Process. *In collaboration with James Olds, Morris Zelditch and Philip E. Slater. 456 pp. 50 figures and tables.*

SOCIAL SERVICES

Bastide, Roger. The Sociology of Mental Disorder. *Translated from the French by Jean McNeil. 260 pp.*

Carlebach, Julius. Caring for Children in Trouble. *266 pp.*

George, Victor. Foster Care. *Theory and Practice. 234 pp.*
   Social Security: *Beveridge and After. 258 pp.*

George, V. and **Wilding, P.** Motherless Families. *248 pp.*

● **Goetschius, George W.** Working with Community Groups. *256 pp.*

Goetschius, George W. and **Tash, Joan.** Working with Unattached Youth. *416 pp.*

Heywood, Jean S. Children in Care. *The Development of the Service for the Deprived Child. Third revised edition. 284 pp.*

King, Roy D., Ranes, Norma V. and **Tizard, Jack.** Patterns of Residential Care. *356 pp.*

Leigh, John. Young People and Leisure. *256 pp.*

● **Mays, John.** (Ed.) Penelope Hall's Social Services of England and Wales. *368 pp.*

Morris Mary. Voluntary Work and the Welfare State. *300 pp.*

Nokes. P. L. The Professional Task in Welfare Practice. *152 pp.*

Timms, Noel. Psychiatric Social Work in Great Britain (1939–1962). *280 pp.*

●   Social Casework: *Principles and Practice. 256 pp.*

SOCIOLOGY OF EDUCATION

Banks, Olive. Parity and Prestige in English Secondary Education: a Study in Educational Sociology. *272 pp.*

● **Blyth, W. A. L.** English Primary Education. *A Sociological Description.* 2. Background. *168 pp.*

Collier, K. G. The Social Purposes of Education: *Personal and Social Values in Education. 268 pp.*

Evans, K. M. Sociometry and Education. *158 pp.*

● **Ford, Julienne.** Social Class and the Comprehensive School. *192 pp.*

Foster, P. J. Education and Social Change in Ghana. *336 pp. 3 maps.*

Fraser, W. R. Education and Society in Modern France. *150 pp.*

Grace, Gerald R. Role Conflict and the Teacher. *150 pp.*

Hans, Nicholas. New Trends in Education in the Eighteenth Century. *278 pp. 19 tables.*

●   Comparative Education: *A Study of Educational Factors and Traditions. 360 pp.*

● **Hargreaves, David.** Interpersonal Relations and Education. *432 pp.*

●   Social Relations in a Secondary School. *240 pp.*

  School Organization and Pupil Involvement. *A Study of Secondary Schools.*

● **Mannheim, Karl** and **Stewart, W. A. C.** An Introduction to the Sociology of Education. *206 pp.*

● **Musgrove, F.** Youth and the Social Order. *176 pp.*

● **Ottaway, A. K. C.** Education and Society: An Introduction to the Sociology of Education. *With an Introduction by W. O. Lester Smith. 212 pp.*

Peers, Robert. Adult Education: *A Comparative Study. Revised edition. 398 pp.*

Stratta, Erica. The Education of Borstal Boys. *A Study of their Educational Experiences prior to, and during, Borstal Training. 256 pp.*

● **Taylor, P. H., Reid, W. A.** and **Holley, B. J.** The English Sixth Form. *A Case Study in Curriculum Research. 198 pp.*

SOCIOLOGY OF CULTURE

● **Eppel, E. M.** and **M.** Adolescents and Morality: *A Study of some Moral Values and Dilemmas of Working Adolescents in the Context of a changing Climate of Opinion. Foreword by W. J. H. Sprott. 268 pp. 39 tables.*

● **Fromm, Erich.** The Fear of Freedom. *286 pp.*

●   The Sane Society. *400 pp.*

Johnson, L. The Cultural Critics. *From Matthew Arnold to Raymond Williams. 233 pp.*

Mannheim, Karl. Essays on the Sociology of Culture. *Edited by Ernst Mannheim in co-operation with Paul Kecskemeti. Editorial Note by Adolph Lowe. 280 pp.*

  Structures of Thinking. *Edited by David Kettler, Volker Meja and Nico Stehr. 304 pp.*

Merquior, J. G. The Veil and the Mask. *Essays on Culture and Ideology. Foreword by Ernest Gellner. 140 pp.*

Zijderfeld, A. C. On Clichés. *The Supersedure of Meaning by Function in Modernity. 150 pp.*

  Reality in a Looking Glass. *Rationality through an Analysis of Traditional Folly. 208 pp.*

Strong, P. Ceremonial Order of the Clinic. *267 pp.*
Urry, J. Reference Groups and the Theory of Revolution. *244 pp.*
Weinberg, E. Development of Sociology in the Soviet Union. *173 pp.*

FOREIGN CLASSICS OF SOCIOLOGY

● **Gerth, H. H.** and **Mills, C. Wright.** From Max Weber: *Essays in Sociology. 502 pp.*

● **Tönnies, Ferdinand.** Community and Association (*Gemeinschaft und Gesellschaft*). *Translated and Supplemented by Charles P. Loomis. Foreword by Pitirim A. Sorokin. 334 pp.*

SOCIAL STRUCTURE

Andreski, Stanislav. Military Organization and Society. *Foreword by Professor A. R. Radcliffe-Brown. 226 pp. 1 folder.*

Bozzoli, B. The Political Nature of a Ruling Class. *Capital and Ideology in South Africa 1890–1939. 396 pp.*

Bauman, Z. Memories of Class. *The Prehistory and After life of Class. 240 pp.*

Broom, L., Lancaster Jones, F., McDonnell, P. and **Williams, T.** The Inheritance of Inequality. *208 pp.*

Carlton, Eric. Ideology and Social Order. *Foreword by Professor Philip Abrahams. 326 pp.*

Clegg, S. and **Dunkerley, D.** Organization, Class and Control. *614 pp.*

Coontz, Sydney H. Population Theories and the Economic Interpretation. *202 pp.*

Coser, Lewis. The Functions of Social Conflict. *204 pp.*

Crook, I. and **D.** The First Years of the Yangyi Commune. *304 pp., illustrated.*

Dickie-Clark, H. F. Marginal Situation: *A Sociological Study of a Coloured Group. 240 pp. 11 tables.*

Fidler, J. The British Business Elite. *Its Attitudes to Class, Status and Power. 332 pp.*

Giner, S. and **Archer, M. S.** (Eds) Contemporary Europe: *Social Structures and Cultural Patterns. 336 pp.*

● **Glaser, Barney** and **Strauss, Anselm L.** Status Passage: *A Formal Theory. 212 pp.*

Glass, D. V. (Ed.) Social Mobility in Britain. *Contributions by J. Berent, T. Bottomore, R. C. Chambers, J. Floud, D. V. Glass, J. R. Hall, H. T. Himmelweit, R. K. Kelsall, F. M. Martin, C. A. Moser, R. Mukherjee and W. Ziegel. 420 pp.*

Kelsall, R. K. Higher Civil Servants in Britain: *From 1870 to the Present Day. 268 pp. 31 tables.*

● **Lawton, Denis.** Social Class, Language and Education. *192 pp.*

McLeish, John. The Theory of Social Change. *Four Views Considered. 128 pp.*

● **Marsh, David C.** The Changing Social Structure of England and Wales, 1871–1961. *Revised edition. 288 pp.*

Menzies, Ken. Talcott Parsons and the Social Image of Man. *206 pp.*

● **Mouzelis, Nicos.** Organization and Bureaucracy. *An Analysis of Modern Theories. 240 pp.*

● **Ossowski, Stanislaw.** Class Structure in the Social Consciousness. *210 pp.*

● **Podgórecki, Adam.** Law and Society. *302 pp.*

Ratcliffe, P. Racism and Reaction. *A Profile of Handsworth. 388 pp.*

Renner, Karl. Institutions of Private Law and Their Social Functions. *Edited, with an Introduction and Notes, by O. Kahn-Freud. Translated by Agnes Schwarzschild. 316 pp.*

Rex, J. and **Tomlinson, S.** Colonial Immigrants in a British City. *A Class Analysis. 368 pp.*

Smooha, S. Israel. *Pluralism and Conflict. 472 pp.*

Strasser, H. and **Randall, S. C.** An Introduction to Theories of Social Change. *300 pp.*

Wesołowski, W. Class, Strata and Power. *Trans. and with Introduction by G. Kolankiewicz. 160 pp.*

Zureik, E. Palestinians in Israel. *A Study in Internal Colonialism 264 pp.*

SOCIOLOGY AND POLITICS

Acton, T. A. Gypsy Politics and Social Change. *316 pp.*

Burton, F. Politics of Legitimacy. *Struggles in a Belfast Community. 250 pp.*

Crook, I. and **D.** Revolution in a Chinese Village. *Ten Mile Inn. 216 pp., illustrated.*

de Silva, S. B. D. The Political Economy of Underdevelopment. *640 pp.*

Etzioni-Halevy, E. Political Manipulation and Administrative Power. *A Comparative Study. 228 pp.*

Fielding, N. The National Front. *260 pp.*

● **Hechter, Michael.** Internal Colonialism. *The Celtic Fringe in British National Development, 1536–1966. 380 pp.*

Levy, N. The Foundations of the South African Cheap Labour System. *367 pp.*

Kornhauser, William. The Politics of Mass Society. *272 pp. 20 tables.*

● **Korpi, W.** The Working Class in Welfare Capitalism. *Work, Unions and Politics in Sweden. 472 pp.*

Kroes, R. Soldiers and Students. *A Study of Right- and Left-wing Students. 174 pp.*

Martin, Roderick. Sociology of Power. *214 pp.*

Merquior, J. G. Rousseau and Weber. *A Study in the Theory of Legitimacy. 286 pp.*

Myrdal, Gunnar. The Political Element in the Development of Economic Theory. *Translated from the German by Paul Streeten. 282 pp.*

Preston, P. W. Theories of Development. *296 pp.*

Varma, B. N. The Sociology and Politics of Development. *A Theoretical Study. 236 pp.*

Wong, S.-L. Sociology and Socialism in Contemporary China. *160 pp.*

Wootton, Graham. Workers, Unions and the State. *188 pp.*

CRIMINOLOGY

Ancel, Marc. Social Defence: *A Modern Approach to Criminal Problems. Foreword by Leon Radzinowicz. 240 pp.*

Athens, L. Violent Criminal Acts and Actors. *104 pp.*

Cain, Maureen E. Society and the Policeman's Role. *326 pp.*

Cloward, Richard A. and **Ohlin, Lloyd E.** Delinquency and Opportunity: *A Theory of Delinquent Gangs. 248 pp.*

Downes, David M. The Delinquent Solution. *A Study in Subcultural Theory. 296 pp.*

Friedlander, Kate. The Psycho-Analytical Approach to Juvenile Delinquency: *Theory, Case Studies, Treatment. 320 pp.*

Glueck, Sheldon and **Eleanor.** Family Environment and Delinquency. *With the statistical assistance of Rose W. Kneznek. 340 pp.*

Lopez-Rey, Manuel. Crime. *An Analytical Appraisal. 288 pp.*

Mannheim, Hermann. Comparative Criminology: *A Text Book. Two volumes. 442 pp. and 380 pp.*

Morris, Terence. The Criminal Area: *A Study in Social Ecology. Foreword by Hermann Mannheim. 232 pp. 25 tables. 4 maps.*

Rock, Paul. Making People Pay. *338 pp.*

● **Taylor, Ian, Walton, Paul** and **Young, Jock.** The New Criminology. *For a Social Theory of Deviance. 325 pp.*

● **Taylor, Ian, Walton, Paul** and **Young, Jock.** (Eds) Critical Criminology. *268 pp.*

SOCIOLOGY OF RELIGION

Argyle, Michael and **Beit-Hallahmi, Benjamin.** The Social Psychology of Religion. *256 pp..*

Glasner, Peter E. The Sociology of Secularisation. *A Critique of a Concept. 146 pp.*

Hall, J. R. The Ways Out. *Utopian Communal Groups in an Age of Babylon. 280 pp.*

Ranson, S., Hinings, B. and **Bryman, A.** Clergy, Ministers and Priests. *216 pp.*

Stark, Werner. The Sociology of Religion. *A Study of Christendom.*
Volume II. *Sectarian Religion. 368 pp.*
Volume III. *The Universal Church. 464 pp.*
Volume IV. *Types of Religious Man. 352 pp.*
Volume V. *Types of Religious Culture. 464 pp.*

Turner, B. S. Weber and Islam. *216 pp.*

Watt, W. Montgomery. Islam and the Integration of Society. 230 pp.

Pomian-Srzednicki, M. Religious Change in Contemporary Poland. *Sociology and Secularization. 280 pp.*

SOCIOLOGY OF ART AND LITERATURE

Jarvie, Ian C. Towards a Sociology of the Cinema. *A Comparative Essay on the Structure and Functioning of a Major Entertainment Industry. 405 pp.*

Rust, Frances S. Dance in Society. *An Analysis of the Relationships between the Social Dance and Society in England from the Middle Ages to the Present Day. 256 pp. 8 pp. of plates.*

Schücking, L. L. The Sociology of Literary Taste. *112 pp.*

Wolff, Janet. Hermeneutic Philosophy and the Sociology of Art. *150 pp.*

SOCIOLOGY OF KNOWLEDGE

Diesing, P. Patterns of Discovery in the Social Sciences. *262 pp.*

● **Douglas, J. D.** (Ed.) Understanding Everyday Life. *270 pp.*

● **Hamilton, P.** Knowledge and Social Structure. *174 pp.*

Jarvie, I. C. Concepts and Society. *232 pp.*

Mannheim, Karl. Essays on the Sociology of Knowledge. *Edited by Paul Kecskemeti. Editorial Note by Adolph Lowe. 353 pp.*

Remmling, Gunter W. The Sociology of Karl Mannheim. *With a Bibliographical Guide to the Sociology of Knowledge, Ideological Analysis, and Social Planning. 255 pp.*

Remmling, Gunter W. (Ed.) Towards the Sociology of Knowledge. *Origin and Development of a Sociological Thought Style. 463 pp.*

Scheler, M. Problems of a Sociology of Knowledge. *Trans. by M. S. Frings. Edited and with an Introduction by K. Stikkers. 232 pp.*

URBAN SOCIOLOGY

Aldridge, M. The British New Towns. *A Programme Without a Policy. 232 pp.*

Ashworth, William. The Genesis of Modern British Town Planning: *A Study in Economic and Social History of the Nineteenth and Twentieth Centuries. 288 pp.*

Brittan, A. The Privatised World. *196 pp.*

Cullingworth, J. B. Housing Needs and Planning Policy: *a Restatement of the Problems of Housing Need and 'Overspill' in England and Wales. 232 pp. 44 tables. 8 maps.*

Dickinson, Robert E. City and Region: *A Geographical Interpretation. 608 pp. 125 figures.*
The West European City: *A Geographical Interpretation. 600 pp. 129 maps. 29 plates.*

Humphreys, Alexander J. New Dubliners: *Urbanization and the Irish Family.* *Foreword by George C. Homans. 304 pp.*

Jackson, Brian. Working Class Community: *Some General Notions raised by a Series of Studies in Northern England. 192 pp.*

● Mann, P. H. An Approach to Urban Sociology. *240 pp.*

Mellor, J. R. Urban Sociology in an Urbanized Society. *326 pp.*

Morris, R. N. and Mogey, J. The Sociology of Housing. *Studies at Berinsfield. 232 pp. 4 pp. plates.*

Mullan, R. Stevenage Ltd. *438 pp.*

Rex, J. and Tomlinson, S. Colonial Immigrants in a British City. *A Class Analysis. 368 pp.*

Rosser, C. and Harris, C. The Family and Social Change. *A Study of Family and Kinship in a South Wales Town. 352 pp. 8 maps.*

● Stacey, Margaret, Batsone, Eric, Bell, Colin and Thurcott, Anne. Power, Persistence and Change. *A Second Study of Banbury. 196 pp.*

RURAL SOCIOLOGY

● Mayer, Adrian C. Peasants in the Pacific. *A Study of Fiji Indian Rural Society. 248 pp. 20 plates.*

Williams, W. M. The Sociology of an English Village: *Gosforth. 272 pp. 12 figures. 13 tables.*

SOCIOLOGY OF INDUSTRY AND DISTRIBUTION

Dunkerley, David. The Foreman. *Aspects of Task and Structure. 192 pp.*

Eldridge, J. E. T. *Industrial Disputes. Essays in the Sociology of Industrial Relations. 288 pp.*

Hollowell, Peter G. The Lorry Driver. *272 pp.*

● Oxaal, I., Barnett, T. and Booth, D. (Eds) Beyond the Sociology of Development. *Economy and Society in Latin America and Africa. 295 pp.*

Smelser, Neil J. Social Change in the Industrial Revolution: *An Application of Theory to the Lancashire Cotton Industry, 1770–1840. 468 pp. 12 figures. 14 tables.*

Watson, T. J. The Personnel Managers. *A Study in the Sociology of Work and Employment, 262 pp.*

ANTHROPOLOGY

Brandel-Syrier, Mia. Reeftown Elite. *A Study of Social Mobility in a Modern African Community on the Reef. 376 pp.*

Dickie-Clark, H. F. The Marginal Situation. *A Sociological Study of a Coloured Group. 236 pp.*

Dube, S. C. Indian Village. *Foreword by Morris Edward Opler. 276 pp. 4 plates.*

India's Changing Villages: *Human Factors in Community Development. 260 pp. 8 plates. 1 map.*

Fei, H.-T. Peasant Life in China. *A Field Study of Country Life in the Yangtze Valley. With a foreword by Bronislaw Malinowski. 328 pp. 16 pp. plates.*

Firth, Raymond. Malay Fishermen. *Their Peasant Economy. 420 pp. 17 pp. plates.*

Gulliver, P H. Social Control in an African Society: a Study of the Arusha, *Agricultural Masai of Northern Tanganykia. 320 pp. 8 plates. 10 figures.* Family Herds. *288 pp.*

Jarvie, Ian C. The Revolution in Anthropology. *268 pp.*

Little, Kenneth L. Mende of Sierra Leone. *308 pp. and folder.* Negroes in Britain. *With a New Introduction and Contemporary Study by Leonard Bloom. 320 pp.*

Tambs-Lyche, H. London Patidars. *168 pp.*

Madan, G. R. Western Sociologists on Indian Society. *Marx, Spencer, Weber, Durkheim, Pareto. 384 pp.*

Mayer, A. C. Peasants in the Pacific. *A Study of Fiji Indian Rural Society. 248 pp.*

Meer, Fatima. Race and Suicide in South Africa. *325 pp.*

Smith, Raymond T. The Negro Family in British Guiana: *Family Structure and Social Status in the Villages. With a Foreword by Meyer Fortes. 314 pp. 8 plates. 1 figure. 4 maps.*

SOCIOLOGY AND PHILOSOPHY

● **Adriaansens, H.** Talcott Parsons and the Conceptual Dilemma. *200 pp.*

Barnsley, John H. The Social Reality of Ethics. *A Comparative Analysis of Moral Codes. 448 pp.*

Diesing, Paul. Patterns of Discovery in the Social Sciences. *362 pp.*

● **Douglas, Jack D.** (Ed.) Understanding Everyday Life. *Toward the Reconstruction of Sociological Knowledge. Contributions by Alan F. Blum, Aaron W. Cicourel, Norman K. Denzin, Jack D. Douglas, John Heeren, Peter McHugh, Peter K. Manning, Melvin Power, Matthew Speier, Roy Turner, D. Lawrence Wieder, Thomas P. Wilson and Don H. Zimmerman. 370 pp.*

Gorman, Robert A. The Dual Vision. *Alfred Schutz and the Myth of Phenomenological Social Science. 240 pp.*

Jarvie, Ian C. Concepts and Society. *216 pp.*

Kilminster, R. Praxis and Method. *A Sociological Dialogue with Lukács, Gramsci and the Early Frankfurt School. 334 pp.*

Outhwaite, W. Concept Formation in Social Science. *255 pp.*

● **Pelz, Werner.** The Scope of Understanding in Sociology. *Towards a More Radical Reorientation in the Social Humanistic Sciences. 283 pp.*

Roch., Maurice, Phenomenology, Language and the Social Sciences. *371 pp.*

Sahay, Arun. Sociological Analysis. *212 pp.*

● **Slater, P.** Origin and Significance of the Frankfurt School. *A Marxist Perspective. 185 pp.*

Spurling, L. Phenomenology and the Social World. *The Philosophy of Merleau-Ponty and its Relation to the Social Sciences. 222 pp.*

Wilson, H. T. The American Ideology. *Science, Technology and Organization as Modes of Rationality. 368 pp.*

International Library of Anthropology
General Editor Adam Kuper

● **Ahmed, A. S.** Millennium and Charisma Among Pathans. *A Critical Essay in Social Anthropology. 192 pp.*
  Pukhtun Economy and Society. *Traditional Structure and Economic Development. 422 pp.*

Barth, F. Selected Essays. *Volume 1. 256 pp.* Selected Essays. *Volume II. 200 pp.*

Brown, Paula. The Chimbu. *A Study of Change in the New Guinea Highlands. 151 pp.*

Duller, H. J. Development Technology. *192 pp.*

Foner, N. Jamaica Farewell. *200 pp.*

Gudeman, Stephen. Relationships, Residence and the Individual. *A Rural Panamanian Community. 288 pp. 11 plates, 5 figures, 2 maps, 10 tables.*
  The Demise of a Rural Economy. *From Subsistence to Capitalism in a Latin American Village. 160 pp.*

Hamnett, Ian. Chieftainship and Legitimacy. *An Anthropological Study of Executive Law in Lesotho. 163 pp.*

Hanson, F. Allan. Meaning in Culture. *127 pp.*

Hazan, H. The Limbo People. *A Study of the Constitution of the Time Universe Among the Aged. 208 pp.*

Humphreys, S. C. Anthropology and the Greeks. *288 pp.*

Karp, I. Fields of Change Among the Iteso of Kenya. *140 pp.*

Kuper, A. Wives for Cattle. *Bridewealth in Southern Africa. 224 pp.*

Lloyd, P. C. Power and Independence. *Urban Africans' Perception of Social Inequality. 264 pp.*

Malinowski, B. and **de la Fuente, J.** Malinowski in Mexico. *The Economics of a Mexican Market System. Edited and Introduced by Susan Drucker-Brown. About 240 pp.*

Parry, J. P. Caste and Kinship in Kangra. *352 pp. Illustrated.*

Pettigrew, Joyce. Robber Noblemen. *A Study of the Political System of the Sikh Jats. 284 pp.*

Street, Brian V. The Savage in Literature. *Representations of 'Primitive' Society in English Fiction, 1858–1920. 207 pp.*

Van Den Berghe, Pierre L. Power and Privilege at an African University. *278 pp.*

International Library of Phenomenology and Moral Sciences
General Editor John O'Neill

Adorno, T. W. Aesthetic Theory. Translated by C. Lenhardt.

Apel, K.-O. Towards a Transformation of Philosophy. *308 pp.*

Bologh, R. W. Dialectical Phenomenology. *Marx's Method. 287 pp.*

Fekete, J. The Critical Twilight. *Explorations in the Ideology of Anglo-American Literary Theory from Eliot to McLuhan. 300 pp.*

Green, B. S. Knowing the Poor. *A Case Study in Textual Reality Construction. 200 pp.*

McHoul, A. W. How Texts Talk. *Essays on Reading and Ethnomethodology. 163 pp.*

Medina, A. Reflection, Time and the Novel. *Towards a Communicative Theory of Literature. 143 pp.*

O'Neill, J. Essaying Montaigne. *A Study of the Renaissance Institution of Writing and Reading. 244 pp.*

Schutz. A. Life Forms and Meaning Structure. *Translated, Introduced and Annotated by Helmut Wagner. 207 pp.*

International Library of Social Policy
General Editor Kathleen Jones

Bayley, M. Mental Handicap and Community Care. *426 pp.*

Bottoms, A. E. and **McClean, J. D.** Defendants in the Criminal Process. *284 pp.*

Bradshaw, J. The Family Fund. *An Initiative in Social Policy. 248 pp.*

Butler, J. R. Family Doctors and Public Policy. *208 pp.*

Davies, Martin. Prisoners of Society. *Attitudes and Aftercare. 204 pp.*

Gittus, Elizabeth. Flats, Families and the Under-Fives. *285 pp.*

Holman, Robert. Trading in Children. *A Study of Private Fostering. 355 pp.*

Jeffs, A. Young People and the Youth Service. *160 pp.*

Jones, Howard and **Cornes, Paul.** Open Prisons. *288 pp.*

Jones, Kathleen. History of the Mental Health Service. *428 pp.*

- Recording in Social Work. *124 pp. Crown 8vo.*
- **Todd, F. Joan.** Social Work with the Mentally Subnormal. *96 pp. Crown 8vo.*
- **Walrond-Skinner, Sue.** Family Therapy. *The Treatment of Natural Systems. 172 pp.*
- **Warham, Joyce.** An Introduction to Administration for Social Workers. *Revised edition. 112 pp.*
- An Open Case. *The Organisational Context of Social Work. 172 pp.*
○ **Wittenberg, Isca Salzberger.** Psycho-Analytic Insight and Relationships. *A Kleinian Approach. 196 pp. Crown 8vo.*

Primary Socialization, Language and Education
General Editor Basil Bernstein

Adlam, Diana S., *with the assistance of Geoffrey Turner and Lesley Lineker.* Code in Context. *272 pp.*
Bernstein, Basil. Class, Codes and Control. *3 volumes.*
- 1. *Theoretical Studies Towards a Sociology of Language. 254 pp.*
2. *Applied Studies Towards a Sociology of Language. 377 pp.*
- 3. *Towards a Theory of Educational Transmission. 167 pp.*
Brandis, Walter and **Henderson, Dorothy.** Social Class, Language and Communication. *288 pp.*
Cook-Gumperz, Jenny. Social Control and Socialization. *A Study of Class Differences in the Language of Maternal Control. 290 pp.*
● **Gahagan, D. M.** and **G. A.** Talk Reform. *Exploration in Language for Infant School Children. 160 pp.*
Hawkins, P. R. Social Class, the Nominal Group and Verbal Strategies. *About 220 pp.*
Robinson, W. P. and **Rakstraw, Susan D. A.** A Question of Answers. *2 volumes. 192 pp. and 180 pp.*
Turner, Geoffrey J. and **Mohan, Bernard A.** A Linguistic Description and Computer Programme for Children's Speech. *208 pp.*

Reports of the Institute of Community Studies

Baker, J. The Neighbourhood Advice Centre. A Community Project in Camden. *320 pp.*
● **Cartwright, Ann.** Patients and their Doctors. *A Study of General Practice. 304 pp.*
Dench, Geoff. Maltese in London. *A Case-study in the Erosion of Ethnic Consciousness. 302 pp.*
Jackson, Brian and **Marsden, Dennis.** Education and the Working Class: *Some General Themes Raised by a Study of 88 Working-class Children in a Northern Industrial City. 268 pp. 2 folders.*
Madge, C. and **Willmott, P.** Inner City Poverty in Paris and London. *144 pp.*
Marris, Peter. The Experience of Higher Education. *232 pp. 27 tables.*
● Loss and Change. *192 pp.*
Marris, Peter and **Rein, Martin.** Dilemmas of Social Reform. *Poverty and Community Action in the United States. 256 pp.*
Marris, Peter and **Somerset, Anthony.** African Businessmen. *A Study of Entrepreneurship and Development in Kenya. 256 pp.*
Mills, Richard. Young Outsiders: *a Study in Alternative Communities. 216 pp.*
Runciman, W. G. Relative Deprivation and Social Justice. *A Study of Attitudes to Social Inequality in Twentieth-Century England. 352 pp.*

Willmott, Peter. Adolescent Boys in East London. *230 pp.*

Willmott, Peter and Young, Michael. Family and Class in a London Suburb. *202 pp. 47 tables.*

Young, Michael and McGeeney, Patrick. Learning Begins at Home. *A Study of a Junior School and its Parents. 128 pp.*

Young, Michael and Willmott, Peter. Family and Kinship in East London. *Foreword by Richard M. Titmuss. 252 pp. 39 tables.*
The Symmetrical Family. *410 pp.*

Reports of the Institute for Social Studies in Medical Care

Cartwright, Ann, Hockey, Lisbeth and Anderson, John J. Life Before Death. *310 pp.*

Dunnell, Karen and Cartwright, Ann. Medicine Takers, Prescribers and Hoarders. *190 pp.*

Farrell, C. My Mother Said. . . *A Study of the Way Young People Learned About Sex and Birth Control. 288 pp.*

Medicine, Illness and Society
General Editor   W. M. Williams

Hall, David J. Social Relations & Innovation. *Changing the State of Play in Hospitals. 232 pp.*

Hall, David J. and Stacey M. (Eds) Beyond Separation. *234 pp.*

Robinson, David. The Process of Becoming Ill. *142 pp.*

Stacey, Margaret *et al.* Hospitals, Children and Their Families. *The Report of a Pilot Study. 202 pp.*

Stimson, G. V. and Webb, B. Going to See the Doctor. *The Consultation Process in General Practice. 155 pp.*

Monographs in Social Theory
General Editor   Arthur Brittan

● Barnes, B. Scientific Knowledge and Sociological Theory. *192 pp.*

Bauman, Zygmunt. Culture as Praxis. *204 pp.*

● Dixon, Keith. Sociological Theory. *Pretence and Possibility. 142 pp.*
The Sociology of Belief. *Fallacy and Foundation. 144 pp.*

Goff, T. W. Marx and Mead. *Contributions to a Sociology of Knowledge. 176 pp.*

Meltzer, B. N., Petras, J. W. and Reynolds, L. T. Symbolic Interactionism. *Genesis, Varieties and Criticisms. 144 pp.*

● Smith, Anthony D. The Concept of Social Change. *A Critique of the Functionalist Theory of Social Change. 208 pp.*

● Tudor, Andrew. Beyond Empiricism. *Philosophy of Science in Sociology. 224 pp.*

Routledge Social Science Journals

The British Journal of Sociology. *Editor – Angus Stewart; Associate Editor – Leslie Sklair. Vol. 1, No. 1 – March 1950 and Quarterly. Roy. 8vo. All back issues available. An international journal publishing original papers in the field of sociology and related areas.*

Jones, Kathleen with Brown, John, Cunningham, W. J., Roberts, Julian and Williams, Peter. Opening the Door. *A Study of New Policies for the Mentally Handicapped. 278 pp.*

Karn, Valerie. Retiring to the Seaside. *400 pp. 2 maps. Numerous tables.*

King, R. D. and Elliot, K. W. Albany: Birth of a Prison—End of an Era. *294 pp.*

Thomas, J. E. The English Prison Officer since 1850. *258 pp.*

Walton, R. G. Women in Social Work. *303 pp.*

● Woodward, J. To Do the Sick No Harm. *A Study of the British Voluntary Hospital System to 1875. 234 pp.*

International Library of Welfare and Philosophy
General Editors Noel Timms and David Watson

○ Campbell, J. The Left and Rights. *A Conceptual Analysis of the Idea of Socialist Rights. About 296 pp.*

● McDermott, F. E. (Ed.) Self-Determination in Social Work. *A Collection of Essays on Self-determination and Related Concepts by Philosophers and Social Work Theorists. Contributors: F. P. Biestek, S. Bernstein, A. Keith-Lucas, D. Sayer, H. H. Perelman, C. Whittington, R. F. Stalley, F. E. McDermott, I. Berlin, H. J. McCloskey, H. L. A. Hart, J. Wilson, A. I. Melden, S. I. Benn. 254 pp.*

● Plant, Raymond. Community and Ideology. *104 pp.*

● Plant, Raymond, Lesser. Harry and Taylor-Gooby, Peter. Political Philosophy and Social Welfare. *Essays on the Normative Basis of Welfare Provision. 276 pp.*

Ragg, N. M. People Not Cases. *A Philosophical Approach to Social Work. 168 pp.*

Timms, Noel (Ed.) Social Welfare. *Why and How? 316 pp. 7 figures.*

● Timms, Noel and Watson, David (Eds) Talking About Welfare. *Readings in Philosophy and Social Policy. Contributors: T. H. Marshall, R. B. Brandt, G. H. von Wright, K. Nielsen, M. Cranston, R. M. Titmuss, R. S. Downie, E. Telfer, D. Donnison, J. Benson, P. Leonard. A. Keith-Lucas, D. Walsh, I. T. Ramsey. 230 pp.*

● Philosophy in Social Work. *250 pp.*

● Weale, A. Equality and Social Policy. *164 pp.*

Library of Social Work
General Editor Noel Timms

● Baldock, Peter. Community Work and Social Work. *140 pp.*

○ Beedell, Christopher. Residential Life with Children. *210 pp. Crown 8vo.*

● Berry, Juliet. Daily Experience in Residential Life. *A Study of Children and their Care-givers. 202 pp.*

○ Social Work with Children. *190 pp. Crown 8vo.*

● Brearley, C. Paul. Residential Work with the Elderly. *116 pp.*

● Social Work, Ageing and Society. *126 pp.*

● Cheetham, Juliet. Social Work with Immigrants. *240 pp. Crown 8vo.*

● Cross, Crispin P. (Ed.) Interviewing and Communication in Social Work. *Contributions by C. P. Cross, D. Laurenson, B. Strutt, S. Raven. 192 pp. Crown 8vo.*

● Curnock, Kathleen and Hardiker, Pauline. Towards Practice Theory. *Skills and Methods in Social Assessments. 208 pp.*

● Davies, Bernard. The Use of Groups in Social Work Practice. *158 pp.*

Davies, Bleddyn and Knapp, M. Old People's Homes and the Production of Welfare. *264 pp.*

AW-7506